THE NEW WINE

Christian Witness of the Family

Carlo Maria Martini

St. Paul Books & Media

Martini, Carlo M.
      [Vino nuovo. English]
      The new wine : Christian witness of the family / Carlo Maria
Martini ; translated by Mary James Berger.
          p.   cm.
      ISBN 0-8198-5131-0
      1. Family—Prayer-books and devotions—English. 2. Catholic
Church—Prayer-books and devotions—English. I. Title.
BX2351.M37   1994   93-51488
249—dc20   CIP

Texts of the Gospels used in this work are taken from *The Alba
House Gospels,* translated by Mark A. Wauck, copyright © 1992 by
the Society of St. Paul,
Staten Island, New York, and are used by permission. All rights
reserved.

All other Scripture texts contained herein are from the *New
Revised Standard Version Bible,* copyright © 1989 by the Division of
Christian Education of the National Council of Churches of
Christ in the U.S.A., and are used by permission. All rights
reserved.

The English translation of "The Angelus" from *A Book of Prayers,*
copyright © 1982, International Committee on English in the
Liturgy, Inc. All rights reserved.

Original title: *Il vino nuovo: meditazioni per le famiglie.*
Copyright © 1992, Edizioni Piemme, S.p.a., Via del Carmine 5, 15033
Casale Monferrato, Italy.

Translated from the Italian by Mary James Berger, fsp
Edited by Patricia Edward Jablonski, fsp

English edition copyright © 1994, Daughters of St. Paul

Printed and published in the U.S.A. by St. Paul Books & Media,
50 St. Paul's Avenue, Boston, MA 02130

St. Paul Books & Media is the publishing house of the Daughters of
St. Paul, an international congregation of women religious serving
the Church with the communications media.

1 2 3 4 5 6 7 8 9   99 98 97 96 95 94

Contents

Presentation

This volume contains conferences, meditations and letters which Carlo Maria Martini addressed to families between 1982 and 1991.

The task of presenting these to readers has been entrusted to married couples, and this is an important sign. It is true that, in our diocese, spouses and families have been involved for many years in pastoral action, in complete harmony with the Bishop. However, it is not customary for them to open the discourse, introducing the readers to the ecclesial and personal ambient in which the addresses of the Bishop have been maturing.

It is precisely here, in our opinion, that we find the importance of the sign. The intention of this discourse is twofold: in a sense we want to present a message which we have welcomed with affection and which we in turn propose to others, just as we share with friends something of value; in another sense, we intend to "respond" to the Bishop, proving to him that his words are valuable to us.

All this has nothing to do with deference to authority. When we believed it necessary to point out to the

Bishop aspects of the pastoral action of the local Church which we thought didn't apply, we did it in a spirit of sincere collaboration. Here we want to acknowledge that the words of the Bishop are existentially important for the life of families and for the life of the society in which the families live and work.

In fact, in reading the material covered in the various addresses, one notes, first of all, the continual references to Scripture, to the risen Christ, to the Eucharist, to faith. We are, therefore, touching the center of life.

This, indeed, is a characteristic of the pastoral approach of Martini. Milan has been aware of it since the beginning of his ministry, when he caused a bit of dismay, initiating a dialogue with the pragmatic, business-minded world of our city by recalling the dimension of the contemplative life. And then came the Word and its primacy, the Bread of life and the Risen One who draws everyone to himself.

There were those who were deeply impressed by the Bishop's words, but also those who were stupefied, as if he had said something incomprehensible.

It was, simply, the beginning of an essential dialogue about things that have the ability to change life—the only things that count.

The line of development is similar in our case.

Little by little as one goes ahead, the essential ties between those existential principles and the most concrete situations of daily life appear more evident. Charity is prominent in all its multiform reality in the addresses on "Becoming Neighbor," referring to the Samaritan in the Gospel.

Work, education, freedom: Martini presents all these values in strict connection with faith in the risen Christ and in the Spirit. He links them also to the drama of the restlessness of many young people, who lack satisfactory reference points in their time of growth.

In particular, the sense of freedom appears as a fundamental option to which each person is called. Beyond what one chooses in the varied contingencies of life, the ability to choose the evangelical way of life is what counts. This is made possible by entrusting oneself to the risen Christ.

The theme is taken up again when the Bishop speaks of the married couple's life and of harmony among family members. In the jumble of possibilities which can make the family a meeting place—but also a den of incompatibility—harmony depends on faith. This is true not because non-believers cannot build their unity by mutually fostering the freedom of each person, but rather because that fundamental option remains the fulcrum of one's whole life for everyone, even for those who tend toward it without being fully aware of it.

Step by step, without ever abandoning this line of intrinsic coherence, Martini addresses the most varied aspects of family life, including those which make it an intimate and quiet place of human richness.

Here we have a book which offers families some prayers to say together, at times of celebration and times of sorrow. Here we also have the celebrated points on the importance of the media in family and social life, with particular reference to television.

It's time for readers to enjoy the texts in person. We only want to add one word: here you will find the outline of a journey that can lead the family to "truly be what it is" (according to the well-known invitation of *Familiaris Consortio*), making it—instead of a dry leaf blown about by the winds—not only a place for the growth of its members, but a center of progress for society.

Piera and Richard Nassigh
for the Commission on the
Family Catholic Action of Milan

CHAPTER 1

Honor Your
Father and Your Mother

Living in the Presence of the Father

The biblical readings from the book of Job and the Gospel of Mark present us with *two very different human situations.* In the first, we encounter a suffering man, consumed by sickness, at the limit of his endurance. In the second we find a narrative about an elderly woman who is miraculously cured of fever and can join in the joy of a festive banquet, serving the brethren.

These two human situations, which apparently are antitheses, have, nevertheless, an interior movement which *unites* them: they are both human stories *lived in the presence of God.*

The lamentations of Job are not self-pitying expressions or anguished questions launched into nothingness. They have a speaker. They resound in the *presence of God's "You."* Even though Job is unsuccessful in understanding God's behavior in the face of his personal suffering, Job is convinced that God is *one who can be spoken to.* Actually, God is the only one who can be spoken to during certain decisive moments in life, because in the unfathomable profundity of his being there is hidden a mysterious capacity for *listening* and *intervening* that surpasses all human expectation and understanding. In other passages of the book, Job openly professes the certainty of God's intervention:

"For I know that my Redeemer lives,
and that at the last he will stand upon the earth..."
(Job 19:25).

And, in the grand, final appearance, God presents himself as the God who is always unpredictable, incomprehensible, unquestionable, not in the sense of intruding as a menace to the life of man, but rather in the manner of a love that has created and continuously recreates life.

This same mysterious, paternal presence is suggested in Mark's account. After having narrated the healing of Peter's mother-in-law and other healings of sick and possessed persons, the evangelist gives us a glimpse of the *profound mystery of Jesus,* presenting his lengthy prayer before the Father in the stillness of the night. *The healings that Jesus works* are the sign and the irradiation of that *divine will of life and love* in whose presence he continuously lives.

Life: A Gift Forever

These perspectives of faith, revealed to us in the Word of God, introduce us to an understanding of the significance of the *Day for Life*, which will be celebrated today in all the Christian communities of Italy.

"Life: *a gift forever*": this is the theme proposed by the Italian Conference of Bishops. The accent placed on "*forever*" sounds like a challenge. At first consideration life *does not always seem* like a gift. There are moments of joy, of activity, of friendship, of prosperity: these we willingly welcome as a gift (even though, to tell the truth, the exuberance which arises at these moments could tempt us to consider these experiences as our possessions, the fruit of our own efficiency). Then come the moments of *inertia*, of sickness, of loneliness, of suffering: these do not seem like a gift, but rather like strange and obscure *intervals* of life to be shortened as much as possible, and then immediately forgotten. And when we are unable to rid ourselves of such experiences, we carry them within as a weight which disquiets us, embitters us, and robs us of the enjoyment of life. How is it possible to *make sense* of these moments too? Here we encounter the message we have derived today from Sacred Scripture. Life is not to be understood only in its external circumstances. These vary, alternating between joy and sorrow. They cannot offer us a definitive meaning. They can only direct us beyond themselves and beyond ourselves toward the mystery from which we receive life. The mystery is given a face and a *name in Jesus*; it is revealed as the Father who calls all his children to the joy of a *profound communion of life and of love*.

In love there are no constraints. For this reason we can say "no" to God, can separate ourselves from God's life and his joy, ending up in loneliness, in incommunicability, in death.

In love, however, there is neither weariness nor resentment. Because of this reality, God has not abandoned human sinners to themselves, but has done everything to call them back to himself, to continually reopen the dialogue of pardon and of hope.

In love there is no fear. Because this is true, in the historical life and presence of Jesus, God had the courage not to place value on qualities that human beings regard as divine prerogatives, qualities such as omnipotence and majesty. In Jesus, God took the risk of not resembling God, in order to reveal to us his true privilege, which is love. He has taken to himself our sin, our pain and our death, to conquer them with the power of love.

While revealing to us the true face of God, Jesus, who lives in the presence of the Father, also reveals our innermost selves to us. Jesus teaches us the true meaning of life. He enables us to understand that life is always a gift: *the joys*, which adorn earthly existence, are welcomed as a sign of the final joy which God prepares in his eternal dwelling; *the sufferings* which, on the one hand, denounce the separation of man from God, on the other, in the light of the cross of Christ, can be transformed by love, can become a path of purification and spiritual matura- tion, can be viewed as a call to share in the innocent and redemptive suffering of Jesus.

Honor Your Father and Your Mother

It is certainly not easy to understand and accept this message of faith. Life's *joys*, especially in this our civiliza- tion of well-being, often, at a certain point, bind and seduce us, hindering us from understanding that they are not the supreme good but are signs of the love of God which he paternally dispenses. Instead, *the pains*, the preoccupations, the sufferings *hurt* us so deeply that it seems impossible for us to find in them a path of spiritual maturation and closeness to God. From a misunderstand- ing of suffering stem many mistaken attitudes toward sick- ness and death, attitudes that sometimes culminate in the tragic act called euthanasia, of which I have spoken in the discourse of last December.

So that faith's message regarding life may beneficially penetrate modern mentality, *I appeal* to you, dear brothers and sisters, who have entered what might be called the *third age.* I have invited you to celebrate the Eucharist with me on this "Day for Life" because I wish to honor, value, and place at the disposition of everyone the patrimony of wisdom which adorns your age and which can reveal to us precious perspectives concerning the meaning of life.

Following the Year of the Child and the Year of the Handicapped, the UN invites us this year to think about the elderly. We have spoken of the child's right to be loved. Evidence has been given of the handicapped person's right to rehabilitation and integration. Now we speak of the elderly person's *right to be honored*, according to the great commandment which resounds in the Bible but which is also summarized in the moral tradition of every civilization: "Honor your father and your mother." What is the meaning of this honor which must be given to the elderly? It certainly cannot be limited to respect, to caring for their food and clothing, to the assistance offered them during sickness. Honoring the elderly means also and above all to acknowledge their authority which is founded upon the authentic values which the elderly bear within themselves. As the father of this community by virtue of the ministry which the Lord has entrusted to me, I wish at this moment to interpret the voices of many *children*, asking you to give us the gift of your authoritativeness.

In your life, which is always getting longer, you have seen many things, have had many experiences, have practiced faith in the most varied human situations, have understood that while ideas, fashions, and styles of life, of society and of power may change, Christ remains forever as the messenger of authentic humanity.

You have experienced the fragility of many of life's joys. You have discovered that these very moments of difficulty and pain, lived in faith, have invited you to retreat within yourselves, to have a purer trust in God, a fuller possession of human gifts, a more intense human solidarity. With this authoritativeness of yours, help us give to our faith the profound and convincing resonance that comes from a long life experience, a resonance which can open up with calm, mature courage to society's

ever emerging problems and the always new tasks of the
Christian community.

Problems of the Third Age

I certainly do not wish to ignore your difficulties. To
honor the elderly person also means to help him or her
consider life with joy, creating conditions for a dignified
and serene existence.

Because of its work schedule, the type of family and
home and the complex forms of social life which characterized it, the society that preceded ours was able to glo-
bally *integrate* the elderly.

Today's society instead encounters grave difficulties.
The new work cycle anticipates retirement and often,
along with this, forced inertia. The concept of the family
and its housing possibilities often make it difficult to
welcome the elderly. The huge generation gap disrupts
the dialogue between the young and the old. Today's
consumerist society marginalizes whomever does not produce or consume certain types of goods. I could continue
the analysis of these difficulties. But I should also recall
the positive aspects: improved health care; the many possibilities for involvement; the means of cultural anima-
tion; the many occasions for volunteer activity for the
elderly in the Church and in society; the new sensitivity
among many families and many young people who,
through civil service or volunteer organizations, are available to meet not only the material necessities but above
all the psychological needs of the elderly.

It is a question of courageously examining the difficulties and the possibilities, so as to build a society capable of genuinely honoring the presence of the elderly.

It would be helpful this year to reflect again on the
document *Pastoral Action for the Third Age*, by Cardinal
Giovanni Colombo, both on its deep, original intuitions

and its concrete directives regarding retirement, shelter, the promotion of culture, and ecclesial service of the elderly.

I myself have already touched upon this subject in the discourse for the feast of St. Ambrose, and I hope to have other occasions in which to delve into the many aspects of the third age.

In the meantime, while I express gratitude, appreciation and approval for the many initiatives which spring up around us, I particularly recommend to all the Christian communities the program promoted by the diocesan movement "Caritas," and the initiatives promoted by the Movement of the Third Age, which for years has been working in our diocese with talent and dedication.

Service of the Elderly

In this my first meeting with you during the Year of the Elderly, I would like, to return to the theme of service, the service which you can render to society and to the Church not only through your activity, but also through that message of life that comes from the serene acceptance of the limitations of age, from abandonment to God even in moments of inactivity and sickness, from courageous and trusting preparation for death.

In the Gospel that was proclaimed today, we are told that Peter's mother-in-law, whose health was miraculously restored, placed herself at the service of Jesus and his disciples. Let us employ all the strength and health the Lord gives us in the service of our brothers and sisters.

The book of Job, instead, has presented the figure of a man who did not renounce his service to God despite illness.

Let us, too, transform the sufferings of life into occasions of service and into a testimony of faith.

In this way we will become messengers of the Gospel

as was Paul, who today in the Letter to the Corinthians said: "I have made myself the servant of all to gain as many as possible. I have made myself weak with the weak; I have made myself all to all" (cf 1 Cor 9:19-23).

In a very similar passage found in the Letter to the Philippians, Paul says: "I know what it is to have little, and I know what it is to have plenty. In any and all circumstances I have learned the secret of being well-fed and of going hungry, of having plenty and of being in need. I can do all things through him who strengthens me" (Phil 4:12-13).

I ask for this strength of Christ for myself and for you in the Eucharist we celebrate together.

CHAPTER 2

Educate Children to the Faith

Is it possible to educate today, or is it an uncertain undertaking that succeeds only once every so often?

This question is often transformed into a sorrowful affirmation that sometimes comes from the lips of parents involved in difficult situations: "Perhaps we have done everything wrong.... Why did this happen?"

This is the anxiety, the suffering which today permeates the desire to be educators.

On the other hand, the education of children is an undertaking that we can take on only with great trust in Providence and prayer; we need a generous, open, free spirit, capable of communicating enthusiasm. If the spirit is troubled, smothered by a multitude of existing impediments, then the first condition necessary for an educator is lacking.

We must therefore be very careful that the list of anti-educational elements present in our society does not make us fearful educators. Persons who live in a state of alarm are unable to grasp the fundamental point of education which consists in transmitting the ability to open oneself up to something greater.

The Setting of Formative Activity: the Great Metropolises

a) The *large metropolis* is the element that determines our formative environment. In this regard I reread the text of *Octogesima Adveniens* of Paul VI (1971, on the occasion of the eightieth anniversary of *Rerum Novarum*), where in the first part, under the title "Christians in the city" it says: "Is not the birth of an urban civilization, which accompanies the growth of an industrial civilization, a real challenge to the wisdom of human persons, to their organizational abilities, to their imagination with regard to the future?"

I believe that the theme of big cities is to be seen from this perspective: education in a big city is not only a necessity, it is not only a source of serious difficulties and dangers. It is, rather, a *great challenge* which can become truly formative because it moves the person to respond to both positive and negative stimuli. One who is educated in a small neighborhood usually finds it harder to acquire a broad mental and cultural horizon and an openness to ideas. The small environment is protected and is therefore without stimuli, without struggles, without choices to make: education remains at a disadvantage.

So, while we think of the large cities—especially Milan—as places of danger, of difficulties, of the gathering of anti-educational forces that threaten to overwhelm the experience of adolescence, we should also consider them challenges to creativity, to commitment, to courage, to choice, to decision. We need to educate not so much *in spite of* society as *in* society, drawing from it the strength to form personalities suited to our times.

Octogesima Adveniens continues: "Aware of this responsibility, may Christians not lose courage before the immensity of the city without a face. Let them remember the prophet Jonah who walked the length and breadth of

Nineveh, the great city, to announce the good news of the divine mercy. In his weakness he was sustained by the power of the Word of the omnipotent God. In the Bible the city is often the place of sin and pride; the pride of a man who feels secure enough to build his own life without God and even to profess himself powerful against God. But it is also Jerusalem, the holy city, the place of the encounter with God, the promise of the city coming down from on high."

This passage of Paul VI emphasizes, I think, the fact that the large city is at once a threat and a promise and incentive. He stresses that the formative task should be equal to these threats and promises. It is not a task for "our free time," a task added on to others. It is a fundamental duty, a battle to be won which demands the united and tireless energy and effort of both family members and educators. I often have the impression that we develop our formative energies only minimally. There are parents who—perhaps out of a sense of delegation, false powerlessness, or excessive reserve—develop only ten or twenty percent of their formative power and do not reveal themselves to their children until they are old, that is, when communication becomes easy and uncomplicated. Instead, if they were aware of how much they can give, they would possess a tremendous formative power, particularly if they settled in the right environment, with all the formative "allies" (Catholic schools, ecclesial communities).

Then the educational influence could become very great. We rightly speak of an "education based on example"; and since, in reality, there are many bad examples, formative activity seems to be condemned to failure. However, we need to remember another truth: the world of the baby and the child is a singular world, in whose view there are certain figures which sum up human experience, while others are seen as "background." The important thing is that there be even a very few examples but so outstanding as to somehow be indisputable as far as the child's experience is able to grasp them.

b) However, in addition to the setting of the city— with its agnosticism, its radical bourgeois or marxist mentality—the child is educated in the environment of the Church, some of whose characteristics are to be noted with careful attention....

Ecclesial realities are not made sufficiently relevant, and, as far as the child is concerned, it's as if they did not exist. So the child lives in an artificial world of dreams, records, music, few friends. For him/her, the city signifies certain life styles, certain persons, certain models, and all the rest is lost in an indistinct background.

Instead, it is the task of the family, the environment and the educators to make ecclesial realities alive for children. This is the great challenge in the relationship between the Catholic school and the local Church (parish, priests...). Children must be helped to live Christianity at all times and in varied situations. It shouldn't be that once they leave their home environment, they find themselves lost and bewildered. Rather, they should be helped to take part in the life of the local Church.

This local Church—with its popular character, its relationships between children, priests and families, and its particular cultural, historical and artistic ambient— allows children to "form an environment for themselves," one which is clearly distinguished by some irrefutable values and some sufficiently clear-cut examples. Then, those who know how to choose will find the strength to substitute an authentic choice for a radical bourgeois tendency or a tendency to respectability.

Often we do not utilize these formative possibilities, but concentrate, instead, on some incomplete educative efforts which leave later moments and experiences uncovered. In acting this way we do not respond to the *challenge* and to the great number of elements that impede or thwart formative activity.

The Journey of Education to the Faith

What does it mean to educate to the faith? It means to educate for a journey; to know how to continually perceive the various stages of the journey; to adapt formative activity to the different successive moments. The journey of faith is, in fact, very long. For young persons it certainly lasts until their engagement, and often the first years of matrimony are still a journey of discovery of the faith. We need to help them make the journey, keeping in mind its different stages. I would like to recall at least two of these stages, the initial ones, which correspond to two stages in the history of God's people in the Bible.

1. The first is the *receptive faith* of childhood, which can last for several years. It is the period in which the baby or child *receives* everything, even God, through the mediation of those "who know everything." Here the parents are of fundamental importance, and often deficiencies that occur in this first stage later appear traumatic. In fact, if the parents do not know how to clearly communicate the reality of God as one to whom the human person trustingly abandons himself, the child is deprived of an attraction to the journey of faith. It can happen, at times, that the parents themselves are still making a journey of discovery, and so what they communicate to the child is, involuntarily, imprecise or deficient. The consequences of such a situation will certainly be serious.

2. At a certain point the first stage of the faith, which is precisely a "receiving," an "accepting," an "entrusting of self," is transformed into *oblative faith*: God is not only the one who does things for me but is also the one for whom I am called to do something. The dynamism of the journey

moves toward an active, operative faith, and this is the most delicate moment. Only if the young person succeeds in perceiving life as a call of God has the formative question been implanted in the very center of his or her being. Only when the young person recognizes life as a call of God can the truth of human existence emerge. Then the youth will be able to make his/her life a response to the call.

All the other ideals of life which do not correspond to a vocational openness lead inevitably to mistaken and therefore dangerous choices.

3. When—through a formative process that uses all the means available—young persons are made aware of their power of freedom to give a personal response that differs from what the current mentality offers, they become very strong. This response is their *own* choice which they have made despite the environment and difficult circumstances. It is true that all this requires much attention and dedication. However, in traveling through the diocese, I have come to know, on many occasions, a great number of young people who make this choice. What is needed is that they come to know one another, that they not be isolated, that they form part of the fabric of a Church that is living and lucid in its expression. Parents too must understand that if, for their child, life is a response to a call, this call can demand everything. The implicit exclusion of what could be the vocation of total consecration is usually harmful in the formative field because it does not allow for that total moral attention which alone is capable of catalyzing youthful energies toward a troubled world like ours. In fact, educating to *faith* means educating to *holiness*: a decisive, resolute Christian holiness that knows how to withstand the storm, and in fact, expresses the best of itself in the storm.

This is not a time in which we can give "half an

education." Precisely because we are living at this moment in time, God will grant that we give the best of ourselves, while respecting freedom and the times. I often meet parents who fear they have failed and yet, in verifying their efforts, one cannot find the cause of the failure. In these cases we need to know how to humbly accept God's moments. We must not believe that everything is lost if a young person moves toward choices that are far from a journey of faith; we need to wait and hope.

Conclusion

It is not enough to educate simply to faith, prayer, and holiness; today, more than ever, we need "holiness of the intellect."

Young persons must be able to "dismantle" the cultural mechanisms that surround them and know how to perceive their emptiness; we need a school that teaches how to reason and to think. Here the Catholic school has a tremendous task, because if it does not succeed in educating to a critical sense of reality, young persons will fall prey to thousands of things. When the educational effort in the school is united to the educational effort of the Christian community, the parish community, then education becomes possible and yields outstanding results. Today we have a notable number of young persons who are more in touch with the reality of the Church and of life than preceding generations were. All this should fill us with hope.

The last thing I desire to tell you is taken from a passage of the "educational plan of the professional schools of Don Bosco," which was given to me. "To avoid dangerous dichotomies between the school's real motivations for choices and the actual carrying out of formative work, it is absolutely necessary to specify the educational plan, to develop it, to share it and to loyally and responsibly assume it together." Young persons are well aware whether or not the motivations for which they are sent to a Catholic school are the same for both parents and school. The choice of the Catholic school, therefore, must not be made by the parents simply because of the seriousness of the studies or the tranquillity of the environment. It is only the ideal of "Christian holiness" which can bring about that profound unity of intentions capable of achieving the best formative results.

CHAPTER 3

Witnesses of the Risen One

I Come to You This Evening

The telephone rings at home....

"Hello? This is your Bishop speaking. I would like to ask you a favor. Would you invite me to supper this evening so we can talk together for a while? I would be happy if all the members of the family were there."

I can imagine the face of the person on the other end of the line.

Some persons would say: "Yes, yes. We would be glad to have you." But then they would begin to worry: "Actually, I have nothing prepared for a guest this evening.... We wouldn't want to make a bad showing! Couldn't we plan for another evening?"

Other persons would excuse themselves: "This evening the children aren't home, we had already decided to go out, the grandparents are expecting us. We're sorry; come another time...."

"Very well. I don't insist," I reply. Also because if I were seriously to accept the invitation, I wouldn't know where to find enough free evenings.

My intention is to tell you that I truly would like to spend some time with you. This time I am doing it by means of this small book, which is given to you by your pastor in my name, together with my greetings for Christmas. If you take the time to read it, you will give me more pleasure than if you invited me to supper.

A Strange Guest

Jesus sometimes had supper with people, even though he often had to refuse invitations because of lack of time. But there was one occasion on which he let himself be invited by persons he didn't know. It happened like this.

Two friends met him on the road. They were very saddened. Seeing that he was going in the same direction, they accepted him, even if reluctantly, as a traveling companion.

While continuing on they started to vent some of their bitterness to him. Jesus listened to them and let them speak so that they could explain themselves well. Then he began. He did not say anything new. But what he said were things that they needed to hear repeated, and which at that moment took on a new meaning. The two listened to him, and were more and more attracted by those words which made them see the events of life, even the darkest, in a new way, one full of hope. It seemed to them that everything that weighed on their hearts was lifted little by little. And so it was that when they arrived home they said: "Why don't you have supper with us?" And they recognized him in the breaking of the bread.

A Race in the Night

At once they jumped to their feet. They left their half-finished supper and began to run toward Jerusalem (a two-hour journey) while evening came on. They wanted to tell the others the unheard-of news. The Jesus who had been killed on the cross three days before, had appeared to them on the way and had broken bread for them.

That leap to their feet, that leaving aside of their supper, that torch-lit race in the dark of the night, never cease to fascinate me.

I see here the model of a journey which our Christian communities and all baptized persons must make.

In past months I have commented on the journey of the two disciples in a longer letter entitled *Partenza da Emmaus* (*Departure from Emmaus*), which outlines the missionary itinerary of our Church. I invite the more committed Christians to confront themselves with that letter. Here I will take up again some of the fundamental ideas, in the hope of almost being able to enter into each home with these words, since, as I noted at the beginning, I cannot come personally as I would like, to bless the children, to console the sick, to urge on the young, and to confer with the adults.

The Full Heart

The profound meaning of the race of the disciples of Emmaus is contained in the phrase which the Gospel of Luke places on their lips: "Weren't our hearts burning within us while he spoke to us on the road?" (Lk 24:32). Jesus has inflamed their hearts and they can no longer contain their ardor: they feel the need to communicate it to others.

Here, perhaps, some of my readers are already stopping, troubled and somewhat self-conscious.

Someone says, I have never found the encounter with Jesus to be so stirring. Perhaps as a child and a young person I felt a sincere attraction to Jesus. I participated with joy in the life of the Christian community, in catechism classes, in prayer. Some of us even served as altar boys. But then little by little we grew cold in our practice of the Faith.

Our coldness may be partly due to the many problems of life that have distracted us. It may also be partly traced to the fact that we have been, so to speak, disappointed by Jesus, or at least by the Church. To us it seems that the Christian faith, so rich in fascination in our childhood, has not succeeded in saying anything truly important about work, the family, the problems of children, social involvement, that is, all the serious questions that accompany adult life.

I want to respect this spiritual situation of not a few of my readers.

However, I ask these brothers and sisters not to immediately close this book. I ask them to go back a bit, for a moment, to that point of the journey of the disciples of Emmaus, the point at which they too were disillusioned and without hope, before meeting the risen Jesus.

"We Were Hoping"

"We were hoping that he was the Savior." This is what the two disciples said about Jesus, when the mysterious traveler met them on the road and wanted to know the reason for their sadness.

We must seek the reason for this disappointed hope.

The two disciples had their own plans and hopes; they were hoping for a Messiah who measured up to their ambitions. They wanted him to be involved in the search for economic prosperity and material well-being. The death of Jesus, condemned as a criminal, was not compatible with these plans: herein lies the profound disillusionment.

However, we must ask ourselves very honestly: were the superficial and restricted plans of these two disciples right? Or was not the plan of God, who is attentive to the material but also to the spiritual needs of all people, more just?

At this point, we should have the courage to shift our attention from the plans of the disciples of Emmaus to our own plans.

We, too, have desires, plans, hopes, to which we cling with great passion, sometimes neglecting to consider the possibility that there is a plan of God greater than our thoughts, but for this very reason more beautiful, more useful for us, more exciting, more capable of giving breath and hope.

Of course it is not easy to face the mystery of this plan. We prefer to stay with things that can be touched and measured.

But isn't it true that our heart feels a strong desire to go beyond concrete and tangible things?

Perhaps we should more often and more attentively examine our experience, which teaches us that our hopes about work, about economic security, about the family, about the success of our children, while bringing us many satisfactions, are also fragile and passing. Many times they disappoint us. But then, what is their meaning?

It is important in these cases not to shut ourselves up in lamenting and bitterness, but to go beyond the difficulties. Why not see in these great though fragile hopes the sign of a mysterious hope that does not disappoint, that hope to which our heart is called?

Experience tells us that the obstinate attachment of persons to their individual plans makes living with others difficult.

Each one thinks of their own concerns and is not aware of the needs of others; from this stem misunderstandings, injustices, struggles, and divisions.

Shouldn't we be convinced that, in order to lead a

morally good and upright life, we must all be open to a Good which is above all and which proposes ideals and duties valid for everyone and forever?

I know that I am offering just a few poor words on a tremendous topic, but it is clear that our desires, our hopes, our very disappointments, the difficulties of our staying together in the family, in society, bring us back to the One who is at the origin of our desires and can heal our divisions. They place us in the presence of the mystery of God, Creator and Father.

Why not speak together more at length about these things, even as a family? Why not discuss them with some competent persons?

Why not do some good reading, which affirms the certainty of faith in God? Why not reread the Gospel, so as to know how Jesus speaks to us about the mystery of God?

I would like to look a bit more deeply into this last question.

"Stay with Us, Lord"

In the common opinion of people there is a great liking for the figure of Jesus.

Everyone knows, at least vaguely, the purity of his message, his preference for the poor and the lowly, the consistency between his life and words, from the grotto of Bethlehem to the dramatic poverty of the cross.

If, then, not being satisfied with a confused remembrance of the catechism, a person begins to read or re-read the Gospel, he or she encounters an unforgettable Person, who has spoken strong words about the important problems of life, a Person who approached each man and woman, from the greatest to the smallest, with a serenity, a tenderness and a clearness that are impressive.

An attentive reading of the Gospel, however, obliges us to go further.

By means of many words and actions, Jesus lets us understand that the particular intensity with which he understood and lived his existence as a man among human persons, comes from a profound relationship with God his Father.

Jesus spoke stupendous words about the merciful and demanding love of the Father. He declared that he wanted always to do the Father's will; in the terrible moments of the agony in Gethsemane he asked the Father for the courage to give his whole life for the salvation of humanity. While dying on the cross he entrusted his life into the hands of the Father and awaited from him resurrection, the fullness of life and joy.

Throughout his life as man, Jesus revealed the mysterious unity that exists between him and the Father. Why not believe in this upright man who is wise and generous, able to cure the sick and raise the dead?

Why not believe that the fully human life that he lived among us, reveals the designs, the desires, the plans of God for all humanity?

Why not believe that God, in his immense love, has come among us in Jesus, and has truly dwelt in our midst on our earth?

Why not believe that God calls us to live near him always, together with the risen Jesus?

Here again I recognize the poverty of my words.

The risen Jesus himself should speak to you as he did to the disciples of Emmaus.

I cannot compress into a few lines the personal itinerary that each of us needs to complete so as to pass from a simple human attraction to Jesus to faith in the Son of God, who saves us through his death and resurrection.

I pray that all may know how to accomplish this

journey, and, if necessary, to begin it anew. I ask Jesus himself to accompany each one of us, as he accompanied the two disciples of Emmaus, so that each of us, at the end of our journey, can repeat their prayer: "Stay with us, Lord, because it's near evening."

In the uncertain shadows of our thoughts about the meaning of life and in the sinful ambiguity of our behavior toward the dignity and freedom of each person, we invoke the presence of Jesus. He is the true man because he reveals to us and communicates to us the love with which God himself takes care of each person.

In him alone do we find the truth and hope for our life.

Witnesses of the Risen One

When we discover that Jesus is the truth, the hope and the salvation of our lives, we are not content to cling to him with all our might, but feel the urgent obligation to communicate our discovery to others.

The disciples of Emmaus ran back to Jerusalem to tell the others about their encounter with the risen Jesus.

If we have truly understood that Jesus is not just any man but the one who knows the full truth about the human person, my truth and that of every person, we cannot remain indifferent to the fact that so many of our brothers and sisters live, work, suffer and die without knowing and meeting Jesus.

We feel driven to become witnesses of the Risen One. In the Gospel Jesus himself invites his disciples to be missionaries and witnesses: witnesses of him who is risen and alive, and who attracts to himself, today, every man and woman in this world.

It moves us to realize that Jesus asks for our free collaboration in helping him to reach other people, and we feel our responsibility to do this. We offer our hands, our voice, our heart to Jesus, so that he can meet every person.

Among Jesus' many words about mission, I want to recall at least two, which seem especially stimulating to me.

The first word is contained in chapter 10 of the Gospel of Luke. There for the first time Jesus sends the disciples two by two into the villages of Galilee to announce the Gospel.

He exhorts them to be poor, sincere, simple, able to accept hardships and misunderstanding, intrepid in giving witness to the Gospel, confiding in God's fatherly help.

In our civilization, so concerned with well-being and success, Jesus traces for the disciple an austere style of life that knows how to adhere to the really essential things even at the cost of going against the current.

The second word is found on the last page of Matthew's Gospel.

Before returning to the Father, the risen Jesus sends his disciples into the whole world. He entrusts them with a universal mission, open to all people.

Our era is witnessing an explosion of global meaning, based on the rapid evolution of the means of communication. However, it is also an era of racial discrimination, of injustices practiced by the developed nations against those on the road to development, of divisions between social classes, of the arms race.

The disciple of Christ finds in the Gospel an announcement of brotherhood and peace to be spread to all peoples and all individuals.

How I wish that these Gospel pages would be reread and commented on in every family!

The Vine and the Branches

In entrusting us with the task of witnessing to him, Jesus offers some suggestions to make our testimony effective.

The first suggestion is to cling closely to his person.

Another passage that could be read and discussed as a family is chapter 1 of John's Gospel, from verses 37 to 51. It describes the first gathering of the disciples around Jesus. Those who have met Jesus speak about him to a brother or a friend and invite them to join the group. However, before inviting the others, the disciple lives an experience of intimacy with the Master.

The Gospel, in fact, narrates that two of the disciples of John the Baptist follow Jesus. He turns to them and asks: "What are you looking for?" They answer: "Rabbi...where are you staying?" "Come and see," Jesus says to them. "So they came and saw where he was staying, and they stayed with him that day" (cf John 1:37-39).

Even the discourses at the Last Supper insist on the necessity of living close to Jesus, of dwelling in him, that is, of assimilating his thoughts and desires.

Jesus explains to the disciples that he is about to leave this world and return to the Father. They themselves will be the presence of Jesus in the midst of his people, under the guidance and with the power of the Holy Spirit. To do this, they must be profoundly united to Jesus.

The image described in chapter 15 of John has become famous: Jesus compares himself to the vine and the disciples to the branches, which must remain attached to the vine so as to bear fruit.

These words of Jesus oblige us to reflect.

Perhaps the sterility in our Christian life comes from the fact that we reduce it to a series of actions to be accomplished, and we do not live this life as a personal relationship of our whole being with Jesus? Who is Jesus, really, for us?

We need to rediscover prayer, especially that prayer which takes as a point of departure some words spoken by Jesus in the Gospel and then seeks to apply them to the reality of daily life.

If we pray like this, we will comprehend what it means to understand Jesus and his life in us.

A precious aid in applying the Gospel to life is offered by spiritual sharings with our brothers and sisters in the faith. I am thinking of conversation with a priest, which enlightens our conscience; but I include also conversation in families, between spouses and between parents and children, about the way to apply the words of Jesus to the problems and circumstances of family life.

We must also be careful of behavior that is contrary to the teachings of Jesus. Sinful behavior separates us from the Lord, makes us branches detached from the vine.

Then we trustingly have recourse to the act of pardon with which Jesus, in the sacrament of Penance, unites us again to himself.

Let us seek the Lord's pardon not only in exceptional circumstances, for serious sins, but also with more regular frequency, for those daily failings which create an opaque barrier between our life and the plan traced out by Jesus in the Gospel.

United Heart and Soul

Adherence to Jesus is nourished and expressed in adherence to the Christian community. The two disciples of Emmaus, after having met the Lord, returned to Jerusalem to rejoin the community from which they had separated themselves with hearts full of sadness.

Community life offers the climate of faith and charity that supports witnessing. The book of the Acts of the Apostles is instructive in this regard. It narrates how Jesus' first disciples bore witness to the Gospel, bringing the good news of the risen Jesus throughout the then-known world.

These are fresh and interesting pages which we read, even today, with wonder and admiration.

At the root of the intense missionary activity of the early Christians we find the life of the community. The believers listen to the word of the Lord authoritatively proclaimed by the apostles; they celebrate the Eucharist with joy; they place their goods in common; they are of one heart and one soul.

This fraternal charity becomes a very powerful call to non-believers.

I know that I am touching on a delicate problem.

Not a few reject the Church because it does not resemble the community of the first Christians and does not seem to correspond to the desires of Jesus. They say: "Jesus, yes; the Church, no."

It is a very complex question which refers both to the life of the Church of our time and to the history of individual persons, who may even have had disappointing and unpleasant encounters with the Christian community.

I limit myself to mentioning a point that is strictly connected with missionary witness. This witness calls for the collaboration of everyone. In order that people in very different situations may understand that Jesus is the truth, way and hope, it is first of all necessary that believers communicate with their words and their lives what they have found in Jesus!

In addition, we need to remember that all Christians receive the gift and the task of giving "active witness." Perhaps many of them are mistrustful of the Church, because they have not yet found their place and their active role in the community, or the community has not had enough imagination to offer them a way of collaborating.

I ask families to reflect on two things.

The first is the possibility, already realized in many

parishes, that groups of families meet to pray together, to discuss their problems in the Christian life, and to seek forms of active presence in the life of the community.

The second is the necessity that children be taught to discover the marvelous variety of Christian vocations which the Church needs in order to carry out missionary witness. I am thinking especially of priestly and missionary vocations and vocations to a special consecration.

Are we certain of doing the best for our children by thinking of their future only in terms of a career and of security? Shouldn't we look with pride, joy and hope at a young man or woman who has the courage to choose a life of commitment and not a life of conformity?

From Door to Door, from Home to the World

Certainly there remains the problem of a Christian community which is not fully credible and which thus alienates people whom, instead, it should draw closer to Jesus.

Criticisms are legitimate and useful, but the most complete and useful gesture is that of offering a humble and serene contribution to the renewal of the community, that its missionary witness may not be dimmed and compromised by too many human limitations. I am thinking especially of the establishment of free, sincere, fraternal relationships among the members of the community.

This kind of fraternity becomes a prophetic model from which relationships with every other person can draw inspiration. Too often we think of the ills of humanity in general and we are not attentive to the sister or brother who is near us, right next door.

Jesus recounted the parable of the good Samaritan who paid no attention to the racial differences which separated him from the man attacked by the robbers, but instead drew near him, so that the stranger became his neighbor.

The mission of Christians is that of creating a close relationship with each person Then when we run into more extensive problems, we will seek to dialogue with our sisters and brothers in the faith and to collaborate with every person of good will, to find each time the most suitable means for denouncing injustice and to aid those who are treated unjustly.

If the family lives these attitudes of charity, then the children will naturally be formed to generosity. The home becomes a window open to the world. Young men and women will feel attracted to active participation in the community. They will become responsible for social and political commitments; they will participate in the various forms of volunteer work and civil service; they might even ask to go to the third world, either to announce the Gospel or to be involved in social work there.

What many young people are already doing assures us that the things said above are not daydreams but real fruits of God's mysterious action in human hearts.

Catechesis

In the preceding pages I have spoken often of the need for deeper study of some questions, of taking up certain topics again, of developing some notes. I could sum up all these tasks of further reflection in the task of catechesis; it is the task I wish to offer as a concrete proposal, as a working synthesis of this letter. In order to understand the importance of catechesis, we might reflect on some of the encounters of Jesus narrated in the Gospels.

For example, chapter 19 of Luke's Gospel describes the encounter between Jesus and Zacchaeus.

Zacchaeus was a tax collector; the people considered

him a public sinner and avoided him. When Zacchaeus knew that Jesus was traveling to Jericho, his city, he felt the desire to see him. Since he was short, he climbed a tree. Jesus made him come down. He wanted to go to his house.

Complaints were heard from the crowd which was scandalized by this gesture of friendship toward a public sinner. Meanwhile Zacchaeus felt reborn: he promised to make ample recompense to the persons he had cheated and to share his goods with the poor.

Jesus concluded by saying that he had come to seek and to save those who were lost. This final expression explains the meaning of the whole episode. Zacchaeus was able to meet Jesus because Jesus sought him out and loved him. However the search Jesus made intersects, increases the value of and purifies the uneasy search of Zacchaeus. It overcomes all the obstacles that prevent this search from attaining its end.

We could also examine the encounter of Jesus with the Samaritan woman, narrated in chapter 4 of John's Gospel. Jesus leads the woman to faith through a long pedagogical journey in which he directs and purifies the superficial or ambiguous desires expressed by the argumentative woman.

We continually find that the encounter with Jesus, salvation of humanity, always brings about a confrontation with the desires a person carries within himself, a confrontation with the often troubled and ambiguous journey that the person is making toward the truth.

In proposing catechesis, the Christian community intends to foster this confrontation, which gives a more knowledgeable and mature character to our faith in Jesus. Unfortunately, in the great majority of cases, catechesis ceases after childhood.

When the yearnings of young people begin to take

shape, when the human search for truth grows into adult-hood and is faced with family and social responsibilities, catechesis becomes more important, yet it is at that point that it is neglected. Then comes the crisis of faith or the persistence of an awkward and childish faith.

I ask adults to reflect seriously on this topic and to collaborate with the initiatives that will be suggested by the Christian communities this year. I am thinking especially of the preparation for the Catechetical Convention that will be held in October of 1984. It will have as its theme, *Catechists as witnesses,* and aims in particular to give impetus to the forms of catechesis done by adults, for adults and with adults. In saying "by adults" I refer especially to that first, fundamental and indispensable catechesis which is the catechesis given by parents to their children right from their earliest years.

A Year of Grace

In this pastoral year 1983-1984, some significant celebrations will offer us the occasion to deepen the themes treated in this letter.

First of all, we are still living in the spiritual climate of the *National Eucharistic Congress* and the *visit of the Pope.* I recall these events so as to thank the Pope for his visit and his precious teaching, and to thank the diocese for its warm and unanimous participation. However, I recall them especially because some urgent tasks stem from them.

The Eucharist permits us to enter into communion with the paschal mystery of Jesus, that is, with a gesture of total trust in the love of God the Father and of unlimited dedication to the service of humankind. How can we reproduce in our personal and communitarian life these attitudes announced and communicated to us by the Eucharistic celebration?

Another event is the *fourth centenary of the death of St. Charles Borromeo.*

Many remember this great Bishop of Milan because of his prayers and penances and extraordinary works of charity. However, we must rediscover him above all as a pastor who deeply loved the Church and promoted an intense and widespread reform, so as to render the Church more qualified for proclaiming the Gospel of Jesus. In particular he concerned himself very much with catechesis. The Catechetical Convention will therefore be a fitting conclusion to the centenary year of St. Charles. The saint's pastoral intuitions will once again be able to stimulate the Church of Milan in the exercise of the mission which the Lord entrusts to it in today's society.

To these celebrations proper to our Diocese are added two events which involve the whole Church. The first is the extraordinary Holy Year proclaimed by the Pope to celebrate the anniversary of the Redemption (33-1983 of the Christian era). The theme chosen by the Pope as the motto of the Holy Year: *Open the doors to Christ the Redeemer,* summarizes very well the itinerary of a rediscovery of Christ and of witness to the Risen One that I have tried to describe in this letter.

The second event of the universal Church is the Synod of Bishops. It, too, concerns the mission of the Church from a particular point of view, that is, the proclamation of God's pardon given to sinful man, closed within himself, separated from others, and inserted in a society full of struggles and anxieties.

We will meditate on this theme in a special way during Lent, discovering the austere beauty of the penitential journey by means of which man receives the peace of God and becomes a builder of peace among his sisters and brothers.

The Prayer of the Family

I have alluded to some extraordinary events which can sustain our commitment. I want to also recall the ordinary events that have a greater effectiveness.

The whole Christian community, for example, gathers for the great weekly appointment of *Sunday Mass*. I invite families to participate in it in an active and constant way, and to extend the climate of faith, joy, and fraternity proper to the Eucharist, to the whole day. May Sunday become once again the day of the Lord, of serene rest, of works of charity, of renewed friendship with our sisters and brothers.

Write to me about your experiences in this regard.

Another appointment is *daily prayer*. Many parents still pray together with their children. Why not find a time for prayer together as a family? It can become a means for regaining serenity, for dispelling arguments, for asking and obtaining pardon.

There are some beautiful collections of prayers for the different circumstances of family life: meal times, joyful events, times of trouble, sorrowful events. By way of concluding, I offer you a family prayer for the parish and the diocese. It would be wonderful if families became used to reciting it at supper time or before evening: adults and children could recite it in turn.

"God our Father, we give you thanks for this family you have given us.

"In the love with which we daily accept one another, help one another, forgive one another, you offer us the image of the love with which you created each life and take care of each person.

"We thank you also for our Christian community, for the parish, for the diocese, in which you make present the signs of the love of Jesus: in the Word, in the Eucharist, in the examples of fraternal love, which the community offers us, and in which our

family finds a model and support to continue to walk in love.

"We ask you, Father, that the relationships between the family and the Christian community may become ever more intense.

"We pray for the universal Church and for the Pope.

"Grant that the Church may more and more resemble a family: that it may foster fraternal friendship, may welcome the collaboration of everyone, that it may be attentive to everyone, especially the families who are without peace, without affection, without bread, without work, and without joy.

"Grant that our family may more and more resemble the Church: may it have faith in you, may it welcome the word of Jesus just as Mary his Mother welcomed it, may it apply the Gospel to daily life, may it help children to respond with joy to your call, may it be open to dialogue and collaboration with other families.

"Grant that the Church and the family be an image of your house, where you await us after our earthly journey."

While I ask families to pray for the Church, I assure all of them of my constant prayers.

Let us entrust our prayer to the Mother of Jesus.

May she who was present at the wedding feast of Cana, who obtained the first miracle from Jesus so as to gladden the beginnings of the life of one family, obtain for all families the joy of Jesus' presence.

Pastoral letter to the families of the Diocese, Milan, November 4, 1983

CHAPTER 4

Let's Go to School *

I Come in Company

This year, too, I come to your house. I come by means of this letter which is brought to you by your priest, who also brings the Lord's blessings and my greetings for a holy Christmas.

I come in simplicity and friendship, without making any noise. I will not even sit down, if you do not want me to. In fact, I come and go somewhat at your discretion. I come each time that you open this book. I leave each time you close it or decide to throw it away.

However, I am certain that you will give me a hearing. And since I know that I do not burden you with the task of preparing a multi-course supper or cups of coffee, I have allowed myself to come as company....

The topic on which I want to converse with you, in fact, should be considered from several points of view, because it is rather complex.... Let's go to school!

---

*Translator's note: With the permission of the Italian publishers, some sections intended specifically for the Italian reader have been omitted from this chapter.

What does this mean? And what thoughts does this invitation arouse in you?

Perhaps you are remembering the desire or the fear with which, as children or youths, you went to school. Perhaps you are thinking of the school attended by your children. Yes, it's about this school that I want to speak with you. It has an important place in our formation. Even if at times they seem simply to put up with it, our children are strongly influenced by school. Some parents fear it, not only because of their concern about its deficiencies and failures, but also because they believe it to be full of problems and conflicts. They consider the school environment to be troubled by political pressures which contrast with the rigorous demands and rhythms of its educational function. At times they believe it alien or even adverse to the education imparted by the family.

On the other hand, the organs of participation at various levels offer families the possibility to intervene, a possibility perhaps not yet sufficiently understood or acted upon....

I will first of all present some of my reflections on the three meanings of the invitation to go to school: to the school of the Gospel, to school with our children, to the school of religion. I will then express your difficulties and questions....

Let's Go to the School of the Gospel

I will begin with a confession.

I began to write these pages by seeking to bring into focus the problem of religion within the sphere of the school. But I soon became aware that this was not enough and it left me dissatisfied. I felt like someone who had to give directives of which he is not totally convinced, something like one who tries to defend the reasons behind the figure of Cinderella. At a certain point I said to myself:

But why? Cinderella will be the bride of the prince! I then sought to dig deeper and I understood that we cannot discuss school and religion in the school without involving the deepest questions of this "bride of the prince" which is the human person, each one of us.

The school is one of the educational realities of society, and education refers to the person to be educated, the motives for which we educate, the values to which we educate. The questions which I posed to myself concerning the school then became questions directed to me as a person, to each one of you.

What does it mean for me to be a person?

How do I live my relationships with others? Why must I respect their dignity? What makes me and others grow? How do I overcome the conflicts between my personal interest and the good of all? What relationship is there between my personal convictions and the opinions diffused around me? Is that desire to communicate, to love and to be loved which inclines my person toward others, sufficiently satisfied in the family, in friendships, in professional and social commitments, or does it go beyond human experiences and direct me toward a mystery, from which my person receives its absolute and inviolable dignity? What does it mean that these aspects of the person must be formed? And who has taught me these things? Who has given me the sense of my inner dignity and of the dignity of each person? Who keeps this sense alive in me, despite the disappointments and trials of life? Who sustains me daily in my weakness, who renews within me the decision always and everywhere to struggle on behalf of the human person, to put the least in first place, to give a voice to those who have no voice? It is your word, O Lord! Your teaching, your school. It is you who have said: "Come to me, all you grown weary and burdened, and I will refresh you. Take my yoke upon you and learn from me, for I am gentle and humble hearted, and you will find rest for your souls; for my yoke is easy, and my burden light" (Mt 11:28-30).

So there is a permanent school to which we are invited, and which daily sustains us in the "work of being a human being": it is the school of the Word, of the revelation of God. It reaches us through the Church, is present in the Bible, is transmitted by the entire Christian tradition in many vital forms (beginning with the family); it is present in many expressions and gestures of our culture, of art and custom. Despite many appearances to the contrary, "the principles of Catholicism form part of our historical patrimony." This patrimony, too, is a permanent school of life.

It is a matter of seeing whether I recognize this fact, and whether I accept the task of deepening it with a conscious decision. And how could I not do it, without arbitrarily renouncing or silencing the most profound questions that press me from within?

I too would like to have in my heart the tenderness and persuasive force of Jesus, so as to say first of all to myself and then to all of you: do not be afraid of God, of his Word, of his school! If you still have not met him, continue to seek him with simplicity, without growing tired. If you think you have met him, do not stop but seek him still, because he is greater than your heart.

In this continual search for a love greater than yourself lies your greatness as a human person. By not allowing yourself peace in this search you will attain true peace. Seek God together with Jesus. Seek him within the history of Jesus, a history so like ours and yet so amazing because of the absolute self-giving that animated it.

I cannot dwell longer on the search for God and on the encounter of God with Jesus. And yet, this is the one truly important thing about which we human beings should really speak. All the rest stems from this and finds in it its true meaning. Even the discourse on the school and the teaching of religion cannot be separated from this basic vision.

I often ask myself why we human persons tend to leave aside conversation about God. Perhaps because we suspect that if God enters into our field of interest and our conversation, he steals something of ours?

Instead it is exactly the opposite! Let us return to the page from Matthew 11:28-30, which I cited earlier, in which Jesus invites us to his school.

The fascination of these words of Jesus does not depend only on the authority of the one who spoke them, but also on the fact that they take into account two realities that we have very much at heart: freedom and culture.

First of all, our freedom, with its creative thrusts, with its search for a happier life for ourselves and for others, with its responsibility toward persons and things.

In inviting us to the school of the Gospel, Jesus does not take away our freedom. He wants to form it to be truly itself. He treats it with respect and simplicity. He presents our freedom with some responsibilities that do not overwhelm it but rather awaken the joy of action. He promises our freedom in a journey toward serenity and peace.

Then there is a second reality which has an important place in our lives: it is the sum total of relationships, of ways of communicating, and of every other activity that unites us with other men and women. In other words, it is the *society* of which we are a part; it is the *culture* in which we live.

So, Jesus takes these things into account too. While he invites us to his school, Jesus wants to free us from the wear and from the burden of the duties that weigh on us. He wants to make us understand the meaning of society and culture. He wants to restore us to our daily commitments and relationships with the uplifted spirit of those who know the reason for the things they do and the meaning of the relationships they live.

Going to the school of Jesus, then, means living a singular experience of formation to freedom. It also means understanding and living better our relationship with society and with our cultural environment. This presence of education and of culture in the school of Jesus urges me to take a step further, that is, to consider how the word of Jesus, through the teaching of religion, fits into the cultural institution of the school. But how does it fit in? Here we must not make false steps or leap over intermediate stages. The school is a place of instruction and culture. What relationship is there between religion and the school?

The question is legitimate and merits attention.

We, therefore, need to ask what the school is, what are its goals, its purpose.

We must come to know a bit more closely that reality which our children attend daily.

Let's Go to School with Our Children

Let us then return to school. Not merely with our mind fixed on the past, with the nostalgia of one who wants to find, in those halls scented with chalk, some remembrance of childhood or youth. Let us return with the attentive spirit of one who wants to understand the voices and problems of the school of today.

It seems to me that this is the characteristic of today's school in relation to yesterday's: it's a school of many voices, at times discordant. It is discussed and raises discussion. Many ideas about the school are debated. Alternative plans are attempted, the students do not learn only what is contained in books but feel able to express the most diverse views on whatever happens. Sometimes we "of the old school" ask ourselves whether these voices are not too many and too confused, whether they are accompanied by a serene formation to a critical sense, based on a real comprehension of the heritage of the past which is indispensable for understanding and expressing views about the present.

We could also be tempted to desire a more tranquil school, which only teaches an occupation and gives some useful notions about how to "make it" in life. But this is a temptation we must overcome. While certain exaggerations are to be moderated, it is good for a school to be a place of debate and confrontation. In fact, this highlights better its characteristic as a place not only of instruction but also of formation.

In order to understand this aspect of the school, we can reflect on a word which is often used to express in some specific way the fact that the school carries out a formative task.

We say that it forms by means of culture. But what is culture?

It is first of all the sum total of the traditions, of the ways of thinking and of speaking, of the social and environmental conditions in which we live. By learning and assimilating these things we reach the point of knowingly and actively belonging to our society, we are "nationalized." However, to achieve this goal, culture must not take precedence over persons. It must rather stimulate the intelligence and respect and foster freedom. Culture must strive to form persons capable of reflection and autonomous judgment.

An authentic culture does not equalize the persons in society but helps each person take part in it with his/her own original resources, leaving one free to criticize, to improve, to enable culture and society itself to progress.

This dynamic and creative way of understanding and

directing culture ought to characterize each and every relationship of society with individual persons. I believe that the school is the most typical place for this to happen. In school the student learns the culture and becomes educated. By means of instruction, that is, the reasoned and critical grasp of the facts that compose their culture, students are progressively enabled to understand the meanings of facts. They thus receive a precious light for cultivating their own intelligence and directing their own freedom, so as to be able to make free and creative choices even in conditions of cultural change and transfer.

I said right from the beginning that the topic of this conversation of mine is complex. Perhaps you are becoming aware that it is also difficult. However, if we have the courage to reflect seriously on these things, we will also be able to better clarify some of the problems discussed.

For example, we can clarify the notion of the so-called neutrality of the school. The school cannot be neutral in the sense that it must limit itself to teaching the bare facts about science in the courses on science, or about history in the courses on history and literature. The school cannot take the attitude that facts do not contain within them a meaning which challenges and questions freedom and conscience, and which asks to be linked with the final purpose and fundamental questions of existence. Even those who believe that only the bare facts are to be given and nothing else, are already taking a position, giving a theory about reality, somehow bringing their own person into play. The school must show the relationship between facts and conscience and freedom. It must demonstrate how facts challenge freedom. It must teach the taste for freedom. It must form students to respect the serious and deeply-felt interpretations which men and women give to the facts in relation to the ultimate values of life.

The school must then leave to individuals, to families, to religious communities—that is, to those institutions concerned most directly with the journey by which individuals mold their own interior freedom—the task of making and guiding the decisions about the values of life.

From this springs a second clarification regarding collaboration. It is very useful for schools and other educational institutions to be acquainted with and to collaborate with one another, so as to better know the different roles of each. This knowledge can help educational institutions to better carry out their respective roles, without invading one another's fields, but rather by fostering and affirming what each one does within the sphere of its competence.

Let's Go to the School of Religion

Why and how does the teaching of religion fit into the "framework of the school's purpose"? It renders a service to the school and its goals. We have seen that one purpose of the school is that of posing the problem of the relationship between scientific and historical data and the meaning that these have for conscience and freedom. Now, conscience and freedom refer to the ultimate, universal and fundamental goods of existence. What conscience and freedom then decide about these goods is the responsibility of the individual persons. But it is a duty of the school to correctly pose the problem. The teaching of religion, which is concerned with these decisive questions and the ultimate purpose of life, helps the school to perform this duty.

The teaching of religion helps the school by entering into dialogue with the other subject matters being taught while conserving its own specific character, which cannot be confused with the scope of the other courses.

The other subjects have their own objectives and

make clear the need to consider the problem of freedom and conscience. The teaching of religion responds to this need and discusses the relationship between conscience and freedom and the ultimate purpose of life. It is, therefore, not by adapting itself to the other subjects but, on the contrary, by differentiating itself from them, in a constant dialogue, that the teaching of religion helps the school achieve its purpose....

For many years the Catholic Church has been carrying out this teaching, although with difficulties and deficiencies. From its own patrimony of faith it can draw clear and valuable points for satisfying those scholastic needs which I have already noted, distinguishing this scholastic means of presenting Catholicism from the other initiatives by which the faith of believers is proclaimed and formed within the Christian community. From its own cultural tradition, from which our European culture was born, the Church can draw a pedagogy and a scientific methodology which have no need to envy those of other cultures....

Naturally, the Church must commit itself to fulfilling this task entrusted to it in the best way possible. In this area there is still much to be done.

We have seen the importance, for the Church and the State, of the teaching of religion in school. What about for children? And families?

Concerning *children*, I would like to quote John Paul II's letter to young people written for the year of the youth: "The period of youth is the time of a particularly intense discovery of the human ego, and of the properties and abilities belonging to it.... Life emerges as the realization of a plan, as *self-realization*.... It is the richness of discovering and at the same time of planning, of choosing, of foreseeing, and of making the first decisions on one's own.... What must I do, that my life may have value and full meaning? The youth of each one of you, dear friends, is a treasure which manifests itself in these very questions. Man poses these questions to himself throughout the span of his existence. However, in youth they assert themselves in an especially intense, even insistent way. And it is good that this is so. These questions demonstrate the dynamic of the human person's development that belongs to your time of life" (n. 3).

How can we not feel the responsibility for this moment of life? And how can we not make the most of the only scholastic period expressly dedicated to answering these crucial questions about existence?

"Why should young people," writes G. Barbiellini Amidei, "refuse, even in the years of doubt and uncertainty, to dedicate an hour of their week of studies, to those who speak to them about the God of the Catholics, or the God of the Hebrews, or the God of the Waldensians, or the God of Luther?"

Concerning *parents*, here too I will recall some words of the Pope: "Catholic doctrine and religious culture, in which young people are instructed within the sphere of scholastic formation, is an element which I dare to call indispensable to modern society, in order that young people may deepen their Catholic faith intellectually and then live it as adults, and that they may then be prepared, in any surrounding, to give the reason for the hope that is in them. An immense work of sensitization of families in which children are of school age, is necessary, that they may not neglect this opportunity which the...school offers. The topic can be the occasion for priests to begin and develop a dialogue even with families that are not as close to the parish but which are not alien to the Church, and perhaps in need of a friendly, motivated word of encouragement" (Letter to Cardinal Poletti, August 5, 1985).

In fact, parents assume a great responsibility in view

of the cultural, spiritual and moral preparation of their children, if they renounce for them the scholastic teaching of religion. In choosing a reduced proposal, in cognitive terms, they place their children in the occasion of living moments of greater discernment with little knowledge of the facts and with inferior means for grasping the meaning of their lives as well as the traditions, history and culture of their country. Aware of their formative responsibility, parents will feel it their duty to have their children benefit from the valid opportunity for reflection and maturation offered by the school. In fact the formative importance of the teaching of religion within the school environment is such that it cannot be replaced by other experiences, not even by the very necessary catechesis given by the parish. What has been said applies to all those, parents and children (even those who at the moment are not practicing their faith or do not believe), who are open to the truth and who for this reason want to combat any kind of ignorance, including religious ignorance. It applies to those who are anxious for a social and cultural dialogue that leads to mutual understanding and collaboration even among persons who think differently.

The teaching of religion in the school can therefore be for everyone—believers, non-believers, the indifferent —a unique occasion for critically examining their own position with regard to religion, so as to be able to make a more conscious, freer and more responsible choice, overcoming the conditionings of the environment.

Families will thus find a way to exercise a new formative responsibility, to give motivations, in their dialogue with the children, for the value of studying the Catholic religion, for a full and harmonious formation of the personality. Even if at times it takes courage to choose religious teaching, especially in hostile surroundings, it will be a valuable choice for the child, for the family and for society. It will be a choice made in the name of freedom.

The reasons that impel children and families to choose to avail themselves of the teaching of the Catholic religion in the school are, therefore, good and convincing ones. They will be even more so if such teaching knows how to offer persuasive programs and if the teachers are always better prepared.

This task does not concern only the teachers of religion. It concerns the leaders of the Christian community, who must create occasions for clarifying this topic and offer rigorous means for the formation of teachers. It also concerns the students and their families: the interest with which they will follow this teaching will be a stimulus for making it more suited to its purposes....

Conclusion

If you wish, you can join me in a prayer for a journey of serenity and peace. We will draw inspiration from the Gospel passage with which we began:

"Lord Jesus, we thank you for inviting us to your school.

"We thank you for the sweetness and serenity with which you fill us when we come to your school.

"May we lead to your school many other families who are tried by difficulty or sickness, families who are in need of bread and work, deprived of harmony and peace.

"May our family become a school of prayer, faith, honesty, moderation, industriousness, and love toward everyone.

"May our choices be carefully considered, courageous, open to the true good of all, respectful of others' choices.

"Assist and guide all those who have responsibility for education and formation.

"Grant that they be aware of the great treasure entrusted to them, and of the immense responsibility they have before you, the Church and society.

"Give everyone a share in your great love for children and young people, for their interior richness and their future.

"Let no one be afraid to hear God spoken of, the God of their fathers, of their culture, of their roots.

"Grant that, following Mary's example, we may know how to preserve and meditate in our hearts the words you speak to us each day.

"May we know how to manifest to everyone the serenity, the kindness, the peace which you teach us in your school. Amen."

Christmas letter to families, Milan, November 4, 1985

CHAPTER 5

The Eucharist
and the Christian Family

The Wedding at Cana in Galilee

The topic of my report is in a certain sense an explanation and a deepening of what I had occasion to say yesterday in the brief homily during the adoration of the Blessed Sacrament in Uhuru Park. The connections that exist between the Eucharist and the Christian family can be drawn from a beautiful page of the Gospel according to John: the story of the wedding feast at Cana in Galilee. Someone might be surprised by this statement. How is it possible to give such importance to a brief Gospel narrative? How can we find in the story of Cana the cross, the Eucharist, the Church and Christian marriage?

In our meditation I would like to answer these questions.

We Begin with the Words from John's Gospel

"On the third day there was a wedding in Cana of Galilee, and Jesus' mother was there. Now Jesus was also invited to the wedding as well as his disciples" (Jn 2:1-2).

In the little village of Cana, on the occasion of a

wedding ceremony, "Jesus did this, the first of his signs...and revealed his glory" (Jn 2:11). The transformation of water into wine is the first "sign" that reveals him as Savior. It is at a wedding feast, when the newly-married couple share the happiness of their love with relatives and friends, that Jesus wants to share his glory with his "friends" (cf Jn 15:15).

In the passage from John, it seems that Jesus wants to remain in the background, that he almost wants to draw back from the request of his mother: "And when the wine ran out Jesus' mother said to him, 'They have no wine'" (Jn 2:3).

The answer that the son gives the mother is at once mysterious and enlightening. Mysterious: "What do you want from me, woman?" Enlightening: "My hour hasn't come yet" (Jn 2:4).

We know that this refers to the supreme hour of Jesus' life and mission, the hour of his death on the cross, when he brings to fulfillment his love for the Church. In giving his body and blood, Jesus gives his whole self for the Church. Therefore the hour of Christ is an hour of love and of self-giving. St. Paul refers to it when he writes: "Husbands, love your wives, just as Christ loved the church and *gave himself up for her*" (Eph 5:25).

The cross is the hour of the Church, the hour of her birth from the wounded side of Jesus. Following a biblical and traditional line, in its *Constitution on the Sacred Liturgy* the Second Vatican Council affirms: "For it was from the side of Christ as he slept the sleep of death upon the cross that there came forth 'the wondrous sacrament of the whole Church'" (SC 5; cf EV 1,7).

Jesus therefore gave his first sign at a wedding feast: a sign which was the anticipation of what would happen on the cross, the beginning of the revelation of the mystery of salvation. We may say that the mystery of Cana sheds light on the mystery of the cross. More profoundly, the mystery of the cross explains the hidden meaning of the transformation of water into wine at the wedding feast of Cana.

John himself shows us, in some details of the narrative, the relationship between the mystery of the cross and the miracle at Cana, and consequently between Eucharist and matrimony. First of all, Jesus reveals himself as the spouse of the new dispensation, replacing the earthly spouse and acting in his place. It was, in fact, the husband's duty to make sure that there was enough wine for the feast. This task is taken on and fulfilled by Jesus who then offers the wine. He offers it in unexpected abundance. At his command the servants fill to the brim six stone jars, each holding twenty or thirty gallons. He offers a quality of wine that excites the wonder and amazement of the head steward, who observes: "Every man first puts out the good wine, then when they're drunk [he puts out] the lesser wine; you've kept the good wine till now!" (Jn 2:10). Now, the wine belongs to the symbolism of biblical revelation. It speaks of that happiness, of that celebration and of that joy which will mark the messianic times, the times of a new creation, when the Lord will prepare on the mountain of Sion "a feast of rich food, a feast of well-aged wines, of rich foods filled with marrow, of well-aged wines strained clear" (Isa 25:6). This feast is the sign that the Lord "will swallow up death forever" (Isa 25:8).

In other passages of the Old Testament the wine indicates well-being and joy, as is suggested, for example, by the flow of sweet wine through the parched hills of Judea (cf Am 9:13; Joel 3:18). Wine is also the symbol of the peace between God and humanity, after the dark hours of exile: "Again you shall plant vineyards on the mountains of Samaria; the planters shall plant, and shall enjoy the fruit" (Jer 31:5; Hos 2:24).

At Cana the wine becomes a symbol of Christ, a symbol of the messianic peace and joy personified in Jesus. In fact, its origin is wrapped in mystery ("he didn't know where it came from," Jn 2:9) just as Jesus says of himself in the discussion with the crowd in John 7:25-30 ("the One Who sent me, Whom you don't know"), and like the Spirit of whom "you don't know where it comes from or where it goes" (Jn 3:8).

Its quality is exceptional: "Every man first puts out the good wine...you've kept the good wine till now!" (Jn 2:10).

Jesus is the most perfect presence, he is the "choice wine" par excellence, the living and personal sign of the full divine benediction (Gen 49:11-12).

The water for Jewish ceremonial washings (Jn 2:6) is contrasted with the wine, a symbol of the definitive reality and the absolute truth.

What Happens to the Newlyweds of Cana?

Jesus frees them from a difficult situation, he does not ask, he gives simply, in great abundance. His presence, therefore, is not to be feared but rather desired. This is true for the marriage of Cana and for those which are celebrated in all the villages and cities—great and small—of the world.

Open the doors to Christ! Do not be afraid of him! This is a cry addressed to all human hearts. Why not make it resound, with a deeper and more intense vibration, in the hearts of a couple at the moment in which they begin their journey of love together? Here is the meaning, so simple yet so extraordinarily rich, of the sacrament of Matrimony, on which the life of the spouses is founded! It is not simply a sacred rite, a liturgical celebration of the Church. In it faith discovers, finds and rejoices in a particular presence, the presence of Jesus, the spouse of the Church and of our souls.

Only in terms of a personal encounter does the believer contemplate, celebrate and live. Christ calls us by name, he meets us and, by means of the sacrament, forms a covenant of love with us.

With what joy and amazement does the great bishop of Milan, my predecessor St. Ambrose write: "You have manifested yourself to me, face to face, O Christ: I have found you in your sacraments" (*Apologia of the prophet David*, 12:58).

The same can be said of the sacrament of Christian marriage. Vatican II reiterated it in the Constitution *Gaudium et Spes*: "For as God of old made himself present to his people through a covenant of love and fidelity, so now the Savior of men and the Spouse of the Church comes into the lives of Christian spouses through the sacrament of matrimony" (GS 48; EV 1, 1472).

Jesus meets the Christian spouses: it is not so much the couple who, in receiving the sacrament, go to meet Christ, as Christ himself who takes the initiative, calls the couple, invites them and makes them participants in his love for the Church.

The sacrament affirms that love of God in Christ who is offered first and without conditions: "So we have known and believe the love that God has for us.... We love because he first loved us" (1 Jn 4:16-19).

The sacrament is, therefore, the living presence of Jesus Christ, the presence of his love which gives itself (as witnessed in the most sublime manner on the cross) and which is diffused among believers by the action of the Holy Spirit. The sacrament is an operative sign of the sacrificial love of Jesus: a *sign* because it reveals, *operative* because he gives it to humanity.

And the fundamental sacrament of this love is the Eucharist. The Eucharist is the sacrifice of the new and eternal covenant, the sacrament, under the form of consecrated bread and wine, of the body offered and the blood poured out. It is the sacrifice and sacrament which generates the fraternal communion of the Church and animates its apostolic and missionary activity until the glorious coming of the Lord.

Every sacrament—and thus Matrimony too—is intimately linked to the Eucharist, and reveals and communicates the sacrificial love of the Redeemer, the love of the Shepherd who gives his life for the sheep.

In his apostolic exhortation, *Familiaris Consortio*, John Paul II explains how the love of the spouses reaches its fullness, its complete truth, by becoming "conjugal charity," which is the proper and specific way in which "the spouses participate in and are called to live the very charity of Christ who gave himself on the cross" (n. 13).

We have already seen that some details of the Cana narrative shed light on the relationship existing between the Eucharist and Christian marriage. The spouses receive the gift of the chosen and abundant wine: the sacrament of Matrimony is a sign and place of a new love saved by Christ on the cross.

Love of the Crucified

In order to define and study the relationship between the Eucharist and the Christian family, it is necessary to reflect on the love of the Crucified. *Familiaris Consortio* defines the couple who are celebrating Matrimony, in singularly incisive terms: "Spouses are therefore the permanent reminder to the Church of what happened on the Cross" (n.13).

I will limit myself to pointing out the fundamental characteristics of Christ's love, as they appear on the cross, in the Eucharist and in the sacrament of Matrimony.

1. *A first characteristic* defines what can be called the precise logic of love, its originating, original, and indispensable truth: the *logic of giving*. Human experience itself demonstrates it in an immediate and indisputable manner: to love is to give, to love is to give ourselves.

Where there is love, there is gift. Where there is gift there is love. By means of love the person tends to become one being *with* the other, and even more a unique being *for* the other.

Love is the interior spiritual energy that animates and sustains the person, and it cannot be otherwise, if to love means to give and if the gift places the one who offers and the one who receives in intimate communion (*a communion of persons*). The logic of giving finds a singular form of fulfillment in love, and likewise in family love.

In marriage the total gift and the communion are profoundly personal. The Council says: "This love is an eminently human one since it is directed from one person to another through an affection of the will; it involves the good of the whole person, and therefore can enrich the expressions of body and mind with a unique dignity, ennobling these expressions as special ingredients and signs of the friendship distinctive of marriage" (GS 49). The Council expresses a universal experience of men and women who love one another in marriage: they do not give only what they "have" but also what they "are."

"This conjugal communion sinks its roots in the natural complementarity that exists between man and woman, and is nurtured through the personal willingness of the spouses to share their entire life-project, what they have and what they are: for this reason such communion is the fruit and sign of a profoundly human need" (*Familiaris Consortio*, 19).

No one has loved us as the Lord Jesus has. No one has given themselves as he has, no on has ever realized a communion as intense and profound as he. The breadth of his love, of his gift, of his communion, is fulfilled in the sacrifice of the cross, of which the Eucharist—"sacrament of love"—is the daily memorial of the Church and in the Church.

"Now before the festival of the Passover Jesus, knowing that his hour had come to leave this world for the Father, having loved his own in the world, he loved them to the end" (Jn 13:1). The words of John are taken up by the apostle Paul who exclaims: "(He) loved me and gave himself for me" (Gal 2:20).

This love to the end, this love made of total sacrificial self-giving, is present and operative in the Eucharist, in the body given and the blood poured out for us. And it is present and operative in the sacrament of Matrimony, a divine instrument for confirming, purifying, saving, and renewing the love of self-giving and communion between Christian spouses.

Referring to the human need for conjugal communion, the fruit and sign of self-giving love, *Familiaris Consortio* states: "But in the Lord Christ God takes up this human need, confirms it, purifies it and elevates it, leading it to perfection through the sacrament of matrimony. The Holy Spirit who is poured out in the sacramental celebration offers Christian couples the gift of a new communion of love that is the living and real image of that unique unity which makes of the Church the indivisible Mystical Body of the Lord Jesus" (n. 19).

Grace becomes a law of life for the spouses; it is the interior energy that calls them, stimulates them and helps them to mature day by day in their communion of love. "The gift of the Spirit is a commandment of life for Christian spouses and at the same time a stimulating impulse, so that every day they may progress towards an ever richer union with each other on all levels—of body, of character, of heart, of intelligence and will, of soul—revealing in this way to the Church and to the world the new communion of love, given by the grace of Christ" (*Familiaris Consortio*, n. 19).

This love, which is self-giving and is rooted in the sacrament by which it is nourished, is then destined to guide, shape and encourage interpersonal relationships between parents and children, brothers and sisters. The love between spouses becomes family love, or rather, paternal and maternal, filial, fraternal.

Love, which is self-giving and communion, germinates and grows not only in ties of flesh and blood but also in those deriving from the love of the crucified and risen Christ.

2. *A second characteristic* of the love of the glorious Crucified Jesus is the *purification and sanctification of humanity*, called to be united in a pure and holy Church. The Apostle writes: "Christ loved the church and gave himself up for her, in order to make her holy by cleansing her with the washing of water by the word, so as to present the church to himself in splendor, without a spot or wrinkle or anything of the kind—yes, so that she may be holy and without blemish" (Eph 5:25-27).

It is the same purpose willed by Jesus for the Eucharist, source of pardon for sins and of holiness. It is the same purpose toward which the sacrament of Matrimony tends with the gift of a purified and sanctifying love. We read from the Council: "This love God has judged worthy of special gifts, healing, perfecting and exalting gifts of grace and charity" (GS 49).

Thus there emerge two aspects of the Christian experience of marriage and family life, intimately linked with one another: permanent conversion from sin and holy and sanctifying reconciliation.

The journey of all spouses and families is often laborious, difficult and disappointing. Among the many evils that threaten and ruin the joy of couples and families, the worst is sin: not only as the inevitable limitation for all human beings, but as a moral disorder. The hearts of spouses, of parents, as well as the hearts of children, of brothers and sisters, are too often hearts of stone, full of greed. The capacity to love authentically, and therefore to give, to be in communion, tends to disappear, allowing egoism to prevail. The other person—husband or wife, daughter or son—is no longer an object of a love that gives but rather an object of an egoism that wants to conquer, to the point of using the other as a thing. The original beauty of personal dignity is disfigured. Egoism divides, opposes, separates: sin becomes the cause of the disintegration of both the couple and the family.

Herein lies the difficulty in understanding one another even within the walls of one's home. A little tower of Babel is erected which brings confusion, misunderstanding, and conflict.

Deep in the heart of each family member, however, remains the lively need to correspond to the ideal of love, to its truth of self-donation and communion. And the desire for reconciliation is born. Only those who make the journey of conversion can be won over by this desire and rediscover and live anew the truth of that conjugal and familial love.

But the path of permanent conversion passes through the Eucharist. By participating in the sacrifice of the Eucharist, spouses and Christian families are in fact called to a daily conversion, with an invitation that is a grace and stimulus to detach their hearts from vain and empty "idols" and direct them to the living God.

Happy the family that, letting itself be guided by the

Spirit, participates daily in the Eucharist! "You hear it said that every time the sacrifice is offered, the death, resurrection and ascension of the Lord, and thus the remission of sin, are symbolized, and yet you do not receive the bread of life every day? Those who are wounded seek a cure. For us, being subject to sin is a wound: the cure is the venerable and heavenly sacrament" (St. Ambrose, *De Sacramentis*, V, 4, 25).

Besides testifying to the need for a permanent conversion from sin, the experience of spouses and of the Christian family testifies to the need for a progressive maturation of love in all its values.

In reality, those who love discover in themselves an uncontrollable need to intensify that love more and more: those who love desire an ever greater, more beautiful and more joyful love. Is it an illusion or a utopia? The Christian faith has no doubts and answers categorically that it is a need of the human heart. God himself wills that spouses love one another and love others with the heart of God, with the love of Jesus. The love of spouses is "human" because it involves the person in his/her entirety, in spirit, affection and body.

In and through this human love, however, a supernatural love is made present and operative, the love of God, Creator and Father, the love of Jesus Christ. It is the love which Jesus lived, in particular, in the giving of himself on the cross and which, through the Eucharist and the specific gift of the sacrament of Matrimony, confirms, purifies, uplifts, perfects and transfigures conjugal and family love. It is the love which becomes "sacrament" or, in other words, a sign and place of divine love.

In 1970, Pope Paul VI said to the Èquipes Notre Dame: "Every Christian knows that human love is a good thing at its origins, and if, just as with any other human sentiment, it is wounded and deformed by sin, it will find its salvation and redemption in Christ. On the other hand, isn't this perhaps what twenty centuries of Christian history have taught us? How many spouses have found the way of holiness in the married life, in this communion of life which is the only one founded on a sacrament! The work of the Holy Spirit (cf Titus 3:5), the regeneration in Baptism makes us new creatures (cf Gal 6:15), so that 'we might walk in newness of life' (Rom 6:4). In this great work of renewing all things in Christ, matrimony—it too purified and renewed—becomes a new reality, the sacrament of the new covenant.... Two Christians desire to marry; St. Paul exhorts them: 'you are not your own' (1 Cor 6:19). Members of Christ, joined in the Lord, their union is made 'in the Lord,' like that of the Church, and therefore 'is a great mystery' (Eph 5:32), a sign that not only represents the mystery of the union of Christ with the Church, but comprises and radiates it through the grace of the Holy Spirit who is its life-giving soul. For it is truly this same love, that is, the divine love, which he communicates to us, so that we may love him and love one another with this divine love: 'Just as I have loved you, you also should love one another' (Jn 13:34). For Christian spouses the expressions of affection are penetrated by this love which they draw from the heart of God. And even if the human source of love threatens to dry up, the divine source is without end, just like the immeasurable greatness of the love of God. We can then grasp toward how intimate, intense and rich a communion marital charity tends. An inner spiritual reality transforms the spouses' life together into what could be called —according to the authoritative teaching of the Council —the 'domestic Church' (LG 11), 'a real cell of the Church,' as our beloved predecessor John XXIII already said during your pilgrimage on May 3, 1959; an essential, germinative cell, the smallest and yet the most fundamental of the ecclesial organism."

3. The last words cited from the discourse of Paul VI help us to understand a *third characteristic* of the sacrificial love of Jesus crucified, who through the Eucharist and the sacrament of Christian marriage lives in the love of the Christian family. This third characteristic is *ecclesiality*, the connection with the Church.

On the cross Jesus loves and gives himself to the Church with a love so intense and a self-giving so profound as to constitute the effective reality of the Church. As the beloved spouse of Christ, the Church is born from his wounded side, it is the living fruit and permanent sign of his self-giving love. St. Thomas writes: "The Church springs from the wounded side of Christ crucified" (*Summa Theologiae*, III, 64, 2, ad 3). As the constitutive reality of the Church, love is presented each day anew in the Eucharist and in the other sacraments.

By participating in the Eucharist, and with the grace of the sacrament of Matrimony, Christian spouses and the family become a domestic Church, a manifestation and, in its own way, a realization of the great Church of Christ. Thus, the twofold and unitive activity of the Church, born of Christ who died and has risen, cannot be alien to the Christian family.

We can consider, first of all, liturgical activity which calls the Church to sing the glory of God. At the same time, we acknowledge apostolic-missionary activity which calls the Church to reveal and communicate the salvation of Christ to all people.

a) In virtue of Baptism and, even more, of the sacrament of Christian marriage, the Christian family and couple have the grace and the responsibility to share with the whole Church its *mission of liturgy and worship*. In other words, there is a kind of domestic priesthood which qualifies and binds spouses and the Christian family as such, for the purpose of giving glory to the Lord, of encountering him in the prayer and sphere of the family, and by means of the typical realities of married and family life.

In this way couples and families become a temple of the Spirit. Joys and sorrows, difficulties and hopes, work and rest, promises and disappointments, birth and death, etc., all become a spiritual sacrifice pleasing to God, in Jesus Christ, through the Holy Spirit.

It is in reference to the concrete, daily life of couples and families that the following passage of Vatican Council II can be understood: "For all their works, prayers and apostolic endeavors, their ordinary married and family life, their daily occupations, their physical and mental relaxation, if carried out in the Spirit, and even the hardships of life, if patiently borne—all these become 'spiritual sacrifices acceptable to God through Jesus Christ.' Together with the offering of the Lord's body, they are most fittingly offered in the celebration of the Eucharist. Thus, as those everywhere who adore in holy activity, the laity consecrate the world to God" (LG 34).

A Christian family that participates in the Eucharist cannot help but love prayer which, in all its forms, finds in the Eucharist—the greatest and most sublime prayer of Jesus to the Father—its beginning and fulfillment.

Adoration "in spirit and truth" continues on its course from Church to home, from liturgy to life. In particular, Christian parents find in the Eucharist the strength and light to help them become teachers of prayer to their children.

This prayer, understood as a dialogue of love and intimate communion of life with God, is the climax of the entire work of education. "It is particularly in the Christian family, enriched by the grace and office of the sacrament of Christian marriage, that children should be taught from their early years to have a knowledge of God according to the faith received in Baptism, to worship him and to love their neighbor" (*Gravissimum Educationis*, 3).

b) Thanks to the Eucharist and the sacrament of Matrimony, the Christian family is not only "the domestic sanctuary of the Church" (*Apostolicam Actuositatem*, 11), but also *an apostolic and missionary community* that shares in the Church's pastoral activity, its mission to be a sign and instrument of salvation in the world. It is an explicit invitation to Christian families to be present and active in the Church, to dedicate themselves to building up the kingdom of God in history.

The Church knows that it has been saved by Christ and only by Christ, and rejoices in this fact. However, the salvific love of the Lord is so effective as to make the Church his collaborator in the work of salvation which continues in history. Likewise, the Christian family is saved by Christ and sent by him as a community of salvation. "In turn, the Christian family is grafted into the mystery of the Church to such a degree as to become a sharer, in its own way, in the saving mission proper to the Church; by virtue of the sacrament, Christian married couples and parents 'in their state and way of life have their own special gift among the People of God' (LG 11). For this reason they not only *receive* the love of Christ and become a *saved* community, but they are also called upon to *communicate* Christ's love to their brethren, thus becoming a *saving* community. In this way, while the Christian family is a fruit and sign of the supernatural fecundity of the Church, it stands also as a symbol, witness and participant of the Church's motherhood" (*Familiaris Consortio*, 49).

The first source of the Christian family's missionary activity is the Eucharist. In fact, while it ensures the most intimate "communion" among the members of the family, it establishes and encourages a greater "openness" toward others. Eucharistic charity which makes them "one heart and one spirit" continues to urge on ("the charity of Christ impels us") the family members to feel the spiritual and material needs of all their sisters and brothers. We can truly say that the Eucharist is the soul of every apostolate.

"The Eucharist is a fountain of charity. In the Eucharistic gift of charity the Christian family finds the foundation and soul of its 'communion' and its 'mission': by partaking in the Eucharistic bread, the different members of the Christian family become one body, which reveals and shares in the wider unity of the Church. Their sharing in the Body of Christ that is 'given up' and in his blood that is 'shed' becomes a never-ending source of missionary and apostolic dynamism for the Christian family" (*Familiaris Consortio*, 57).

Naturally, it is not possible to go into detail about the different ways that families and Christian couples can participate in the apostolic and missionary work of the Church. It suffices to recall how the various works—from evangelization and catechesis to participation in the life of liturgy and prayer, from charity towards our brothers and sisters in the faith to charity towards everyone, especially the "least," from the various forms of service in the Church to the task of building a more human society— can be summed up in one fundamental task: *to give witness to and bring communion into one's own surroundings.*

Communion is born and grows in and with love. Love is the "heart" of conjugal and family life, and thus spouses and families are the first builders of that communion of love which constitutes the root and foundation of social life, whether in the civil community or in the ecclesial community itself.

Christian spouses are called to this witness by the grace of the sacrament. This grace binds them indissolubly with the same bond of love by which Christ, the spouse, is united to the Church, making it his bride and his body.

In the Eucharist the family discovers the originating source of its communion of love, the example and commandment. "In this sacrifice of the new and eternal Covenant, Christian spouses encounter the source from which their own marriage covenant flows, is interiorly structured and continuously renewed" (*Familiaris Consortio*, 57).

The covenant of love between God and his people is revealed, lived and presented to the world in existence itself and through the covenant of love between spouses and in families. This is the Gospel that humanity wants to hear, because love makes us live. Humanity wants to live, grow in life and spread it!

The task of the couple and of the family in the humanization of the world becomes irreplaceable. It is their mission "to guard, reveal and communicate love" (*Familiaris Consortio*, 17) in the first place by the witness of their lives.

There is no family, however poor or weighed down with difficulties, that does not possess within itself a tremendous resource of love. There is no family that can feel exempted from the task of "humanizing" the world with the strength of love alone.

In a deservedly famous passage, Tertullian, the ancient Christian writer of Africa, has expressed well the greatness of the married life lived in the love of Christ. While rereading it, let us think of the many Christian couples who, in our country and throughout the African continent, still give witness today to these words.

"How can I describe the happiness of a marriage celebrated by the Church, confirmed by the offering, sealed by the blessing announced by the angels and which the Father sanctions?

"What a beautiful couple formed by two believers, united in one hope, in one ideal, united by the same way of life and the same availability!

"Both brethren and servants of the same Lord, without any division either of flesh or of spirit, they pray together, kneel together and fast together.

"They exchange teachings, exhort and support one another.

"They are together at the sacred celebration, together at the Lord's supper, together in trials, in persecutions, in joy.

"For them there is no danger that one might hide from the other, avoid the other, or be a burden to the other.

"With good will they visit the sick, and help the needy. They give alms generously, carry out their daily tasks tirelessly. Certainly they do not know what hidden signs of the cross they might be!

"They give thanks without any reserve, they bless one another. They recite psalms and hymns with alternate voices, they compete with one another to see who can better sing the praises of God.

"In seeing and hearing this, Christ is pleased and bestows his peace on those spouses. Where there are two of them, there, too, is Christ" (*Ad Uxorem*, II, 9).

Mary the Woman

We conclude our meditation on the intimate bond between the Eucharist and the Christian family by returning to contemplate the scene of the miracle at Cana. Among the "disciples" who "believed" in Jesus and accepted the manifestation of his "glory," there is Mary. She is the first to believe, and she believes with the most fervent faith. More than any other disciple she is intro-

duced into the understanding of the "sign" and participates in the salvific love of her Son: "His mother said to
the servants, 'Do whatever he tells you'" (John 2:5). Even
in the supreme hour of the cross, she will be near Jesus,
both as one redeemed and as co-redemptrix.

The presence of Mary at Cana is an invitation to
rediscover the special role which, according to the eternal
plan of divine love and the diverse demands of history,
women play in marriage and in the family, in the Church
and in society. Mary intervenes serenely and courageously. It is an implicit but clear exhortation to decisively
overcome the unacceptable expressions of women's inferiority with regard to men. Woman must discover, together with the irreplaceable values of motherhood and
education in the family, the many gifts God has offered
her for the good of the family and of all humanity.

At Cana Mary is a model of the style of *sharing*: she
discovers the uneasiness of the spouses and makes it her
own, their suffering becomes hers: "Jesus' mother said to
him, 'They have no wine'" (Jn 2:3). These words are not
simply an affirmation or observation. Rather they mean:
"We have no more wine."

This intense participation of Mary in human suffering is still true today, in the face of the difficulties, sorrows, trials, and even the tragedies of the family. She is
the mother of the Church and is also mother of the
domestic churches.

We can thus invoke her by praying:

*"O Mary, we want to entrust to you all Christian families.
Help them to live again the love to which Jesus bore witness by
giving himself on the cross and which he unceasingly offers in the
Eucharist to spouses, parents and children."*

Report to the International Eucharistic Congress,
Nairobi, August 12, 1985

CHAPTER 6

How to Become Neighbors

To the Young People of the Parish: Who Is My Neighbor?

Dear young people:

The freshness and spontaneity of your letter impressed me; however, it also embarrassed me somewhat. It is not easy to answer. You turn to me as to an expert on charity, wanting to know what concrete action you can take, at your age, to "become neighbors."

It all started some weeks ago when your pastor, in concluding the year of catechesis, invited you to prepare to publicly renew your profession of faith next year. Your pastor rightly explained that faith finds its fullest expression in charity. He spoke to you about the many pastoral initiatives of our diocese which center around the theme of charity. He also told you that the Archbishop wrote a letter entitled: "Become a Neighbor." This is why you turn to me as to an expert. I would not want to disillusion you, but I do not believe myself to be an expert, in fact, I believe that no one in the world is an expert on charity. The Holy Spirit is the only real expert. He slowly introduces into the experience of charity those who pray much and let themselves be guided, in the dialogue of faith, to listen ever more closely to his voice. Here, you see, the suggestions which the pastor gives you are—for many of you—set against the background of a serene moment in your life. At home, even if there is some friction, you feel welcome. You have simple and joyful relationships with friends. You nourish a trusting openness toward the world of educators. But I wait to see you some months from now: a lot will have changed in you!

You will feel that your relationships with other young men and women are troubled and upset. You will find it hard to speak at home of yourself and your problems, and will close up like a clam. You will begin to be suspicious of the guidance that your educators offer you. I imagine you will find a justification for all this. You will say that your parents are oppressing you, that they don't want you to grow, that they would like to push you back into the world of childhood. You will say that priests no longer understand you, that they continue to suggest a form of education that does not take into account the new and important experiences you are having. And so you will be tempted to shake off all formative relationships, while feeling from time to time the great need for conversation, confidence and direction.

The reasons you will give do have some truth to them, but they do not touch the heart of the problem. They only shed light on some external aspects or some consequences of the real problem. And the problem is this: you are changing! Your life which up to now has been fairly smooth has been affected by new encounters. Your way of desiring has become restless and complex. In the end you yourself do not understand what you want at times.

The risk that can arise is to consider all that is hap-

pening within you as a "given" and not as a stimulus to a
formative commitment. The very word "formation" makes
you wrinkle your nose because it seems to introduce some
external constraints and laws into a reality of desires and
searches that you want to live in originality, freedom and
spontaneity.

But will it be possible to realize such spontaneity by
rejecting formation and the educational effort? Will a
desire that is not critically evaluated, not corrected, not
formed, succeed in really remaining free and authentic?
Could it not happen that the desire leads to what seems
the easiest, what gives immediate success, that which allows us to do what everyone else is doing without too
many scruples? Yes, it could happen. This is why it is
important to be convinced that the new life which ex-
plodes in adolescence is not to be abandoned to itself and
its own impulses but must be given a lot of attention.

I will seek the assistance of a biblical example. You
all know the parable of the prodigal son, narrated in the
fifteenth chapter of Luke. As the son returns, it is enough
for the father to see his profile from far away, and at once
he knows it is his son. He runs to meet him, throws
himself on his son's neck, and organizes a great celebration. The older son, instead, is irritated by the return of
his brother and doesn't even want to go into the banquet
hall.

The father gave this very intense, very merciful, very
generous welcome because in his desires he always thought
of his younger son. He kept the memory of this son's eyes,
his words, and his gestures. The older son, instead, did not
reserve even a small corner of his feelings for a vague
remembrance of his brother. A desire cultivated with constancy generates a constructive encounter while a neglected desire causes miserable pettiness to explode.

In whom, then, should the prodigal son have more

trust: the father or the older brother? Certainly in the one who, having kept him in his heart, intimately understands his actions and desires, even if they are wrong.

I am coming to the conclusion. If, at your age, it is important to foster a serene and mutual dialogue between yourselves and your educators, it follows that the basic closeness (being neighbor) required of you should begin with those who, while they might weigh on you somewhat, or appear possessive or oppressive at times, have the gifts of wisdom and love to offer you formative incentives.

Now you will say that the Archbishop abandons you to yourselves, takes sides with the adults, is apprehensive about you. I hope that you understand the seriousness of what I have said to you. If you still have some doubts, we could talk about them together, even during the next pastoral visit. Let us keep the dialogue open and entrust it to mutual prayer.

To Juliana, a Widow: On the Solitude of the Elderly and Being Neighbors

Dear Juliana,

Your letter sheds light on one of the most serious problems of our society: the problem of the elderly. You present it with great delicacy and serenity; basically, you feel you are privileged. Your children never leave you by yourself, they welcome you into their families for long periods of time. But your thought turns to the majority of those your age who are tossed about in family situations that are less comfortable, less welcoming and serene, people for whom homes are hard to find and to live in with sufficient satisfaction.

There is some concern about yourself, too. Now your health is still fairly good, but what will happen when, either gradually or suddenly, you lose your independence?

Here we touch on the problem of a different conception and structuring of family life. It is not necessarily a matter of reintroducing the ancient patriarchal family, but neither can we be content with those restricted forms to which families are being reduced in western countries.

We also need to emphasize the need for social health care structures which reach the families and offer adequate assistance to the growing number of elderly persons in present society and, even more importantly, in the society of the future.

Each of these topics would take up many pages. I limit myself to some observations that you make on the theme of solitude, which you note as a serious threat to the life of the elderly person. The serenity which characterized the first lines of your letter permits you to achieve a particular refinement in considering the subject of solitude.

For you it is not only a matter of hours spent alone and a renunciation of forms of social life to which you are accustomed. You describe solitude in more subtle terms: it means understanding that the world of the family, of society and, even to some extent, of the Church in which we are immersed is no longer a world for us, it no longer completely "fits us" and we no longer "fit" it. We almost become persons without a world, without a society, without communication between what we carry inside us and what is lived, proclaimed exteriorly.

I would begin by explaining that solitude, which is certainly painful especially in its initial impact, can also contain a secret richness which must be discovered. This solitude of yours can also draw on your gift of wisdom. You are now able to approach persons and events from the perspective of this "wisdom," your capacity to savor, to weigh, to appreciate things. You have seen some myths dissolve over the long years of life. You have recognized the pettiness of many proposals which at first glance seemed serious and generous. You have learned to perceive what is truly important and lasting within the great and small events of life.

Is this wise way of looking at life usually characteristic of young people or adults? Does everyone enjoy this simple and spontaneous profundity in communicating what has been lived, discovered and suffered? No. This is why solitude comes: not because something has diminished within you but because something has arisen in you that is so great, so beautiful, so new that it is not yet understood in all its tremendous fruitfulness.

Perhaps at this point we can see what it means for the elderly to "be neighbor" to others. It means not resigning ourselves to holding everything inside, but finding every opportunity to communicate to others this wisdom which has matured in the heart, not being surprised that others are at first unable to understand even remotely this new way of seeing reality.

Do not bury yourself in solitude; do not become discouraged over misunderstandings. Continue instead to become a wise and gentle neighbor to your family members and to everyone else you meet.

For both the young person and the adult there is a mutual duty to "be neighbor." There is the duty to remain close to the elderly not only out of pity, or to appease one's conscience, or to offer help, but to learn from them the wisdom which is like the fullness of the autumn season, rich in colors and shades.

I am very grateful to you for what you have taught me and I ask for myself, too, the wisdom which God has granted to your years.

To Stephanie: No Excuses for Not "Being Neighbor"

Dear Stephanie,

Perhaps my letter will take you by surprise. In fact, it is not a response to a letter of yours or to a specific question.

It is my own initiative, in which I want to tell you with meditative calm some things which I would have liked to tell you more hurriedly yesterday evening after the Mass celebrated in your parish during my pastoral visit.

I first met you while conversing with the youth group, and then I saw that you were chosen by the group to present an intention for the prayer of the faithful. I don't remember the exact words, only the sense. You were asking that each young person might know how to give of their own time and energies for the service of their brothers and sisters in the Christian community and in society.

I obviously appreciate every effort by which young people seek to overcome even a small part of their egoism. But yesterday it was a prayer in which, in some way, you meant to outline not only the journey of small human struggles against egoism, but an ideal of Christian life for which you invoked the grace and blessing of the Father.

It is on this point that I want to reflect with you. Please excuse my directness, but that prayer was mistaken because it did not treat of the ideal of Christian life. When dedication to others is in question, we cannot speak of having to give a little or a lot. Interpersonal self-giving is of its nature absolute and unconditional.

A deeper consideration of the relationships between persons should help you understand that they do not require only this or that thing, this or that service so that one can evaluate the time and energy that must be employed to meet their needs.

The human person needs many things, an explicit sign of a friendship, an interest, a welcome, none of which can be exhausted in the concrete action performed but must surpass it to become the fruitful root of other, new actions and of other more intense services.

You seriously believe this, and are thus capable of finding the reason for the absoluteness which accompanies the self-giving of one person to another. You know that each person is not a measure of the good of others, but together with the others, with humility and commitment, seeks that mysterious and divine good dwelling in each person, conferring on him or her an absolute dignity, a drive toward freedom, a desire for the infinite. In fact, you do not believe only in a generic God, but you have had the incomparable gift of knowing the God of Jesus Christ, that is, the God who in Christ has given himself totally and radically to man, to the point of death on the cross: the God who has willed that we be with him in the fullness of the resurrection.

Perhaps you are frightened by these very demanding ideals. Perhaps you are unable to grasp the full meaning of some of the words I have written to you. With this in mind, I want to outline for you some steps of a journey you could make in the direction which, with much fraternal concern and simplicity, I have just indicated.

The first step is that of beginning to look at all the persons you meet with new eyes, not thinking only of some need they have or some pleasing or displeasing aspect. Too often we have already labeled the person whom we see every day. It happens to all of us, even to me. We are lazy and we hold to the truth of our first judgment, expecting only to confirm it, not to change it. Worse yet, when we meet someone, we immediately think of something we can get out of them, spurred on by the often unconscious impulses to self-centered exploitation of others which arise in our hearts. This is why new eyes are needed. They allow us to look at others, not superficially or greedily, but with attention to the hidden questions of the one whom we meet.

The second step is to make the resources of your faith bear greater fruit. You know that the God of Jesus has spoken to us in Jesus and that this living word is preserved in the Christian community. Seek to confront yourself often with this word. Choose a passage from the word of God each day and let it motivate your daily behavior. You will see how many jolts, how many changes, how many crises will result from this practice.

The third step is to acquire—with humility, with strong adaptability, and also with much creative responsibility—the good habit of accepting others, of greeting them, of paying attention even to their smallest needs, of exercising that mutual pardon which, though mixed with many defects, you will often see practiced in your family and Christian community.

A fourth step is that of welcoming, as a powerful sign of the Holy Spirit for the young people of our time, those various initiatives which all together come under the title of voluntary service. I cannot explain the juridical aspects and concrete functioning of these initiatives. Undoubtedly you have heard of them. Perhaps you have already done something of this type. I see in all this a real school that prepares for a new way of responding, even on an international level, to the problems of relationships between persons.

Finally there is the last step, which seals and gives authenticity to the rest of the journey: it is that of understanding the relatively stable, complete and concrete way in which you can live and offer your whole life as a total gift of yourself to others. This very important phenomenon is referred to with a word that unfortunately has become ambiguous. It is the matter of a "vocation," which some consider a privilege for certain categories of Christians.

I cannot speak to you at length on this topic. I cannot tell you what means to use to discover and cultivate your own vocation. I only tell you that each baptized person is called by God to live not only for him or herself but for others. Each of us is called to live our vocation for others after the example of Jesus and with the power of the Holy Spirit, in a concrete form of life which is the same for all in the fullness of faith and the heroism of charity. This vocation differs for each one according to the tasks and functions he/she carries out in the Christian community so as to realize the mission of the Church in the world. The important thing is that each one can say that the road chosen is the most sincere, most prayerful, most deeply-felt and fruitful way of belonging to others rather than to self.

For you who live this season of youth, being neighbor means all this. I ask that you not become frightened, but be enthusiastic about the concern for others to which you are called.

To Alice, Whose Husband Is Seriously Ill

Dear Alice,

With this letter I would like not only to converse with you, but almost to enter into your home so as to spend a moment of comfort and prayer with your whole family. I enter on tiptoe and with a bit of embarrassment. I know that your husband has been ill for some time and has now reached the point where he has been rendered completely immobile; only his obstinate will to survive sustains him.

From the letter which you have written to me, I am able to envision all the affectionate care, the acts of patience and of courage with which you and your children surround the sick one. But at a certain point in your letter, I see some anguished questions appear: "Why this interminable illness? Does it still make sense to live like this, can't we somehow shorten a life which seems to have lost every human quality?" These are formidable questions.

The problems that these questions raise are numerous and involve many interacting elements. For example, to answer them properly, we would need to make the dialogue between morality and science more fruitful. We would need to improve the public structures of hospitals and other institutions which make possible the care of the incurably ill, without placing the whole burden on the families. We would also need to recreate more supportive and fraternal relationships among different families (without useless laments for the ancient patriarchal family) so that the weight of the care of these sick persons, shared by friendly families, may become more bearable.

I am unable to dwell on these very serious topics. I limit myself to a brief word about a phrase which you have written almost fleetingly in your letter.

You say that the most difficult suffering that you are experiencing at this time is that of no longer being able to communicate with your husband. Different persons have written the same thing to me about their seriously handicapped child. I would like to invite you, very fraternally, to reflect on the real dimensions of human communication. Try to remember the times in which communication with your husband seemed rich and gratifying. Think also of the very simple word with which we ask a family member for a glass of water or for some other service. Normally we feel the need to add "please"; in this way we impress on the communication among persons a dynamism that goes beyond the simple exchange of things that are useful to us. Even a glass of water is no longer something which turns the person asked into an instrument to serve us. Rather, it becomes a gift which we await with hope and trust from the favor and selflessness of the other.

Think then of the deepest, most serious, most decisive communications you have shared with your husband by means of the mysterious dialogue of love, of the exchange of ideas about future plans for the family, of confidences about the good things or concerns regarding the behavior of your children. Who knows how many times, during these dialogues, these exchanges, and these communications, you understood that only silence allowed you to truly communicate. And, since you are believers, you also understood that only hands joined in prayer became the mysterious point of encounter between your hearts and your thoughts.

In short, you felt truly close only when you knew how to recognize and respect a distance that there is between persons, a distance which is filled by the one closeness that never lessens, closeness to God. Now communication with your husband is made only of long periods of silence and hands folded in prayer. It may seem that you are separated by a great distance, while in reality you are achieving the greatest closeness. You are living a mysterious fullness of communication which gives meaning to everything that you, your husband and your children have said to one another throughout your lives, and which also gives meaning to this long period of suffering and agony. The communication you are living is the most real because it is totally selfless, it does not seek anything from the other. In fact, I dare say that this communication becomes the convincing verification of all the others, it clarifies whether the preceding communications masked some subtle interest or whether they were always enlightened from within by the desire for gift, for self-giving, for selflessness.

I have written these words to you with much suffering, because I know that words can become useful or troublesome at certain moments in life. Now I too will cease talking. I will remain close to all of you, and make myself your neighbor with a presence composed of silence and prayer.

To Joseph, Who Just Returned from the Hospital: Closeness in Sickness

Dear Joseph,

First of all I thank you for having accepted my invitation to write to me after your stay in the hospital. When I came to see you during your illness, I was able to exchange only a few words with you. It is a torment for me as bishop always to have to run here and there without being able to remain with others as long as I would like. The few words you spoke to me, however, interested me very much; this is why I invited you to put them in writing. And now that I read them in your letter, I find them even more interesting.

The letter does not speak of the meaning of sickness and suffering, or of the problem of renewing hospital structures, even though these are serious problems and should be treated when speaking of the need to be close to one who is ill. I myself will not speak of these problems, also because they seem out of proportion to the few lines of this letter.

In addition, you do not present illness (as many other persons consider it) as an interval in life, a kind of parentheses to be closed as soon as possible because there is nothing good inside. Most people think that good things are only to be found at home in the more normal and active moments of life. You, instead, write to me about some discoveries you have made within the time and rhythm of your illness.

What you tell me has to do with closeness. Your letter

sketches for me a kind of twofold, converging closeness. There is the initial closeness to others which you experienced: illness has provided you with new insights into yourself and others.

A first approach to these insights, still somewhat superficial and basic, is the discovery that we need others. You especially, who are used to acting autonomously, have sometimes felt tempted to pretend to be able to do everything by yourself. Your illness, instead, has made you understand that at times you can do nothing without the dedicated help of others.

More interesting still is a second discovery: there is a sense of fraternity, a crumbling of social, cultural and economic barriers between persons who share the same experience of illness. They become friends quickly; they let go of labels; they help one another. They trust one another in many things. Because of these shared experiences, the period of illness becomes lighter and less monotonous.

There is a third approach which I find difficult to express. I will attempt to describe it this way: it involves drawing closer to what is more truly human in each of us by means of a simplification of the many things which complicate and even falsify our daily existence. This approach to reality involves a rediscovery of something simple and fundamental which enables us to feel truly human, even when many methods, which at first seemed indispensable for convincing ourselves to live a life truly worthy of a human person, fail.

Those who are believers can say that this approach is a rediscovered relationship with the mystery of God, who is no longer simply the God of rituals, laws and ecclesiastical customs, but "my God, the Father who loves me, who is always close to me, who has given himself a face and a name in the life and words of Jesus. But even those who do not believe explicitly draw close to something humanly

intense and mysterious which creates a real distance between the rhythms of daily life and the deeper rhythms
that nourish the thought, the paths of the intelligence
and the desires of the heart.

In view of these very beautiful discoveries, I see delin-
eated the second type of closeness to others which traces
the journey by which the various persons involved in the
area of health care must learn to draw close to those who
are sick. I am thinking especially of the hospital environment. Here too there are enormous problems of scientific research, of constant updating of personnel, of more
linear and effective modes of assigning duties; I am not
able to discuss such vast topics. In line with what you have
written to me, I see outlined a very important task for the
doctors, nurses, and volunteer workers who have access to
the wards. First of all, they should not make the reality of
the patient's need for them a burden, but should treat
the patient with great respect, preserving the dignity of
his/her person in every way. Then, whatever their religious belief, they should create the conditions in which
each sick person can intuit at least something of what you
have written to me in your letter.

And now I come to myself as bishop, and I make
reference to all the members of the Christian community,
in particular, priests, men and women religious, extraordinary ministers of the Eucharist for the sick, chaplains of
hospitals. What you have said awakens in me much remorse
and a great sense of responsibility. The Christian community, in the variety of its members and charisms, needs to
seriously consider the reality of illness. It needs to educate
persons to "live" their illness, to be very near
to and to be neighbor to those who are ill, whether at home
or in the hospital, so that the time of illness not be wasted
but rather become the "favorable" time, the time in
which a special visit of God is felt in the history of one of his
children.

I want to be well understood. I am not wishing that anyone be ill, not even myself, and I wish that you, Mr. Joseph, may truly be well. The last word of the Christian is always hope, victory over evil, the resurrection. What I want to wish everyone, however, is that, when it comes, the time of illness may truly become an experience in which we feel the victory of the love of God over all the forms of evil that torment our lives.

I send you a warm greeting. Farewell until we meet again, outside of the hospital.

To the Family of Laura and Francis: Closeness and Family

Dearest Laura and Francis,

Thank you for having helped me to reflect on the letter Become a neighbor, not only by participating in the various parish initiatives, but by sending some observations directly to me, just as many other families have done.

In your letter I find a theme that also appears frequently in the others. Your reaction to the pastoral program, "Become a neighbor," oscillates between two poles.

First you write that you feel profoundly shaken and almost put in crisis by what I have said in the pastoral letter and by all the initiatives which have grown up around it. It seems to you that you do too little, that you are far from that shining ideal of charity and generosity which has been placed before you.

However, you then conclude by saying that, honestly, you do not know what more you can do. You are not able to take more time for others from the already intense rhythm of your family life. You suggest that for you, "to be neighbor" means to continue to do what your family has done until now.

I am happy that there is in you this tension between

uneasiness and reconciliation. Such tension generates desires, new motives for discussion between parents and children, efforts to participate in charitable activities which, perhaps, laziness and superficiality may have caused you to neglect.

However, you write from a kind of erroneous perspective. You examine yourself on how you have been a neighbor to others only from the viewpoint of what you have "done." First you say that you need to do more, then you conclude that it is sufficient to do what you are already doing. I think that we must not limit ourselves to doing. For a family, "being neighbor" does not immediately concern the level of "doing," but touches, rather, the level of "being." That is, "being neighbor" touches upon that profound mystery of closeness that is the meaning and foundation of the family's existence and from which also arises the obligation "to do."

Perhaps the simplest way of illustrating this mysterious closeness, typical of the reality of a family, is to return to the moment of your parents' marriage. They married one another before God, during the Eucharistic Celebration, in the presence of the Christian community. The presentation of themselves to God, if it was lived with sincerity and due preparation, signified an act of trust, of abandonment: "Father, we are here at your disposition. Speak to us. Speak, through us, to all the children whom you love."

This availability explains the linking of your marriage with the Eucharist, because in the Eucharist the paschal mystery of Jesus is made present, in which the Father, with a supreme and definitive word, the word of love which allows itself to be placed on the cross, has told us how much he loves us.

So, when one wants to do the will of the Father, he must celebrate the Eucharist, he must dwell in that paschal love which Jesus lived on the cross and which he makes present in the Eucharist of the Church. And here is where the presence of the Christian community comes in. Your marriage was not only yours, it was the new word by which the love of God the Father and of Jesus Christ, celebrated in the Eucharist, speaks again to the believers of today, believers who rightly await the marvelous opening of God's lips through the opening of your married life.

On the other hand, during the preparation for Matrimony, you were told that it is a sacrament, that is, it is like an aspect, an irradiation, of that one, full, fundamental sacrament which is the Eucharist of Jesus. Now you understand what it means for you "to be neighbor." Before being a program of actions that you can or cannot perform, "being neighbors" means becoming aware that your family, in its formation and its continuation as a Christian family, is a witness, a living image, a sign of the closeness which God willed to establish with humankind through the paschal mystery of Jesus and the gift of the Holy Spirit.

Your first task as a Christian family, as a custodian of the closeness of God, is to offer to all your sisters and brothers in the faith and to the whole world, even if it does not understand, the witness of God who is gift, who has divested himself so as to be able to dwell with us, who has willed that we remain in an indissoluble union with him.

Don't think this is an easy task. In our time, forms of family life are imagined and proposed that too greatly resemble a temporary commitment to living together, a work contract, a sharing of life that can be begun and ended at will. The clear, strong and courageous witness to what a family is according to God's plan, becomes not so much your way of "being neighbor" as your unique, exclusive, and irreplaceable commitment to keeping alive the closeness which has been given to you and of which you are witnesses.

Certainly all this will lead to action so "that they'll see your good works and glorify your Father in heaven" (Mt 5:16). Therefore all the initiatives which strive to bind family groups together are to be welcomed with much understanding and hope. All initiatives which prepare family groups for the work of visiting and assisting families in difficulty, should be welcomed in the same way. Unfortunately, there are many families in trouble because of work or home situations, disturbing financial problems, psychological breakdowns caused by the pressures experienced in trying to raise children who are difficult to educate. For them it is a great encouragement to find families who are available to give immediate assistance, to help in the search for work, to offer solid support, to help them return to a more serene social and economic life.

"Becoming neighbors" means all this, but everything must depend on "being a neighbor." And, whether the urge to become neighbors stems from our intimacy with God or from the desire to be of service to our brothers and sisters, both motivations depend on that mysterious, precious and irreplaceable moment, perhaps difficult to find in the demanding schedule of daily life: the moment of family prayer.

It is especially that moment of prayer which has as its reference point the Word celebrated and assimilated with all our brothers and sisters in faith in the Christian community. But prayer becomes capable of stimulating all the aspects of personal and family life only if it is taken on, savored, and made an object of the communication of faith between parents and children. Prayer must be the moment when all join hands and express to God the deepest sentiments of the heart: thanksgiving for the gifts received, repentance for having guarded this gift too superficially, the proposal and commitment to change one's life, to pardon one another more, to be more understanding and accepting of one another within the family.

Thus the closeness given by God will shine as a noted characteristic of a family born before the altar. At those moments know that among your joined hands there are also those of your bishop.

To John, Who Is Physically Challenged: Become Neighbor by Forgetting Oneself and Dedicating Oneself to Others

Dear John,

Your letter came to recall and strengthen the long friendship between us. I thank the Lord for having given me some time to work with physically challenged persons, acquiring experiences which have greatly marked my life. In your last letter you thanked me for the pastoral program, "Become a neighbor." You suggested some interesting initiatives by means of which groups of physically challenged persons want to actively participate in the journey which the Church in Milan is making, whether by reinforcing the bonds among the members of the groups, by rendering charity among the group members more intense or by strengthening a new sensitivity which, in recent times, our Christian communities are beginning to show toward persons who are physically challenged.

These are all very beautiful things and they are certainly included in the great concert of initiatives and activities of this biennial pastoral program dedicated to "becoming neighbors." However, I would not be truly sincere with you and I would misinterpret the close friendship which unites us, if I stopped to appreciate the initiatives you recount to me and did not go to the root of the problems. You see, John, the initiatives of which you speak can also be ambiguous. They can mean that you have overcome the personal problems relative to the physically challenged person, problems related to the limitations imposed on you, to the uncertainty they cast on your future. The initiatives you describe can thus be the sign of a person who has become transparent, so free of self as to be able to dedicate himself with simplicity and disinterestedness to the problems of others. However, these initiatives could also hide a very subtle and camouflaged confirmation of the will to display oneself, to feel important, to know that one is capable of doing many things despite the handicap which troubles one. But you might say to me: all this is neither just nor true! Haven't I also the right to feel independent? Yes, it's true that you do, but that's not all that is at issue, and it would be too little if the exercise of this right were the dominant incentive for action.

Excuse me if I use such harsh language with a friend like you. But, precisely because we are friends, I think I am able to speak to you with this vigorous frankness and explain myself more fully.

For physically challenged persons, "becoming neighbors" requires a long journey in which I too want to be present with my prayers and my help. It is almost inevitable that the many realities which are shouldered by physically challenged persons and which weigh on their future, make them almost unswervingly preoccupied with themselves. It is inevitable that they ask themselves: "Was I truly accepted by my family, despite the great efforts they made to disguise their understandable disappointment? In the educational environment I frequented, did I receive only pity or was there real appreciation of my person despite my handicap? Doesn't society, which on the level of official programs is carrying out an intense program of socialization for physically challenged persons, then end by rejecting us because it favors ways of living, ideals and projects which we are not capable of sharing in? And then, who will think of me when my parents are gone? And, while my parents are still living, is it right that I continually burden them? Shouldn't I be able to have that autonomy from the family to which every adult person aspires?"

These are legitimate questions that cannot be totally eliminated from one's heart or from one's thoughts about the future. And yet, I believe that with a patient work of self-acceptance and of victory over the many problems which disturb relationships with persons of the same age and with adults, with a serious abandonment to the plan of God, with some real hope in the expression of St. Paul: "It is more blessed to give than to receive" (Acts 20:35), these questions might be relegated to the background. It is possible, instead, that in the space of the heart, in moments of prayer and in relationships with others, a sincere forgetfulness of self be allowed to prevail, so as to give oneself simply and solely to others. This seems to me to be the real "closeness" which a physically challenged person is called, with the help of God, to attain. The many actions which contain a real orientation toward others but which do not have this detachment from self at their basis, may give immediate satisfaction and even be of real help, but they do not resolve the true problem.

I said before that this closeness is achieved with the help of God, which comes through mysterious ways that link each human person to the mystery of the Father, but which at the same time manifests itself through the solidarity, serenity, understanding and acceptance which families and communities know how to show to physically challenged persons. Here we close the discussion of how individual Christians and communities can become neighbors to their handicapped brothers and sisters. All this goes beyond our personal letter. I know that there is a great movement in our Churches, I know that they are going forward with generosity and intelligence, even if there are still some disturbing signs of backwardness. I myself have spoken, even in detail, of the obligation of the Christian and of communities, in the publication: *Dare a ciascuno una voce* (*Give Each One a Voice*), which is a collection of some interventions made on the occasion of the international year of the handicapped, proclaimed by the UN.

Without dwelling on these initiatives, in keeping with the discussion I have offered, I must ask my sisters and brothers in the faith, and myself first of all, that what is done for physically challenged persons not be limited to alleviating some uneasiness and bringing some support to families particularly burdened, to finding work or serenely occupying free time. Let them strive above all to create that mysterious climate of a real, convinced acceptance of physically challenged persons, so that they no longer have any problems with accepting themselves and are thus able to truly forget themselves and divest themselves so as to think only of others. Only in this way can a person be successful and happy.

Dear John, I hope that with this exchange of ideas, we have taken a small step on the journey of closeness to others. We ask the Lord that our steps not tire but advance strong and secure, even if the road to be traveled seems to be a difficult mountain path. The Lord will walk with us.

To the Family of a Parish in the Suburbs: Becoming Neighbors by Closing the Door?

Dear Friends,
      This letter will be a bit longer than the others. But it concerns a question, not an easy one, that you posed to

me during the pastoral visit. You asked me whether we live closeness even if at times we risk closing the door in someone's face.

I will explain myself. You have told me that in the area of your suburbs, there are persons going around who introduce themselves into your home with manners that are very kind but insistent. They seek to persuade you to read their magazines, their books, implying that you do not know the truth, that what is being said in your churches is wrong, that only by going along with them will you have real happiness. And when you courteously tell them that you have your own convictions and intend neither to renounce them nor to discuss them, they return with insistence and without giving up.

Certainly, if "becoming neighbor" is difficult for everyone and with everyone, even with our dear ones and with those with whom we share the faith, as has appeared in the preceding letters, what does it mean to "become neighbor" to one who seeks to take away our faith?

Sometimes it is our friends, fellow students, associates at work or at the office, who try to draw us away from our faith. But you posed the question especially about members of those religious movements who carry on an intense campaign of proselytizing, to the point of constituting a real "offensive of the sects." Among these sects, the one that is most active and has the greatest success in our country and even in our diocese is that of the Jehovah's Witnesses.

Certainly many of us have heard them spoken of. Many of us have personally experienced their insistence at the doors of our homes, and we know how difficult it is to politely turn them away. Are we to "become neighbors" to Jehovah's Witnesses, too? In what sense, in what way? Many people are disoriented; many do not know how to conduct themselves when confronted with such a situation.

Of course we remember the words of Jesus recorded in the Gospel of Luke: "But to you who are listening, I say, love your enemies, do good to those who hate you, bless those who curse you, pray for those who insult you. To the one who strikes you on one cheek, offer the other cheek as well, and from the one who takes your cloak, don't hold back your tunic" (Lk 6:27-29). But what about the one who tries to take away our faith?

The teaching of the Jehovah's Witnesses is not only contrary to that of the Catholic Church, but is also contrary to that of the other Christian churches. In fact, they deny the most fundamental Christian truths, such as the triune God, the divinity of Jesus Christ, the personhood of the Holy Spirit, the existence of the spiritual soul, so much so that we must ask if they can still consider themselves Christians. There is no doubt, therefore, that adherence to this movement is an apostasy from the Christian, not only the Catholic, faith. The truth of the faith is in question.

Now we all recall in this regard the serious admonitions of Jesus with respect to "false prophets": "Watch out for false prophets who come to you in sheep's clothing, but within are savage wolves. By their fruit you will know them!" (Mt 7:15). And further on, with regard to false apocalyptic expectations, he repeats: "See that no one leads you astray; many will come in my name saying, 'I'm the one,' and they'll lead many astray.... And then, if anyone says, 'Look, here's the Messiah!' or 'Look there!' don't believe it. For false messiahs and false prophets will rise up and will produce signs and wonders to lead astray, if possible, the chosen ones. But see to yourselves; I've told you everything ahead of time" (Mk 13:5-6, 21-23).

Let us listen to what a holy bishop, Ignatius of Antioch, said to the Ephesians (n. 9): "I have heard that some have come among you from lands below, bringing a perverse teaching. But you have not allowed them to sow in your midst; in fact, you have plugged up your ears so as not to hear their words."

Charity, then, must meet with truth. "Charity and truth seek one another," I wrote in the letter, *Become a Neighbor.* The truth of charity and the charity of truth are always to be sought.

The truth of charity consists in truly seeking the good of the other. We are not neighbor to a drug addict by loving his illness, but by helping him to get well, and much less do we too take drugs with the excuse of being better able to understand him. We do not help sinners by committing sin. Sin is not a positive technique because it is an element of opposition and division within the heart as well as within society. Therefore we do not truly love the sinner if we do not hate the sin.

The truth of charity poses the fundamental questions about the true idea of the human person and about the true idea of God, for which reason—as I wrote in the letter, *Become a Neighbor*—"the passion for human needs is strictly linked to the passion for the truth."

From this we understand that the first charity is that of the truth. Jesus made himself our neighbor by communicating to us, with his person, his life and his death, the truth about God and about ourselves: "Grace and truth came through Jesus Christ" (Jn 1:17). Because of this supreme charity Jesus was killed: "But now you're trying to kill me, a man who's told you the truth he heard from God" (Jn 8:40). Jesus consecrated himself and his followers to this truth: "Make them holy in the truth; your *word* is truth. Just as you sent me into the world, I, too, have sent them into the world. And I consecrate myself for their sake that they may be made holy in the truth" (Jn 17:17-19). We need, therefore, to stand firm in the truth and resist falsehood and error. It is not possible to build any truth for the human person if we begin from a lie or a denial.

The apostles were well aware of this responsibility of theirs. In writing to the Christians of Galatia who were upset by the meddling of false brethren, St. Paul declares: "We did not submit to them even for a moment, so that the truth of the gospel might always remain with you" (Gal 2:5).

In the second letter to the faithful of Corinth, Paul notes that lack of courage can cause one to present the truth of the Gospel falsely, something he never did: "Therefore, since it is by God's mercy that we are engaged in this ministry, we do not lose heart. We have renounced the shameful things that one hides; we refuse to practice cunning or to falsify God's word; but by the open statement of the truth we commend ourselves to the conscience of everyone in the sight of God" (2 Cor 4:1-2).

I wanted to quote here the text of various biblical passages since the Jehovah's Witnesses' unique rule of faith is the Bible.

But a little reasoning is sufficient for understanding that we do not love persons if we leave them in their error. If someone should want at all costs to convince us that two plus two equals five, no one, I believe, would think they had to accept what the person was saying in order to show that they wished him well, too. We are to be neighbors to persons, not to the error that they may be teaching. Sometimes, becoming neighbors means that instead of opening the door we have to close it.

The apostle St. John was very decisive in this regard: "Everyone who does not abide in the teaching of Christ, but goes beyond it, does not have God; whoever abides in the teaching has both the Father and the Son. Do not receive into the house or welcome anyone who comes to you and does not bring this teaching; for to welcome is to participate in the evil deeds of such a person" (2 Jn 9-10). We cannot remain indifferent or inactive, underestimating the seriousness of the danger.

Of course, to close the door does not mean to slam it. It is not necessary to defend the faith by offending charity. The very proclamation of the truth which constitutes the Gospel comes about "in charity." The truth of the Gospel is manifested precisely in love. Truth is situated in charity. Therefore in exhorting the Christians of the communities of Asia Minor not to be "children, tossed to and fro and blown about by every wind of doctrine, by people's trickery, by their craftiness in deceitful scheming," he concludes by saying: "But speaking the truth in love, we must grow up in every way into him who is the head, into Christ" (Eph 4:14-15).

Charity should lead to helping those who are wrong to understand and correct their error: "speak the truth to our neighbors, for we are members of one another" (Eph 4:25). This is not always possible; in certain cases it is not even opportune, and in the case of the Jehovah's Witnesses, when they are insistent and do not leave your homes, it is truly not the time for discussion. The extreme casualness with which the Witnesses pass over their most serious errors, for example the many prophecies made by their leaders about the end of the present century which have not come true, does not invite us to open a serene dialogue with them. Unfortunately, a true religious dialogue with them is often practically impossible, given their sectarian mentality. We must not believe that those who go over to the Witnesses become more religious and better believers: fanaticism and sectarianism are not true religiosity. However, charity is able to save the subjective good faith and the sincerity of those who, unfortunately, join the Witnesses.

Above all charity teaches us that it is always our duty

to pray and it is always possible to hope, and therefore—
as St. Paul says—to be "kindly...patient, correcting oppo-
nents with gentleness. God may perhaps grant that they
will repent and come to know the truth" (2 Tim 2:24-26).

There is an urgent need to "become neighbors"
among ourselves, especially to the most simple and defenseless, who are most open to the threat of the
Jehovah's Witnesses.

To become neighbor, then, means to intensify the
work of catechesis, to deepen the study of the Bible, to
increase knowledge of Church history, because religious
ignorance and attacks against the Church form the most
suitable ground for the seed of the Witnesses.

At this point someone might say that to become
neighbor is actually very complex. This is true, because it
involves more than a simple act of goodness. It is a new
and original way of living, one which only the Good Samaritan Jesus could reveal and communicate to us. In the
end, to become neighbor even to those who persecute us
in order to upset our faith means to let ourselves be
reached by Christ and filled with his redemptive love.
Having become like him we will speak his truth even
without words, but "ready to make your defense to anyone
who demands from you an accounting for the hope that
is in you; yet do it with gentleness and reverence. Keep
your conscience clear, so that, when you are maligned,
those who abuse you for your good conduct in Christ may
be put to shame" (1 Pet 3:15-16).

I greet all of you with much affection.

Eight family letters, Milan, November, 1986

CHAPTER 7

To Become Neighbor in the Family

I thank you, dearest families, for having come to our cathedral this evening for an encounter which I believe is important. It refers to the approaching liturgical feast of the Holy Family, and to the subsequent celebration of the ninth Day for Life, but it is also an encounter to which I look with particular attention and hope, as to an anticipation of what we want to live in the next stages of the pastoral journey of our Church. I speak of it with some emotion and also with some trepidation, because it is the first time that I am stating the future diocesan program in an explicit form. We will be called to question ourselves on the educative spheres and means for forming a community animated by charity. The family certainly is one of these spheres.

For this reason, dearest parents and children, I am grateful to you for your availability and your participation in this moment of reflection and prayer....

John Paul II has spoken a special word of appreciation for the zeal of pastors who are making admirable efforts to prepare young people to form their own families. Then, among the various problems that trouble the Church today, he recalled the situation of the family, emphasizing the parish's role and duty toward it.

Let us listen again to his exact words: "In particular, given the widespread nature of the parish and the concrete effectiveness which it still possesses in the fabric of human life, it is especially on the parish that we need to base ourselves in opposing the destructive activity which threatens the essential cell of all civil society, the family."

In light of these suggestions I would like to begin this evening a reflection that may help us discover the link between the theme of the family and its life and the basic themes of the diocesan pastoral, especially the journey of charity, which has characterized and concluded our itinerary of these past years and which now needs to be more precisely and concretely realized.

Therefore, using a terminology we are already accustomed to, we will question ourselves and verify ourselves on "becoming neighbor in the family." In the Christmas letter I sent to families, I offered some practical illustrations; here I will seek to propose a broader theoretical reflection, listening with you to the word of God which has been proclaimed from the Letter of St. Paul to the Colossians (3:12-4:6).

Charity and the Word of God

St. Paul exhorts the Christians of Colossae to live those virtues which spring from having risen with Christ, holy because chosen and loved by God. These virtues are summed up in *charity*: "Above all, clothe yourselves with love, which binds everything together in perfect harmony" (Col 3:14).

In the light of charity the Christian virtues are described in different ways and with delicate modulations. The faithful are urged to show themselves rich in that mercy which is tender and knows how to sympathize with others; rich in generous goodness, humility, meekness, and kindness, a kindness that does not judge others severely; rich in long-suffering patience. If they should have reason for feeling offended and for complaining about others, let them know how to expand their charity by bearing with one another and being ready to forgive, after the example and for the sake of the Lord.

From this profound and constant attitude arises that peace which is a gift of Christ and which internally and externally characterizes the conditions of life of the members of the community, that peace to which we are all called.

As nourishment, means and guarantee for keeping alive this fervor and fire of charity, there is on the one hand the constant appeal of the word of God, which is always present in the midst of the faithful and dwells in abundance among them, and on the other hand, incessant prayer: "with gratitude in your hearts sing psalms, hymns, and spiritual songs to God" (Col 3:16).

In view of such rich appeals which describe some essential connotations of the Church's life, we want to apply the exhortation of St. Paul to that particular and real figure of the Church: the Christian family.

According to the teaching of Vatican II, in fact, the family is called the "domestic Church," a real cell of the Church, the smallest and yet the most fundamental cell of the ecclesial organism, as Paul VI said (cf Paul VI to the Èquipes Notre-Dame, May 4, 1970). For *Familiaris Consortio*, the family is "a Church in miniature" (domestic Church)..."a living image and historical representation of the mystery of the Church" (FC 49).

And all this "means that there should be found in every Christian family the various aspects of the entire Church" (*Evangelii Nuntiandi*, 71).

It is therefore possible to emphasize what we have rediscovered in the passage from the Letter of Paul to the Colossians, and apply it to the Christian family. The content of these reflections of mine, in which I wish to develop the theme, "becoming a neighbor in the family," is articulated in this way. It is a specific task of the family community:

a) through the witness of the closeness of God;

b) through the mutual love among family members;

c) with a specific life-style between the spouses;

d) in the service of life, whether as the transmission of life or as the education of children;

e) finally, through the care of the seriously ill, the elderly, and the physically challenged present in the family.

Closeness of God

Let us begin with what is fundamental. "Becoming a neighbor"—which does not immediately concern the level of doing but rather the level of being—intersects that profound mystery of closeness which is the meaning and foundation of the family's entire existence. And so, the first way of letting ourselves be formed and molded by charity is to be faithful to the plan of God as a family, to be sign and sacrament of God's love for the world, sign and sacrament of Christ's love, a witness and living image of the very closeness of God.

It is the first and irreplaceable task of a Christian family, even more so today when forms of family life are imaged and proposed which unfortunately do not much resemble the images of God's love but rather resemble a temporary living together, a work contract, a sharing of life that can be begun and ended at will.

Mutual Love

A second level: in order to be able to offer the witness of fidelity to God, to be a sign and instrument of his love, each family must live this love within itself. This is the first path of charity, as the Pope reminds us in *Familiaris Consortio*, when he says that the first task of the family "is to live with fidelity the reality of communion in a constant effort to develop an authentic community of persons" (n. 18).

Love is to be lived between husband and wife, between parents and children, among brothers and sisters, between relatives and family members.

Love implies harmony, warm understanding, mutual serenity, the ability to laugh, to understand, to encourage the ideas of others; an absence of mutual prejudices, the overcoming of distances, of reticence, of diffidence, of those upsetting moments which often come to disturb family relationships; an ability to carry on an exchange, sharing, and mutual enrichment between the different generations.

The family needs to live a love which is described with those rich and realistic nuances suggested by the apostle Paul in the passage to the Colossians and which recalls us to faithful listening to the word of God in the family, to prayer in the family, as a source of nourishment and security.

It is thus a matter of making room for these precious and irreplaceable moments and spaces, even in the demanding schedule of daily life and even amidst the practical difficulties that can arise. It is the meaning of the "desert moment" applied to the family, the "desert" of which we spoke in our last encounter in the cathedral, for the first Fridays of the month.

It is a matter of finding—all together—the courage, strength and joy to join hands and express to God the deepest sentiments of our hearts. Among the many possible ways of praying as a family and of listening to the word of God as a family, I recall here those three simple ways which I suggested in my Christmas letter for 1984, *Teach Us to Pray as a Family*: to pray together with the words we know; to pray together one of the psalms; to pray together a page of the Gospel.

A Specific Life Style Between Spouses

Within this general discussion, there comes the following dimension: to consider the exact position of the spouses with regard to "becoming a neighbor." Here, too, the very simple points given by the Apostle sustain us: to love and respect one another "as is fitting in the Lord" (Col 3:18b), that is, in the most authentic Christian spirit which, in the Letter to the Ephesians (Eph 5:25-33), is deepened with respect to the mysterious relationship of love between Christ and the Church.

"Becoming neighbors," as applied to husband and wife means, once again, love, charity and tenderness in all their multiple, realistic facets. It means a profound communion, reciprocal understanding, the sharing of each beautiful or sad event of their experience, a cordial sincerity, a total respect and at times even silence as an opportunity for communion and communication that is innate to the truest and most inexpressible realities.

This mutual self-giving and acceptance concerns everything that the spouses "possess" as well as what they "are." For this reason, the content of the gift is the totality of their being, composed of spirituality, affectivity and corporeity.

From this flows a rich and enriching style of life, made up of moments of encounter, dialogue, prayer, and discipline of body and spirit. It is here that we introduce the topic of the natural methods for the regulation of births. They are something more than a method and technique, for they initiate and develop a style of life which interprets the very relationship of love between spouses, in all its entirety and globality, in terms of the intrinsic characteristic notes of human married love. In other words, the natural methods presuppose, first of all, the mutual receiving of the spouses in the totality of their persons; in this specific sense, they can and should be seen as a concrete way of husband and wife "becoming neighbors."

Service to Life

Another dimension of "becoming neighbor in the family," on the part of the parents, is what we can call service to life.

a) In the first place, service to life is the transmission of life itself, according to the words of John Paul II in *Familiaris Consortio*.

As in other spheres of human existence, we witness here a widespread diffusion of a so-called "culture and morality of desire." Thanks to this culture, whatever is ardently and irresistibly desired imposes itself absolutely, therefore becoming necessary. In the context of the transmission of life, there are two opposing outcomes of this logic: either the exclusion of the child by any means because it is unwanted; or the right to conceive and bear the child by any means which modern genetic engineering places at our disposal.

At the root of this "morality" lies one's own desire to get what one wants, at any cost. Faced with this logic of desire, the task of the Christian family is to rediscover the truest meaning of the transmission of life.

In this regard Vatican II has said: "Children are really the supreme gift of marriage.... The true practice of conjugal love, and the whole meaning of family life which results from it, have this aim: that the couple be ready with stout hearts to cooperate with the love of the Creator and Savior, who through them will enlarge and enrich his own family day by day" (*Gaudium et Spes*, 50).

Some emphases arise from this, full of meaning and great potential for the life of today's family, that family of which you are called to be witnesses and privileged ambassadors to the people. Transmitting a new life is cooperating with God in the creation of a new existence. Giving life to a child is a sign and fruit of the encounter between the love of God and the love of the spouses. It is thus a characteristic and original means for witnessing to and making present the love of God who gives and communicates himself in the creation of a new human being.

It is a real opportunity for giving flesh to the foundational and original dimension of "becoming neighbor in the family." If a further emphasis is opportune today, in our present-day [society] on the way toward an ever more dramatic and widespread aging, "becoming neighbor" is expressed in the invitation to families who are able to be more generous in the transmission of life.

The child who is born is, then, a *gift*. The gift is not refused but welcomed with joy. From this very simple consideration we cannot but draw an open condemnation of the practices which reject, deny or eliminate such a precious gift. Human life, even at its origin, is to be respected and saved, in the clear knowledge that it "has its beginning in the eternal love of God, who has willed it in time for an eternal destiny" (cf *Message of the Italian Episcopal Conference for the Ninth Day for Life*, 4).

To respect and defend human life, at its origin as well as at its conclusion, is, among other things, a real and effective action on behalf of peace. The affirmation and question of the Italian bishops resound in a very clear and challenging way. I now propose them again to you and to the whole diocese: "Peace is not destroyed only by the frontiers of war and of acts of violence; it is also betrayed wherever, legally or secretly, killing is done without arms and under the guise of freedom or of compassion.... Then, what peace is there if we do not choose both to defend and to promote each life and all life, from the moment of conception to its natural conclusion?" (2).

Finally, the gift of life is never a right. It must be accepted as a gift. It happens that some ways of speaking about the "right to a child," almost as though this right were something due us at any cost, risk turning the baby into a thing, an object, no longer recognizing the child as a person and a gift. So, too, if the child is a gift, we are called to accept this gift as it is given to us, without predetermining it through means that do not respect the human meaning of the creative act. From this line of reasoning we could begin further critical reflections on the various operations of genetic manipulation, which we do not intend to look at more deeply here and yet which are of great importance and relevance for family, social, civil and political morality today.

b) Service to life finds its fulfillment and perfection in the education of children. *Familiaris Consortio* also recalls this (n. 36).

In this regard we must, unfortunately, note two different and opposing forms of behavior which, though prescinding from subjective intentions, represent either forms of an early surrender of the educational task on the part of parents or forms of possessiveness.

In fact, we often find ourselves face to face with actual renunciation of the duty to educate, accompanied by discouragement and frustration about the initial difficulties with children in continuing the educational dialogue. On the other hand, at times we also encounter real forms of manipulation and restriction of the child's freedom, especially when the children manifest the serious and well-considered desire, even as adolescents, to direct their own life toward some kind of commitment to self-giving and charity or in a vocation of special consecration.

At times these and similar attitudes can be psychologically and even sociologically understood and explained in view of the diminished number of children, and yet they cannot be justified. They can be new ways of arousing the exasperation of the children, that exasperation of which St. Paul clearly wrote: "Fathers, do not provoke your children, or they may lose heart" (Col 3:21). Along this line, with all the strength which comes to me from the Lord, I would like to ask all Christian parents not to hinder but rather to deeply respect, or better yet, to share and accompany with warm and trustful joy the journey of those children who intend to verify and follow a specific vocation to the priesthood, to religious consecration, or to missionary life.

To all parents, then, I would like to direct an appeal that they watch over the growth of all the dimensions of their children's lives, not only the physical and bodily, not only the intellectual, but also the affective, spiritual and religious, in a harmonious and hierarchically structured way, and not in a unilateral way that makes an absolute of some dimensions to the detriment of others.

How many times I am told, during visits to the parishes, that the children are occupied with this or that, in various sports, without ever having time for catechesis! This means ignoring the most serious duty in the education of one's children.

Finally, parents are called to live their educative mission through daily, concrete actions. These range from the witness of a consistent Christian life to a daily life style marked by selflessness, service and hospitality; from the assumption of the formative task in a serious and authentic way (including all the opportunities for collaboration with the school and the parish) to a cordial and constant dialogue with the children, living moments of joy and fun with them.

c) A necessary good for any family that wants to fulfill

its formative obligation is certainly that of the home, a good home that is suitable and secure for everyone.

This is one of the most serious problems for not a few families. It is a problem that appears again and again on the front pages of newspapers, and has not yet found a definitive solution. On the contrary, it is a problem which remains more difficult and unsolved than ever. Herein lie the expectation, the uncertainty and the dismay of many families who live in the same house, of young people who postpone their marriage because it is impossible to find a house at an affordable price, of many other poor families forced to live in unhealthy and unsuitable lodgings. There is especially the bitter reality of evicted families.

Returning from the conference "Become a neighbor," and from the day of solidarity, we are more than ever convinced of the actual possibility of introducing a political charity redeemed by Christ, on the part of Christian laity and social and political workers of good will, so that with consistency and openness we may thoroughly address this great problem.

I turn to these workers, too, that this urgent need may be met. A decisive will is needed to take in hand the politics of housing, bringing together politicians, administrators, city leaders, contractors, and engineers of the area.

For our part, we will ask our social-economic observation team, which has already competently handled some difficult and delicate problems, to help us provide evaluations and suggestions for the Christian communities.

Care of the Sick and the Aged

The final stage of what we call service to life reminds us that the life of a family community often experiences moments and situations of suffering and sorrow. These can manifest themselves in the presence of the seriously ill, the handicapped and the elderly. In such circumstances, the possibility of living as neighbor opens up for everyone, as I already noted in the booklet, *Become a Neighbor*.

For the sick, becoming neighbor can mean living one's own situation as a mysterious but real moment of God's closeness and presence. How often have I found the greatest riches of charity, affection, kindness, and of even human maturity, in visiting families with sick, handicapped, suffering members!

In this way, suffering can become a true, and at times a rediscovered, means of drawing closer to the mystery of God. It can also be a means of drawing closer to the mystery of the human person, in the rediscovery of one's need for others. Suffering facilitates a more open and easy bonding with others, a bonding that supersedes all barriers and distinctions.

Sick persons, who experience all these realities in the depths of their being, mysteriously and often silently but nonetheless truly, know how to communicate to the others whom they meet, and especially to their dear ones, whatever is most authentic in their suffering and in their entire life. If this is true for the elderly and the sick, for the young and healthy it means welcoming these very rich lessons of life. From such an attitude there will arise the ability to remain close to others, the determination not to exclude anyone, not to let oneself be overcome by fear. Those who enjoy good health will feel urged on to seek and re-create more supportive and fraternal relationships among different families, so that the burden of the care for the sick and for those elderly members who are not self-sufficient, may be shared.

We have reached the end of our brief discussion on "becoming neighbor in the family." It is a discussion that has simply begun to describe the Christian family which, in journeying with the Church which lets itself be molded by the love of God, wants to be formed by that same charity.

There are still many topics which remain in the shadows and yet which have been dealt with by means of fruitful discussions and valid suggestions in the various institutions that work on behalf of the family. These discussions highlight the relationship of families among themselves, of families with the Church and with society, and the relationship of the Church, the parish and society with families.

For this evening it suffices that we have begun to speak about some of the relationships within the family, as relationships of authentic "closeness" and of real participation in the ability to love that belongs to God—that love which has been communicated to us in the great mystery of Christ and of the Church.

May the Holy Family of Nazareth, whose feast we will soon celebrate, protect and inspire all our families, that they may know how to grow in evangelical love in the midst of the joys and difficulties of life.

Meditation to families, Milan, January 23, 1987

CHAPTER 8

Work, the Family and Solidarity

Dearest working people, once again on the vigil of the feast of May 1, I would like to express my warmest greetings to each of you, and to thank you for having come.

Along with you, I greet each one of your families, the associations and movements you represent, the pastoral labor groups who carry out their mission with and for you. I also intend to address a greeting and remembrance to all the persons, realities, and associations that constitute the vast world of work.

This meeting for reflection and prayer follows other encounters for the feast of the worker, as well as the various opportunities I have had to meet with many working men and women. In addition, by means of the specific theme—"Work, the family and solidarity"—we are linked both with the reflections for the sixth Day of Solidarity and with the indications given for "becoming neighbor in the family," which I began to offer last January for the feast of the family.

The relationship between work and the family has

been underscored many times in the teaching of the Church, with regard both to considerations of a general nature and to more local and specific problems, such as the topics of the working wage or the work of mothers of families.

In his encyclical *Laborem Exercens*, in addition to offering wide-reaching indications about wages and the relationship between woman and work, Pope John Paul II introduces an interesting and original approach to work and family, from the point of view both of the subjective dimension of work and of education in the family. In this context he affirms that "work constitutes a foundation for the formation of *family life*, which is a natural right and something that man is called to. These two spheres of value—one linked to work and the other consequent on the family nature of human life—must be properly united and must properly permeate each other" (n. 10).

This allusion to the need for a proper union and a proper mutual permeating of the values linked to work and those linked to family life, suggests some reflections which we might develop together this evening. In the light of some prospects and of some new facts which seem to be emerging today, these reflections concern:

1. the style of solidarity in families and among families;

2. the family's role in education;

3. the forms of organization of work and the actualization of a family policy that do not break up the family but rather foster its closeness and stability.

The Style of Solidarity in Families and Among Families

Today the family feels more and more strongly the influence of the environment that surrounds it: because of its economic subsistence which has need of others, the process of cultural formation which takes place largely

outside of it, and the powerful means of social communication which enter into the family, influence it and, in
large part, determine its needs and aspirations.

On the other hand, however, never as today is the
family in a position to influence society, not only on the
political level but also, under certain aspects, on the economic level.

A long period of time passed in which industrial
development and the growth of employment in organizations very distinct from the family seemed to annul its
importance with regard to the economic-productive profile, and in which the persistence of economic unities
based on the family was considered by most as a sign of
backwardness. Today there is a re-evaluation of the economic role of the family.

For example, various experts in social analysis emphasize that the family has been able to exercise a role of
support for those members who are without work or who
seek employment. In fact, on the one hand, young people
remain tied to their families for a longer time because
there, at least, they are able to survive, thanks to strong
solidarity within the family world, which absorbs some of
the difficulties linked to unemployment, to lack of housing and to other economic problems. However, there is
the risk of a merely functional and utilitarian exploitation
of the family, as well as a passive adaptation to a kind of
survival without any actual prospects.

On the other hand, even in situations in which the
family, with its varied relationships between relatives and
friends, somehow succeeds in acting as an agency of support for those seeking work, often with positive results,
the family can only offer a jobless member security when
it is not in its turn marginalized from the market and,
therefore, weak and in serious economic difficulties. In
these latter cases, the possibility of successfully finding

employment is very limited. Here, too, we are faced with the risk that a relatively poor and weak family will be unable to give support; this gives rise to further problems and tensions.

The economic importance of the family is being re-evaluated today because the family itself has again come to be recognized as an economic-productive subject. This recognition has come about with the rediscovery of the small, family-run business, especially in the areas of new industrialization. The wider recognition given to the importance of various forms of "submerged economy" has also contributed to increased interest in the family as an economic unit.

On the one hand, this re-evaluation of the family's economic role emphasizes the positive contribution which the family knows how to offer the complex world of work along with the family's own great resources of solidarity. On the other hand, however, this re-evaluation sheds light on some new problems which also have to be faced according to the objective criteria of justice, charity and solidarity.

From this follows a positive and immediate way of "becoming neighbor in the family," which is to share everything one has at home, even at the cost of some personal sacrifice, so as to alleviate the difficulties of family members who are still unemployed, in addition to offering every possible assistance in the search for employment.

I also believe it is a duty to stimulate a correct kind of economic leadership on the part of the family; this is one way in which family members can help the development and progress of the whole of society.

At the same time, however, I cannot help expressing a concerned disapproval of the lessening of a more wide-spread solidarity which may continue to affect relationships among families and within the broader social context.

It is a matter of recovering the taste for a fuller solidarity, of reliving the meaning of so many past social struggles. In fact, withdrawal into any kind of corporatism, even family-style, is not acceptable; rather, we are to reconcile solidarity within the family circle with solidarity within the spheres of society, trade unions and politics.

In particular, then, this solidarity should be manifested toward the weakest categories and families, overcoming a sufficiently widespread mentality which holds that the important thing is to achieve a certain security, at least for one's own family, even if this be to the detriment of others. This mentality may go even further by hastily accusing these other families of being incapable of commitment and vitality and of being the cause of their own poverty.

As we are faced with these dangers, I renew the appeal which I addressed to you last year on this occasion, "to give a voice in the world of work to the weakest groups, by insisting on giving them a specific social and even contractual dignity."

In addition, I make my own some expressions of John Paul II during his recent trip to Argentina: "Wherever there is a father or mother who, because of their circumstances, cannot fulfill their duty of providing the means of subsistence so as to live in a dignified way with their dear ones, it is there that the solidarity of working men and women should reach.... You must not allow your efforts to be transformed into a kind of group or class 'egoism'.... Support for the weakest will be a proof that your solidarity is authentic."

The Formative Role of the Family

Among the various risks connected with the re-evaluation of the family's economic role, I underscored that of the protracted presence of young people in their families, often without motivation and without serious prospects for the future.

Beginning from this observation, it seems to me that the formative role of the family is immediately called into play, as the place of relationships, of acquaintances, of habitual practices in life, as the place in which it is possible to form one's own points of reference, one's own motivations, one's whole personality, even in what concerns the meaning of work and professional orientation.

I have already dwelt on these formative responsibilities on other occasions. In particular, I refer to the message for the sixth Day of Solidarity, in which I asked parents, "while legitimately aspiring to the social advancement of their children, to free themselves from the exaggerated cult of degrees in higher studies, linked to a prejudice against manual labor." I emphasized that "the witness of a healthy balance between commitment of life (especially in the family) and commitment to work, on the part of the parents, would prove to be valuable" in relation to the perception of a certain image of work. I invited parents to equip their children "even morally, to face the often harsh trials of life by offering them values and ideals which withstand the ups and downs of personal and social fortune."

This evening, continuing the reflection on this delicate relationship between family and work, I would like to offer some further simple considerations.

In the first place, the family is asked to find the way, even amidst all the difficulties, to become the most suitable sphere for the experience of values such as selflessness, dialogue, socialization, and acceptance of others. This all forms a part of the typically humanizing, personalizing and socializing role originally belonging to the family. At the same time this special role is linked to the typical meaning of work as a humanizing reality that helps persons be more completely themselves, apart from success and career, in the ability to relate with others, to share choices and conditions, to establish moments of participation and socialization, all opening onto a vast horizon of solidarity.

In the second place, the family is asked to give its own contribution to overcoming that mentality which sees work as an accidental reality unrelated to life, one that is to be kept separate from the warp and woof of the daily, normal interests of existence. In other words, in the face of a certain widespread tendency to consider work both as something purely instrumental (with little or no intrinsic value) and as a marginal reality (which cannot be an object of real interest and desire), and consequently, in the face of the tendency to communicate nothing about one's own work experience, the family, within its own sphere, must be able to offer a rich and enriching logic of communication.

This is carried out by means of a more open and total communication of one's work experience and one's professional commitment, through a more constant dialogue about the contents, problems, difficulties, discoveries and joys of one's own work.

Finally, the family can always exercise an effective role with regard to the professional choices of its members. Included here is the emphasis, which I have already expressed at other times, on the value found in formation to service, to the ability to sacrifice and to solidarity, in view of the choice of professions that are especially laden with social commitment and real service, as for example, the education of children in trouble, the work of nurses and prison assistants, etc.

Forms of Work Organization and Family Policy

Everything I have been saying can be seen first of all as beginning with the commitment and responsibility of individuals and of families. But it is likewise true that, for a more realistic realization of these prospects, the promotion of an adequate and courageous family policy is needed, as well as an organization of work which begins first of all with respect for family needs.

It is thus necessary and ever more urgent that competent citizens mature and be helped to mature, who will become involved in labor unions, in economics, in culture, in institutions so as to foster a true social and economic policy in favor of the family. It is families themselves who must become the protagonists of this family policy. The Pope affirms this explicitly in *Familiaris Consortio*: "Families should be the first to take steps to see that the laws and institutions of the State not only do not offend but support and positively defend the rights and duties of the family" (n. 44).

Now can we affirm that it is always thus? Can we passively accept that the interpretation of permissive laws in the area of the transmission of life be broadened so as to allow the practically arbitrary suppression of every life? What do we say when we are faced with the autopsy-like examination of a living human body, which no law in the world has been able or will ever be able to make lawful? The actualization of a clear policy in defense of all the values of the family and of life is a serious duty within the competence of all the social forces of business, trade unions, parties, institutions. To all of them goes my pressing appeal to do everything possible for the actualization of a correct and explicit family policy.

Among the rights of the family that should be recognized is that of an organization of work that does not break up the family itself. This is how the Charter of Family Rights expresses it: "Families have a right to a social and economic order in which the organization of work permits members to live together, without hindrance to the unity, well-being, health and stability of the family, and with the possibility for healthy recreation" (article 10).

In this context it is a question of overcoming a kind of rigid and standardized planning in the organization of work. Moreover, the social-economic tendency itself is going in this direction. The diffusion and decentralization of productive units throughout the territory, the creation of business satellites or of labor units, the renewal of emphasis on local businesses or offices (fostered by the versatility and flexibility of new electronic and computer technologies) tend to promote a greater elasticity in the organization of work and a closer relationship with the reality of the family. Herein lies the real possibility for an increased flexibility in working hours and therefore greater opportunities for harmonizing the demands of work with the demands of family life or, simply, the demands outside of work. Obviously, the various forms suggested (flexible daily hours, part-time jobs, job-sharing, a reduced work week) are not sufficient in themselves to assure that more time be given to the family. Other, more personal and fundamental motivations are needed. The greatest possible flexibility in the organization of working hours, however, provides some necessary and not insignificant conditions!

Another problem specifically concerns the work of women in general, and of mothers of families in particular. While in Argentina, John Paul II said: "Put an end to a labor system that forces the mothers of families to work many hours outside of the home and to neglect domestic affairs." In the light of n. 23 of *Familiaris Consortio*, which I invite you to meditate on once more, we need to react to a sufficiently widespread mentality which sees work (especially work in a large industrial enterprise) almost exclusively as a real emancipation, especially for women, and minimizes or misunderstands domestic work and the work of a mother. It is a matter, on the one hand, of finding all the concrete means and forms of work which, because of their hours, their rhythm, and their organization, are such as to allow both the fulfillment of the functions most typically linked to motherhood and insertion in the working world for those who wish it. On the other hand, it is a question of acknowledging, even financially, the value which the mother's work at home has both for the family and society. In this way, the woman who, whether by free choice or because of the objective needs of the family situation, intends to dedicate herself entirely to the life of the family, may do so without fear and frustration and in such a way that her family may live with dignity.

Obviously, a final consideration is raised here concerning the working wage. This wage—as the Charter of Family Rights recalls—could also be given to domestic work. However, it "must be sufficient to establish and maintain a family with dignity, whether by means of a suitable salary, called a 'family salary,' or by other social measures, such as family allowances" or the already mentioned wage for domestic work (art. 10). While there have been praiseworthy initiatives at various levels in this regard, I believe that there is still much progress to make; to go ahead, we first of all need to sensitize public opinion and to study specific structures.

In conclusion, as I have already said in my address for the last Day of Solidarity, "an unavoidable ethical-political fact appears: that institutions, which regulate work or issue from work, be transformed in a way that enables the family carry out fully its dynamic role in society which is on the threshold of the year 2000."

It is a matter of truly regaining and respecting the family in the working world; otherwise it is not possible even to respect the person and consequently his dignity and primacy with regard to work itself!

Reflections on the eve of the feast of St. Joseph the Worker,
Milan, April 30, 1987

CHAPTER 9

Letting Ourselves Be Formed by God in the Family

Introduction

I wish to express a heartfelt thanks to you who have come to this encounter on the vigil of the Feast of the Holy Family, as representatives of all the families of the diocese.

Your presence indicates, in fact, that you feel the urgent need to pursue the way which John Paul II recently emphasized when he said: "The holiness of the family is the master way, the necessary course to follow in order to build a new and better society, to renew hope in the future in a world burdened with so many menaces" (Angelus message of December 27, 1987, on the occasion of the liturgical feast of the Holy Family).

The words of the Pope echo those pronounced by the recent Synod of Bishops on the fundamental importance of the family a reality in which first of all and above all the baptismal holiness of the Christian is expressed, and in which Christian vocations are formed.

The Holy Father continued: "Tomorrow's society will be what the family is today. Unfortunately, the family today is subjected to all kinds of dangers by those who try to tear apart its fabric and to undermine its natural and supernatural unity, by breaking up the moral values on which it is founded, with all the means which the present permissiveness of society makes available, especially the mass media, and by denying the essential principle of respect for the sacredness of every human life, from the first moment of existence."

To make a commitment to the family therefore means entering into conflict with all the forces that threaten the unity of the person and of society. It does not mean simply a pastoral work of information and instruction, nor merely of encouragement. We also need to combat the forces of the world, of egoism, of individualism, of a naturalistic vision of life, which continually assault that which the family represents as a masterpiece of God, as a sketch of the final masterpiece of God, the heavenly Jerusalem, the unity of all peoples in Christ.

We are gathered here to pray and to prepare ourselves for this spiritual combat, to renew our courage, especially the courage of those who are directly engaged as pastoral workers and of all those who, as parents, daily live this challenge and these responsibilities.

So we feel the need to invoke the intercession of our holy patrons, especially of blessed Cardinal Ferrari, who is buried in this cathedral. I ask him to pray for me and for you, and to accompany us in the struggle against the spirit of the world, the counter-evangelical spirit, the spirit of disintegration and of division at work in history, today as yesterday. This year we want to carry on this struggle within the pastoral journey begun some months ago: *the journey of education.*

As I have had many occasions to affirm in the pastoral plan: *God Educates His People,* the family is the first, natural and immediate sphere, in which the dimension and the responsibility for educating are called to express and manifest themselves. I therefore ask of the Lord the grace to be able to reflect with you, at this moment, on the *educational mission entrusted to the family*, the mission of which the family is made capable, by the gift of God, in a troubled and hostile world.

Naturally, we must remind ourselves that God is the first educator, and thus the family itself is called to let itself be formed by him in docile and attentive listening to his word: "Hear, O Israel." For this reason we begin from the passage of Deuteronomy (6:1-9), which constitutes the synthesis of the spirituality of the people of God, and which the Hebrew people still recite every day, as a moment that sums up everything they have lived throughout the centuries.

"Now this is the commandment—the statutes and the ordinances—that the Lord your God charged me to teach you to observe in the land that you are about to cross into and occupy, so that you and your children and your children's children, may fear the Lord your God all the days of your life, and keep all his decrees and his commandments that I am commanding you, so that your days may be long. Hear therefore, O Israel, and observe them diligently, so that it may go well with you, and so that you may multiply greatly in a land flowing with milk and honey, as the Lord, the God of your ancestors, has promised you.

"Hear, O Israel: The Lord is our God, the Lord alone. You shall love the Lord your God with all your heart, and with all your soul, and with all your might. Keep these words that I am commanding you today in your heart. Recite them to your children and talk about them when you are at home and when you are away, when you lie down and when you rise. Bind them as a sign on your hand, fix them as an emblem on your forehead, and write them on the doorposts of your house and on your gates."

May this text, which characterizes and accompanies the entire historical experience of the people of God, enlighten us and help us understand what it means to say that the family lets itself be educated by God by becoming an educator itself.

The Leadership of the Family

In reflecting on the words of Deuteronomy we can note how, according to God's educational style—at once personal and communitarian—the responsibility for listening is entrusted to the chosen people as a whole: "Hear, O Israel." However, it is also entrusted to each individual Israelite, and in particular to the family. In fact the singular and plural forms of the personal pronoun "you" are intertwined, and the command is given with the specific obligation to hand it down from father to son: "you and your children and your children's children.... Keep these words that I am commanding you today in your heart. Recite them to your children and talk about them when you are at home."

The connotation of family is, on the other hand, in harmony with the whole history of events of the people of God; it is the history of the genealogies—from Adam to Jesus—which from generation to generation, by listening to the Word, preserve and increase the heritage of the holy law, of God's instructions of love for his people.

This first reflection suggests to us the idea of the *leadership of the family,* of the reality of the family in the history of Israel, a leadership which still stimulates us today.

In view of the effort required by the educational task, especially as soon as the first serious difficulties arise, as well as the fears, uncertainty and complexity linked to the various factors of change, the family can never abandon itself to resignation, to the sense of the inevitable, to fear, or to fruitless complaints. Instead, it is called to renew the awareness of knowing itself to be the protagonist of divine action, which has its roots in God himself, in his fatherhood and in his love.

a) Parents are thus called to fully assume their own responsibility as educators.

If this very serious duty (cf. *Gravissimum Educationis*, 30) is qualified as a right and duty that is "essential, since it is connected with the transmission of human life" (*Familiaris Consortio*, 36b); if it is "original and primary with regard to the educational role of others, on account of the uniqueness of the loving relationship between parents and children"; if this educational bond is "irreplaceable and inalienable, and therefore incapable of being entirely delegated to others or usurped by others," then parents can carry out this task as a real "ministry of the Church" (*Familiaris*).

They must therefore accept it with faith and trust as an obligation which God has placed in their hands, suiting it to their strength, that they might succeed in fulfilling this mysterious, almost creative, task that arouses free energies of love in the children.

It is true that today in many families, all this appears very hard and at times even out of proportion to the cultural, psychological and physical strength of the parents, to the point of leading to forms of discouragement, resignation and delegation to others.

But it is here that the educational action of the community and of pastoral educators should intervene, action which I would qualify as the action of consolation: to give consolation, to give comfort, to give courage to families who too often find the task of educating difficult and who are tempted to give up.

The ministry of consolation does not only consist in

recalling the proper and irreplaceable, original and primary duty of the family, but in showing that the educational mission is a gift. *To educate is beautiful*, even if it is hard, and it is—as St. John Bosco would say—"a matter of the heart" (cf. *God Educates His People*, 26). It is thus strictly connected to matrimony which is founded on love, which grows and is perfected in love, and which is the root of the possibility and ability to educate.

To educate is a *beautiful gift* because parents, who are married in Christ, have been made participants of the very love of God the Father, of Christ the shepherd, and of the maternal tenderness of the Church. From this springs my warm and pressing invitation to *trust* and *serenity*.

God is with you in your educational ministry, he accompanies you, leads you by the hand, makes you capable of loving and of educating as he loves and educates.

Let us seek to spread this message and to express this encouragement. In recalling the responsibility and urgency of the family's educational mission, let us never neglect to emphasize that it is possible and beautiful, that God fulfills it first of all and helps us to carry it out every day, that God counsels us and suggests the best ways, comforts us in dark moments, and gives us the strength to wait with patience for better times.

b) The family's role as the protagonist in education thus means completely taking on educational responsibility for its members with the awareness that it is a gift, a joyful and beautiful thing, a matter of the heart, and for this reason something to be welcomed with trust and generosity.

However, there is a second meaning which I would like to express with a concise phrase: *to become parents.*

Educational responsibility brings human freedom into play and demands preparation, formation, confrontation and commitment. If it is true that one becomes a parent at the moment of the child's birth, it is likewise true that one truly becomes a parent day by day; in fact, one begins to become a parent even before the birth of the children, and in some way even before marriage. Already during the time of engagement, persons can and must educate themselves to the educational task and to awareness of the choices it involves. This formation must then proceed in a permanent way by means of listening, comparison with the experience of others, deepening of some specific educational topics, and in difficult cases even with recourse to experts, and with participation in "classes on parenting." We have some schools that prepare persons for social and political tasks. Why not attempt to establish some schools for parents?...

Thus, persons become parents as they become more aware of and perhaps even more competent in the various responsibilities of life. Several days ago at Brussels, I took part in a meeting of some bishops from the great European cities. We sought to listen to one another in the desire to understand what it means to be bishops and to study how we can help ourselves to assume and live our pastoral responsibility. For bishops, too, become such on the day of their episcopal ordination, but then each day they must learn how to become bishops, and so the exchange of experiences, the comparison of initiatives, etc., is important.

And so, this day by day learning occurs at all levels of responsibility. It is wonderful that it also takes place in that first cell of social responsibility which is the family, in which the practice of comparison, and even the establishment of some type of school for parents can give courage and comfort, can open horizons, remove the anxiety of blind alleys and dark paths, and restore serenity and trust.

With the strength that you parents will know how to rediscover in your married/family life, and with the maturation which you will know how to achieve more and more, you will be able to carry out your ministry and to bring about an essential, not a secondary, contribution to the growth of society.

c) To be protagonists means, in the third place, *to exercise that role even outside of the family, in one's multiple relations with society*, not from a wrong or presumptuous pretense, but rather in the name of truth. If, in fact, the family is the first cell of society, it must rediscover this role so that the whole of human, social, national and international life may be ordered more according to the values of solidarity, justice, love, generosity, disinterestedness, selflessness, industriousness, and brotherhood, which are the original values of the family (cf *Familiaris Consortio*, 42-43). This involves pouring out the values rediscovered in family experience on all levels, even on the planetary level. Therefore, those dedicated to pastoral work for the family have the duty not only to look after what concerns the family itself, but also to spread family values and promote the protection and affirmation of such values within society.

In this sense it is urgent that all families completely fulfill their role in society by overcoming isolation and remaining open to the world. It is certainly a role that can be expressed in various ways, from the creation of a public opinion that is more attentive to the values and problems of the family and of life, to the witness of some virtues and styles of life that can be a model and example for social relationships, to the direct contribution to the promotion of a genuine family policy in collaboration with other educational agencies existing today.

With regard to this last, I would like to urge Christian parents to new forms of collaboration with the Christian community and, in particular, with the parish and with all those pastoral initiatives (whether already in existence or to be renewed or begun again) which are directed to the preparation of young people for married life and, more generally, to the choice of their personal vocation.

Likewise, I also believe it necessary to renew the awareness and strengthen the will and the longing for a direct and responsible involvement in the structures and in the scholastic organisms that call for participation. This attention is to be ever more careful, critical, intelligent and active, especially in those moments which seem to be marked by a certain tiredness, distrust, and lack of motivation and commitment.

To be protagonists in the field of education thus means to exercise the role of protagonist even outside the family. To be such a protagonist requires involvement in everything from the formation of public opinion to life styles and politics, in collaboration with the Christian community and the school, aiming for what we could call, in its totality, a *global education to peace.*

The family is a fundamental place for education to peace, for educating persons to overcome social aggressiveness. From the family a truly evangelical lifestyle can arise, which then becomes the choice of children and young people and so part of the tradition of society. One of the topics I propose to discuss in the next pastoral year concerns children ages twelve to sixteen and, in particular, the so-called problem of "flight," of young people distancing themselves from Church after Confirmation, after having made their profession of faith. This problem demands great attention, which is not easily resolved with a formula, which makes families, churches, parishes suffer very much, not only in Italy but also to some extent throughout all of the western world. The roots of this problem probably lie in the family and in the initial years of one's education. During this period, fundamental choices are made which are either pro-life and pro-society, or which are potentially rebellious choices that favor an attitude of non-acceptance toward life and society.

With regard to this point, the family has some basic responsibilities, even if it is not aware of them.

The consequences of a child's first years will be revealed later when the youngster is able to make choices. These future choices are influenced by the child's first years and by his/her environment of acceptance.

d) Finally, the leadership of the family also concerns all forms of social deviance, especially among youth, and deviance within the sphere of the family.

I am thinking, on the one hand, of the phenomena of violence, of the maltreatment and sexual abuse of children, of the many cases of sexual violence by which our area is, unfortunately, marked; and on the other hand, of the ever more dramatic proportions which drugs are assuming in the world of the young.

These are phenomena which confront and challenge so many realities, not only at the level of social assistance but also at the levels of planning, acceptance, sharing, and civil, social and pastoral prevention. At the same time, these phenomena are linked to the employment, economic and housing situations of the family. They are related to the quality of the parent-child relationship, to the atmosphere of real union and love in the family, to the importance which the family itself assumes and can in fact assume in the social structure.

Here again lies the need for the family to recover its role as protagonist, both within its own confines and in relation to the society in which it lives.

Forms Which the "Educational Leadership" of the Family Assumes

We can now look, at least briefly, at the forms which this educational leadership of the family assumes, letting ourselves be guided by the text from Deuteronomy.

a) First of all, *sharing the faith* within the family sphere: "Keep these words that I am commanding you today.... Recite them to your children and talk about them when you are at home" (Dt 6:6-7).

In my pastoral letter, *In Principio la Parola* (*In the Beginning Was the Word*), I recalled that today, unfortunately, our ordinary daily conversation rarely deals, simply and seriously, with topics related to the faith. We are often silent about these realities, especially in the family. And I said: "If the family succeeds in gathering around the Word of God, either by discussing what was proclaimed in church during the liturgy, or by systematically reading passages from the Bible, it will find an inexhaustible source of precious messages about family life itself, about the experiences the family passes through in the various stages of life, about the events that take place in today's world" (*In Principio la Parola*, V, 3).

I also remember having then indicated, in the booklet *Insegnaci a Pregare in Famiglia* (*Teach Us How to Pray as a Family*), some concrete means for prayer: beginning from a biblical text—a page from the Gospel, a passage from the Old Testament, a psalm—reflecting in silence and then letting both parents and children express in prayer their reactions, searches, suffering. It is a way of sharing the faith in a simple manner.

b) Sharing the faith is not lived only in explicit dialogue on topics of faith and in moments of prayer together, but is rendered concrete *in the daily experience of choices* made at each stage of our existence and in all the areas of our life.

In fact, the text of Deuteronomy says that you will talk about the commandments "when you are at home and when you are away, when you lie down and when you rise" (Dt 6:7).

All the possible coordinates of time and space are included here to indicate that the transmission of the Lord's precepts is not something just for a moment, but something that concerns each moment of each day of life.

It is urgent, then, that the communication of the faith and of other Christian values be bound up, for example, with respect for life, with the meaning of love, with the right understanding of sexuality, and that it daily express itself in a right relationship between faith and life. It is not a question of something to be done on extraordinary occasions, even though these are an incentive. To communicate our faith means living the simplest choices of the day with an attitude of faith. Our faith influences our conversation about the family, relations, the parish, the Church and society; our decisions to make or not to make certain purchases; our planning of vacations; our way of spending Sunday, or of responding to the different requests that come from school or work.

All these aspects of our existence are called to become a channel of visual communication of truth, justice, uprightness, goodness and faith. In the ordinariness of life, the questions and choices of parents and children—problems, desires and difficulties—are able to truly enrich the maturation of family life itself.

c) Finally I would like to recall the *importance of signs and actions* in the educational task of the family. "Bind (these words that I am commanding you today) as a sign on your hand, fix them as an emblem on your forehead, and write them on the doorposts of your house and on your gates" (Dt 6:8-9).

Even today we see these signs on the hand, on the forehead, on the doorposts of the houses of Jewish families who remember this precept.

But what does it mean, in reality? It means that we

must rediscover the simplicity of some visible signs, of some actions. For example, placing some signs of our faith in a visible spot in our home: *the crucifix*, or a religious picture, a candle or another sign which is a reminder of Baptism, the book of the Bible. When I enter a house to visit the sick, I at once take note of the distinctive signs of the style, the faith, and the daily life of the family.

Among the actions, I mention again *family prayer* every evening, at least a brief prayer before supper. It was not by chance that for Christmas I prepared a small booklet entitled *Preghiere Brevi per la Cena* (*Brief Prayers for Suppertime*), and I recommended children especially to introduce it into their families.

In addition to prayer, other simple yet eloquent actions can and must be carried out—such as acts of caring, of charity, of help, of celebration—which local and family tradition already live or would be able to point out and suggest.

Life as a Blessing

Before concluding the reflection, I offer you a final important consideration which brings us from the Feast of the Family to the Day for Life, which we will celebrate in a few weeks.

Educational leadership finds the condition for its possibility and its continual stimulus in the presence of children. In fact, thanks to this presence the family is continually reminded to question itself about its role, about its way of fulfilling itself, about the choices it makes, about its life style.

In this sense, too, each life that is born and grows within the family nucleus is a precious and enriching event; *it is a blessing.*

Today Christian couples meet with many difficulties when faced with life: the growing problem of sterility; the regulation of fertility; the fear of possible defects and of different forms of illness; even the perception of children as a possible threat to the harmony of the couple; the unwillingness to redimension some pretended needs within the overall tenor of life; the specter of an unhappy existence; the threat of a total destruction of humankind, or of living in an environment that is irremediably polluted.

The temptations are many. The most frequent, right from the beginning, is to delay—sometimes for years—the birth of the first child, or even to reject it by every possible means. From such an attitude stems a culture preoccupied only with a supposed quality of life, a culture which forgets that, while such a concern is certainly important, legitimate and to be shared, it is not the first and absolute value. There also arises a mentality that sees in contraception and abortion, both regarded as a means for regulating births, the most suitable way of resolving the problem.

In the face of these ever more widespread tendencies, the Christian conscience cannot remain indifferent. Therefore, with the whole Church in Italy and with all the Churches, especially in the countries of the West, we see the opportunity and urgent need to promote a broad strategy in favor of life and to appeal to consciences and public opinion confronted with the widespread mentality against life which pervades society, thanks to the conspiracy of silence.

From this point of view, we cannot fail to express once more our negative judgment on having recourse to contraceptive practices, to abortion and to everything which fundamentally expresses violence, rejection of life, and an inability to face responsibilities with the courage that comes from faith and from trust in the love God has for the human person and his future.

We are, in fact, persuaded that every human being, from the beginning to the end of his or her earthly existence, according to his or her intrinsic dignity as "person," is essentially valuable and is neither instrumental nor subordinate to other ends and values.

While with John Paul II we believe that the "unconditional respect for the right to life of each human person already conceived and not yet born is one of the pillars on which every civil society rests" (cf *Address to participants in the convention for studies on "The right to life and Europe,"* December 18, 1987), we are aware that in "some situations, renouncing abortion and welcoming the child can also demand a high price in terms of a renunciation of well-being. But the gain in terms of 'meaning,' not only for the parents but for the whole of society (which must contribute to bearing the burden) is vastly superior" (cf my article: "Respect for Values," *Avvenire*, January 30, 1986).

Above all, it is important that parents rediscover and are helped to rediscover that life is the great gift which God entrusts to the responsibility of man and woman, called to the dignity of being procreators, participants in the very act of love by which God brings a new person into the world.

The passage from Luke that we have listened to (Lk 1:39-45), as well as the words, "Blessed is the fruit of your womb," which have been drawn from it because of their clear Marian tone in view of the upcoming tenth Day for Life, clearly suggest to us that, from the moment Christ is born of Mary and has chosen this way to come among us, each human life is definitively blessed and welcomed by God's mercy.

Each human life is a gift and a blessing. Even the prophet said it, in the poetical passage which was read at the beginning of this encounter: "Your children are not your children. They are the sons and daughters of the great desire which Life has in itself. They do not come from you but through you" (Gilbran, *The Prophet*).

I therefore address to Christian families the invitation to rediscover this value. And you, dearest workers in the pastoral activity for families, I recommend that you help families rediscover it.

In this task the twentieth anniversary of Pope Paul VI's encyclical *Humanae Vitae* on the regulation of births, can be of assistance, together with the various structures which later arose from it to sustain the journey of the couple, structures such as centers for methods of natural family planning.

But it is especially by means of a journey of faith, fostered and supported also by the various experiences of family spirituality, that we can and must recover and at the same time witness to the value of life as a gift blessed by God.

Conclusion

All of us are asked to take part docilely and responsibly in the plan of God: "Hear O Israel."

As it did for Mary and Joseph, this response involves reflection, humility, and searching, so as to understand well what God is asking of us with regard to the educational task, what God is asking of parents with regard to the duty of procreation, with regard to new lives.

Let us pray together to the Holy Family of Nazareth that they may help and sustain us on this journey which is decisive for human history.

Meditation for families, Milan, January 23, 1988

CHAPTER 10

Toward an Education to Freedom and Vocation

Introduction

This is now the third consecutive year that we have met together in the cathedral—parents, children, associations, the Family Commission of Catholic Action, parishes, and ecclesial groups—for a moment of reflection which is also intended to be an expression of gratitude and encouragement. Gratitude for what you do and for who you are; encouragement in all that you are doing so that your families may be the privileged place in which God loves to dwell and act, the place in which love is guarded, revealed and communicated.

Many times during these months dedicated to the journey of educating, I have thought of families. Sometimes I have been reminded of the theme by the letters I have received: letters which spoke of beautiful realities, and others, instead, which spoke of sorrowful and tragic events, of difficulties that are, humanly speaking, insurmountable.

I would have liked to be able to do what I said in the first pages of the Christmas letter, *Don Bosco ci scrive* (*Don*

Bosco Writes to Us): "to listen to you personally, to take part in your conversations, to explore together with you the meaning of this life, which at times is so dark and mysterious...to pray with you."

Because of the practical impossibility of fulfilling my desire, I now seek to sow at least the seeds of a reflection which I then entrust to each one of you, that you may read it in its entirety, discuss it and draw from it some working conclusions for parishes, the communities, family groups, all those realities and institutions that are involved in this journey.

I would like, that is, to dwell with you on a topic which I asked be kept in mind during the various Diocesan Days, beginning from the Day of Solidarity to the Day for Life, to Palm Sunday of Charity, to the Assembly of Sichem: *the difficulties of youth* and its relationship to the *family sphere.*

I am thinking of the many phenomena of violence, of mistreatment and abuse of minors, of sexual violence; I am thinking especially of the phenomenon of drugs, as well as of the difficulties linked to the employment, economic and housing situations of the family, and of the quality of parent-child relationships.

From this springs the title of the reflection: "The youth-life-drugs problem: a challenge for the family and other educational spheres."

The Phenomena of the Unrest of Youth

The spread and the dramatic character of some of the forms of unrest among young people are witnessed by all and arouse concern.

On Christmas Day alone there were 28 drug-related deaths in Italy; in 1988 in Milan, the number of deaths was more than double that of the preceding year. In Italy in 1988, 4,000 sick persons were reported as suffering from

AIDS, with a very high percentage of them living in Milan.

And then there are forms of unrest that are more hidden and widespread. These arise from a state of malaise and from the undefined suffering of young people, in which, however, moments of serious marginalization come to a head.

Divorce and separation among young couples are on the increase. In fact, statistics show that the percentage of separations and divorces is greater in the first ten years of marriage. Also of concern are anti-life attitudes.

All this cannot but remind us of our responsibility and call for our prayer and the commitment of the diocesan community which you represent, in not passively accepting the forms of unrest among youth.

Need for Recovery and Prevention

No one can remain indifferent in the face of the emergency produced by such phenomena.

1. The personal and social *recovery* of those who live in these situations of degeneration is important. Their recovery calls into play various social, civil, political, ecclesial, educational, and legislative realities. In this regard, volunteer work is to be encouraged and fostered anew by the intelligent coordination of the various forces at hand and of cooperation with the social services present in the area.

Direct involvement of families is also possible. It is a matter of educating ourselves and thinking of ourselves as open families, attentive to the needs of others, capable of offering hospitality and welcome, open to forms of adoption and of custody, involved in associations, co-operatives, communities of support, recovery and solidarity. The testimony we have heard has underscored that which is verified in all these cases: beyond and within the individual experiences, there is the joy that overcomes the resistance, fatigue, difficulties and discomfort of choosing to help troubled youth.

But such choices cannot be improvised; they require preparation, a daily education. They require the humility and the courage to face failures. In my letter, *Itinerari educativi* (*Educational Itineraries*), I spoke often of needing to be ready to meet failures, with the trust that they are never definitive because the love of God, which has been communicated to us, makes us capable of fidelity and constancy.

In addition, such choices are sustained with the help of associations, educational and even consultative organizations. Thanks be to God I can affirm that, in our diocese, such "open" families are not few. For the most part they draw no attention, but their presence is of great importance, and I wish that by coming to know them other families may be motivated to decide to live in the same way, each according to its possibilities.

2. The means which are promoted and used to assist recovery are not enough. In fact, *education and prevention* are indispensable, making every effort to hinder the fall by working on the root causes of the unrest.

Among these causes we can point out one that synthesizes them all: the loss of the sense of life's meaning, of the meaning of one's existence.

Young people who are involved in various forms of unrest—especially if they reach a certain "safety level"—betray, with a look or with words, that they have not received or have lost that which can give value to life, and that they do not, therefore, have sufficient motives for facing daily difficulties. Their days are characterized by dissatisfaction and discontent. The primary task for everyone is therefore to present and to witness to the meaning of daily existence, the taste for living and the reasons for living.

The Responsibility of the Family

This urgent need calls on each family with all its responsibilities, to distinguish the roots of unrest in a complex, difficult situation within the family itself.

In the letter, *Don Bosco ci scrive (Don Bosco Writes to Us)*, I cite a phrase of the saint, which I was tempted to correct or tone down, but which I preferred instead to quote exactly. He says that the family is *always* at the root of the serious deviances of young people. In reality, deficiencies in education and the disintegration of families play a very large part in the problems of youth.

At the same time, however, I believe that it is both necessary and wonderful to emphasize that there are still many, many families who know how to fulfill their role and their responsibilities and do so by means of daily witness and formation. They know how to base and renew their commitment on the native resources that derive from marriage and from participation in the love of Christ, which is communicated to them in the sacrament of Christian marriage and in the life of faith. And they know how to draw energy from an intelligent and continual communitarian journey of growth in the rediscovery and assumption of their duties. Your numbers and the attention with which many of you—families whom I want to greet now in a special way—are accompanying children who are in the seminary or in a novitiate or religious formation group, are an eloquent sign that many are still capable of fulfilling their responsibilities and of responding effectively to the daily challenges of society.

Indeed I would like this to be given more notice in the parishes, where I often meet young people who complain that they do not have adult models of the Christian life.

At times we think of the adult as an isolated being, a kind of particular example of holiness, inserted like a stranger in the ordinary life of the people. Examples of lay adult holiness, instead, are found first of all in parents, in the families.

I would also like to clarify a point: reminding families of their responsibility does not mean blaming them. Public opinion and the mass media penalize them too easily. It is not right to ask the family to rediscover itself and to carry out its functions while leaving it alone with its responsibilities, only to later identify it as the scapegoat for all the ills of our society.

Rather, the family should be helped and supported at all levels, cultural and educational. It should be assisted in problems at home, with provisions of a political, economic and social nature that truly foster family life. It is likewise necessary that we question the way in which the family is presented and proposed by the mass media, and that we be vigilant in the face of attempts to legitimize, on a cultural and even juridical-legislative level, family models that are not founded on a stable union.

The ecclesial community itself is involved. I renew the appeal, which I addressed to it in the pastoral program of this year, to promote an attentive family pastoral plan and to suggest educational means, particularly to accompany married couples, by means of the experimentation that is being carried out in educational programs for parents (*Itinerari educativi*, 22, 45-46).

In the attempt to help families assume their responsibilities, I would like to suggest some considerations which seek to shed light on how the specific contribution they are called to offer may be a contribution to an education to freedom and vocation.

An Education to Freedom and Vocation

1. First of all, *all education* is, of its nature, *liberating*. The liberty that accompanies education is purified by

means of a continual and patient work of discernment, a liberty respected and promoted with wisdom and prudence, one open to accepting risks.

In this context, it is opportune to recall the importance of fostering greater responsibility in children and young people, in the conviction that "those who do not learn to satisfy their own existential needs, naturally, without harming or exploiting others, will never be responsible persons.... To make children responsible persons, it is certainly useful to accustom them to face the difficulties of life, its stress, its failures, avoiding the tendency to resolve every problem for them and to smooth out all obstacles, as some parents, who are too anxious and solicitous, believe in doing" (*Don Bosco ci scrive,* 12).

To educate means to teach freedom and to communicate the fundamental values that are linked to the development of freedom: the sense of justice, acceptance, dialogue, availability, selflessness, and profound solidarity. Our society needs this today.

2. But in order that freedom be real, it must be open to all the plans of God, it must be understood as *a response to a plan* in which he calls us to be conformed to the image of his Son, Jesus. St. Paul has reminded us of this in the passage from the Letter to the Romans which we listened to: "Predestined to be conformed to the image of his Son" (Rom 8:29).

This is the plan which gives meaning to life. It is a question of recognizing and welcoming this plan, first of all in the family. Here is where real freedom and maturity lie. The twelve-year-old Jesus, who remains in Jerusalem to concern himself with the things of his Father, affirms his true identity as Son of God (cf Lk 2:41-52).

To educate, therefore, means to help others live according to the plan of God, so that each can recognize and follow his or her own vocation. All formative action thus possesses an intrinsic vocational dimension, and the family is called to be the privileged sphere in which each one may freely decide to live according to the divine plan. How beautiful it is to hear parents say that, by growing with the vocational journey of the child, they also grow to new dimensions in comprehending the mystery of God, of joy, of freedom! How sad, instead, in visiting the parishes, to come to know families who oppose the desire of a son or daughter to choose the religious life or the priesthood!

So that families may be open to educating to vocation, it is important that they experience moments of prayer together, of listening to the Word, of silence. In the last several years I have sought, by means of some booklets, to stimulate prayer in families, and I entrust to you once more the task of using and diffusing them. May you be apostles of this prayer from which many vocational responses spring forth.

In addition to prayer, we need a climate of attentiveness to what is happening; not a narcissism centered on self, but attention to the needs and requests that come to us from others. Then all the vocations will be able to flourish: matrimony—which is an authentic call of God and, as such, is announced and rediscovered; consecrated life in the priesthood, religious and missionary life, and in the secular Institutes, as well as the choice (though without a public and institutionalized form of consecration) of the virginal life for greater dedication to the Church. There is also the vocation of those who find themselves in a state of involuntary celibacy, which, however, is transformed in an appeal of God to personal freedom.

Encouragement and Comfort to Parents and Children

In concluding, I would like to express a word of encouragement and comfort to parents and children, that they might assume their responsibilities.

1. To parents: you cannot live your tremendous responsibilities alone. You must avail yourselves of the collaboration of other educational realities, beginning from the church and school, and of opportunities for sharing with other couples and families.

In addition, seek to question yourselves about the values in which you intend to educate your children, drawing inspiration from the suggestions we listened to in the book of Tobit.

It would be wonderful if, during the year, together with the other diocesan educational bodies, parents and their older children and other couples attempted to specify some fundamental points for an educational plan. Valuable indications could result because they came from the parents themselves.

And I want to tell you again not to become discouraged over failures, about which many suffering parents often write to me. Act in such a way that failures cannot be attributed to your negligence, but seek to envelop them in a journey of greater love. Prepare yourselves for those unexpected or unforeseen choices which could also place you in the situation of not understanding right away, as happened to Mary and Joseph. Even in this case, do not refuse to journey and keep such events in your heart; make your suffering a means by which to guarantee the freedom of your children. Let yourselves be questioned by the choices of your children, and do not fear to accompany their journey with anxious and trustful joy, including the journey of the priestly, religious or missionary life.

2. To children: you too are subjects and protagonists of the educational task and you cannot only complain or demand from others, just as you cannot pretend to do everything by yourselves.

If you want to be free, if you want to feel truly valued, if you rightly ask for much love on the part of those who are older, remember that these desires have to be made to grow in the right direction. Open your eyes and look well! "Before you there are always two paths: one which leads to true freedom, dignity, love and joy, to life: it is the path of the Gospel which Jesus has shown us; the other, instead, confuses with its deception, leading you to slavery, misery, loneliness and unhappiness.... Think seriously about it and listen to your conscience" (*Don Bosco ci scrive*, 27-28). Believe that your parents, your catechists and teachers are real friends. Consider Jesus as the friend and master who is always close to you. With him you will no longer be afraid of anything. "Be his followers, listen to him, pray to him every day, imitate him by practicing his beatitudes" (*Don Bosco*, 28).

Dearest Christian families, I have offered you some reflections within the framework of the serious unrest that plagues young people today, an unrest which has many causes. I am certain that when families, together with the whole Church, commit themselves to an educational activity capable of allowing the freedom of persons to mature and of helping them to discover and live the plan of God, they offer what is most necessary so that life may have meaning and thus be truly lived.

To educate, remaining in the school of God the educator, is the most serious way of assuming our responsibilities, of being attentive to today's problems and tragedies, of offering our contribution for the good of human persons and of society.

May Mary, our Mother, the teacher of Jesus and of the Church, assist us on our journey, assist our work as Christian families, assist the family pastoral plan of our diocese so that it may be courageous in responding to the serious challenges of the modern world.

Meditation for families, Milan, January 21, 1989

CHAPTER 11

Getting Along in the Family

Dear Friends,

It's still Christmas! A feast everyone looks forward to, even if some—due to loneliness, mourning, or division in the family—would prefer to set it at another date. But I wish that everyone who reads these lines may experience a moment of joy.

And do you know what I want to wish for you in particular this year? "That you may get along well together!" I wish that we may together build greater harmony everywhere, and in families first of all. This will be the intention of my prayers to the Son of God who has made himself the brother of all, and who wants us to live in harmony and peace.

I can hear someone immediately object: but we do get along well, we love one another! We don't need these wishes! I already know that this may be the initial, spontaneous reaction, and it is right that it be so. We have it so much at heart to get along well that it is hard for us to admit, to ourselves and especially to those whom we don't know well, that agreement among us at home is not perfect.

However, when we reflect calmly on our daily relationships, on the meaning of certain silences, on the bitterness that lies behind some arguments over trifles, on the degree of irritability that pollutes the domestic atmosphere even more than the automobile exhaust fumes in the streets, we willingly admit that getting along in the family is not always easy, and that if we did get along well at home everything would be much simpler.

But then, what should we do? How can we understand the deeper reasons behind the smallest daily disagreements which, to some extent, poison our lives? How can we enter into the intimacy of our soul so as to find, treat and heal the wounds we bear inside because we have hurt one another, if by nothing else than by our neglect, rudeness, weariness, or lack of self-control?

I do not want to preach to you here; that is something I should do first of all to myself. But I want to invite you to read some pages of the Bible with me, pages in which we discover precisely how difficult and yet how beautiful it is to get along well in our families.

To be a brother or sister is one of the four fundamental dimensions of the human person, together with that of being son or daughter, husband or wife, father or mother. In this letter I am speaking especially of the brother/sister dimension. I do it in my role as your brother, an older brother for many of you. Paul VI used to tell the bishops that we must become the brothers of our people as well as pastors, fathers and teachers. This counsel holds also for parents, teachers, educators and priests.

One final word: when I say getting along *"in the family"* I am not giving this term a restricted meaning. I mean, rather, to say that the difficulties between brothers and sisters of any age, between husband and wife, between cousins and relatives of any degree, the difficulties, that is, of living together in the family and among rela-

tives, are not so very different from the tensions which
cause opposition among groups in the Church, in political and other parties in society, and among people who
differ in race and cultural background.

If we learn to discern and heal the conflicts in the
family, we will also be able to see and heal, day by day, the
small and great personal and social conflicts that arise in
the parish, at work, in school, in the office, in the market-
place, in the stadium, in government, on the continents.
The laws of human pacification all have something in
common. The biblical precepts for the overcoming of
individual conflicts have a symbolic character, that is, they
also signify and shed light on the relationship between
groups, races, and nations. These precepts also shed light
on relationships within the Church, for example between
conservatives and progressives, between associations and
groups of different tendencies, between young and old,
between pastor and assistant pastor, between priests and
laity. Even the relationships between Hebrews and Christians, those two groups of brothers so closely united and
at the same time so in need of ever greater understanding, receive light from the pages of the Bible.

So, a fruitful reading of the Bible can help us in the
search for ways of getting along better in the family, in the
Church and in society!

Six Stories about Brothers

In biblical history there are many accounts about
brothers whose human characteristics are repeated in every generation, right up to our own. By reading these
accounts intelligently we can, in fact, perceive in the individual and particular cases of those times, images that are
typical of our daily life.

I remind you that the words "brother" and "sister"
have in the eastern language—and had even in Jesus'

time—a much broader meaning than we give them. For the people of the Bible, brother and sister refer not only to those who are born of the same parents, but to any relative: cousins, nieces and nephews, aunts and uncles. The words can also signify a friend, companion, or colleague. This detail might convince those who are an only child to continue reading this letter. On the other hand, even the only child, sooner or later, seeks anxiously and insistently for someone to be brother or sister to him/her, because of the innate need that every person has for a fraternal relationship. A person has no peace until he or she finds someone with whom this special relationship can be shared.

From the many biblical stories of brothers and sisters I have chosen six which seem to me to reflect very well our daily relationships and behavior. I will begin with the one that the Bible, too, narrates first.

Why Do We Hurt One Another? (Gen 4:1-16)

Often this question arises in our hearts. We could, in fact, understand (not justify) arguments and tensions where there are conflicts of interest or something similar. But at times, dissent between brothers and sisters (or parents, or friends, or companions at school and work) breaks out even where we see no motive for contention: both persons are good, both have their own position and their own personal success. And yet they find it hard to put up with one another, they criticize and oppose one another. Temperament? Fate? The first biblical story about brothers, which is also the story of mortal hatred between equals, helps us to enter dramatically into the heart of the problem.

Cain and Abel had many things in common: parents, environment, home, upbringing. However, they were unable to reconcile their differences: the oldest and strongest was Cain, the youngest and weakest was Abel. The first was a farmer and the second a shepherd. Their professions expressed different mentalities and cultures.

Both offered God the products of their work. But Cain had the impression that he was not being heard and accepted as was his brother. In fact, he convinced himself that God was distinguishing between persons and preferred Abel. Cain did not bear in mind that God is a Father. Cain saw Abel as a rival. He lost his peace and the joy of living, and allowed envy, jealousy and hatred to break out in his heart.

Out in the country, far from the eyes of others, Cain raised his hand against his brother Abel and killed him. Then the Lord said to Cain: "Where is your brother Abel?"

He said: "I do not know; am I my brother's keeper?"

And God replied: "Your brother's blood is crying out to me from the ground!"... Cain said to the Lord: "My punishment is greater than I can bear!"

But why didn't Cain know how to control the hatred and violence as soon as these arose in his soul? Why didn't he take into account the fact that the well-being and happiness of his brother were also his?

And why should we experience vexation, rebellion and anger when our neighbors are appreciated and praised, when they succeed in their undertakings and things go well for them? Why must we rejoice when things go badly for them?

The envious person is able to cover his/her feelings with the presumed pride of the other and to justify these feelings with various reasons.

Only in the end did Cain realize that envy of and violence against his brother did not resolve his problems or satisfy his needs. On the contrary, they increased them.

Conflict of Interests (Gen 13:2-18)

Fortunately, tensions as serious as those between Cain and Abel are rare. They are, instead, very frequent on the level of races and peoples, where envy and the sense of inferiority or superiority break out into fratricidal wars.

But we are speaking first of all of the family sphere. Now we will consider what is perhaps the most frequent cause of disagreements and divisions between brothers and sisters and between friends: conflict of interest. Two persons get along well, love one another, speak to one another willingly, go around together. But, at a certain point, coldness, silence, and distrust arise, which then break out into disputes, arguments, and separation. What has happened? Let us listen to the second biblical story which features an uncle and a nephew: Abraham and Lot.

Abraham was a man who had made his fortune. From the little he had, he became a cattle-raiser, a respected and esteemed man. His nephew Lot, who was an orphan, had followed him in his migration from the far east toward Palestine; he always shared in Abraham's work and his successes. At a certain point, he began to have his own herds and his own men to work them.

Little by little, the interests that had been the same began to diverge. The Bible lets us understand that the fault was not primarily Abraham's, for he was an upright and peaceful man. It was probably not even Lot's, who had great respect for his uncle. It was their herdsmen who fought. We know how cruel and tragic arguments between herdsmen can be, over a well, some pasture land, a path to travel, a real or supposed theft of herds. And so Abraham and Lot, who had lived in genuine harmony and a peaceful union of interests, were set in opposition to one another.

What could Abraham do? He could insist on his rights, claim his priority, have everything placed again under his command. Instead he showed himself to be wise and understanding. He perceived that at a certain point it was not worthwhile to obstinately maintain certain rights.

There are families who, because they have insisted on their rights for years and decades, have poisoned their blood, have spent huge sums in litigations, and meanwhile the goods that they were contending have remained fruitless! Before beginning arguments over interests, it is well to ask ourselves: is it worth it? And above all, what do Christians do when they recognize that, on the one hand, they have claim to some rights, although these are not always guaranteed, while on the other, they are certain of losing peace, love, harmony, and even health and good humor because of the disagreement? And what then of the harm done to the soul, to faith, which is numbed when we don't succeed in living in peace?

Abraham said to Lot: "Let there be no strife between you and me, and between your herders and my herders; for we are kindred. Is not the whole land before you? Separate yourself from me. If you take the left hand, then I will go to the right; or if you take the right hand, then I will go to the left" (Gen 13:8-9). Abraham let Lot choose the best pastures. The history that follows lets us see that it is precisely the richest lands chosen by Lot that will be struck by the punishment that destroys Sodom and Gomorrah. Abraham had given up some of his rights, but in fact obtained the most lasting pasture lands!

Abraham invites us, not to automatically renounce our rights in case of a disagreement (it is not always licit to do so), but:

1. not to sharpen the causes of a dispute out of motives of self-interest;

2. to know how to be big-hearted and to willingly seek a friendly settlement rather than a quarrel, even with the help of some wise person who is a friend of both parties;

3. not to make a difference of interests a motive for rancor, bitterness and hostility;

4. to know how to give in, knowing that God will not

fail to reward those who have a good heart.

"If it is possible," says St. Paul, "so far as it depends on you, live peaceably with all" (Rom 12:18). And again: "Do not be overcome by evil, but overcome evil with good" (Rom 12:21).

Love and Hate (Gen 25:34; 27:32-33)

There are cases in which, among brothers and sisters, there is neither complete understanding nor complete antipathy, but a mixture that is difficult to understand even for those who are experiencing it. It is a matter of an alternation of sympathy-antipathy, of love-hate. In fact, one has the impression that the two feelings and the two passions do not exclude one another but are intertwined. Persons hate one another because they love one another, and vice versa. A third biblical story can help us enter into this mystery of the human psyche.

Esau and Jacob were twin brothers. Because of this they had many reasons for feeling themselves united and in agreement. However, they were not the kind of twins who resemble each other in everything. On the contrary, there were not a few differences between them: their physiognomies, intelligence, characters, interests and abilities were different. Esau was the father's favorite, while Jacob was the mother's. Yet they had some feelings in common: they loved one another and hated one another with the same ease and frequency; they sought one another in order to immediately flee from one another. Their mother had understood this even before they were born, because she felt them struggling in her womb even though they were so close.

Jacob, clever and pretentious, took advantage of the hunger of his brother and of the blindness of his father. Esau, because of his impatience and superficiality, lost his rights. The mother was no longer able to reconcile them; they had to separate so as not to kill one another. The family appeared to be torn apart, the children discontented and angry, the parents disappointed and discouraged.

But at a mature age, the two brothers returned to seek one another. And they found one another: "Now Jacob looked up and saw Esau coming, and four hundred men with him" (Gen 33:1). He was very afraid.

His twin brother could have become furious and a war to the death could have broken out between them. But Jacob, having been taught by God, went to meet his brother, bowing down to the ground and humiliating himself at least seven times. Then "Esau ran to meet him, and embraced him, and fell on his neck and kissed him, and they wept" (Gen 33:4).

Finally the tension in their souls was released, fear disappeared, revenge vanished. They wept over their history, pardoned one another for their mutual wrongdoing, forgot the curses and exchanged blessings. Humility was able to transform the pleasure of pride and the desire for vengeance into the joy of pardon and the exchange of goodness.

An Impossible Reconciliation (Gen 37-50)

It is wonderful to see the reconciliation of two brothers such as Esau and Jacob. But there are cases in which reconciliation seems almost impossible. This happens when there have been actions that were so crushing and so offensive that one is tempted to say: "Enough, I am finished with them forever!" Is there hope even for a situation like this? This is the problem faced by the last account in Genesis, that which narrates the relationship between Joseph and his brothers.

They were eleven sons of the same father but of different mothers, with one sister, Dina, the protagonist of a story of kidnapping and violence.

Joseph was the next to the youngest son, born of the woman whom Jacob loved most. At seventeen years of age, he was a shepherd in the service of his brothers. But between him and them there was no harmony and their relations were not good. The motives were the usual: he was the favorite of his father, who clothed him better than he did the others; he reported the behavior of his brothers to his father; he was a great dreamer, and his dreams were interpreted by his brothers as projections of his ambition and mania for greatness. Their inability to dialogue with Joseph in a friendly way, to clear up their differences and dissension, their low level of tolerance and support in his regard, their refusal to recognize and criticize their own envy and to accept the reality of the facts, led them to nourish a savage hatred for Joseph.

One day when Joseph went to find his brothers to give news of them to his father, "they saw him from a distance, and before he came near to them, they conspired to kill him" (Gen 37:18). Then Judah said to his brothers: "What profit is it if we kill our brother and conceal his blood? Come, let us sell him to the Ishmaelites, and not lay our hands on him, for he is our brother, our own flesh" (Gen 37:26-27).

Some Midianite traders passed by and the brothers sold Joseph for twenty pieces of silver. He was taken into Egypt and immediately sold to one of Pharaoh's officials. But the Lord was with Joseph and, despite difficulties and sufferings, he became the most powerful man in the Egyptian kingdom.

Stricken by a terrible famine, Joseph's brothers were sent by their father into Egypt in search of grain. They appeared before Joseph without recognizing him. They bowed down to the ground before him.

Though Joseph recognized them, he pretended he did not; in fact, he treated them with severity and accused them of espionage. It seemed that the time had come for him to take revenge for the evil done to him. But Joseph

did not take revenge: with great pedagogical tact he
helped his brothers become aware of the fault they had
committed against their father and against him.

He led them gradually to repentance and to a generous love for the family and in particular for their father,
who lived for his children. When he saw them converted,
he revealed: "'I am your brother, Joseph, whom you sold
into Egypt. And now do not be distressed, or angry with
yourselves, because you sold me here; for God sent me
before you to preserve life.'... And he kissed all his brothers and wept upon them" (Gen 45:4-15).

When Even Pardon Divides (Luke 15:11-32)

The fifth story I want to recount to you is the well-
known story of the prodigal son, one of the most beautiful parables narrated by Jesus.

The protagonists, together with the father, are the
two brothers: the youngest who left home slamming the
door, determined not to return; and the elder who remained in the family serving his father.

But one fine day the spendthrift son reappeared,
reduced to misery. It was a return as much hoped for by
the father as it was unexpected and undesired by the
elder brother.

In fact, the latter, when he came to know about it,
did not want to go into the house. He refused to meet his
brother, and accused the father who had pardoned him
and had prepared a great feast. The elder protested: "But
why? This isn't right. He made his own choice; let him go
back to where he has been until now."

The father responded: "But why? He is my son, he is
your brother!" The father in the parable did not get involved in a lot of rationalization. He helped the older son
discover the reality and accept it. The prodigal son, whatever he may have become and whatever he had done,

always remained the life of the father and mother; he was always an integral part of the life of the family and of the community.

Certainly it becomes inconvenient in these cases to remind ourselves of that real, genuine, unalterable bond that unites us to a sinful and guilty brother. We experience this especially in the sphere of the largest of human families, in which we would want to punish those who have done wrong without seeking first of all their real good. Only conscience, enlightened by the revelation of Jesus, can convince us that the good of the other is always my good, also, our good, and so is his trouble. Only the real love of pure goodness can move us to embrace a guilty brother. We must learn from Jesus not to continually observe the other so as to judge and condemn him but to love and pardon, to help and rehabilitate him.

It Is Beautiful to Remain Together as Brothers

(Psalm 133; Acts 2:42-48; 4:32-35; 5:12-16)

That some brothers and sisters live together in harmony, collaboration and peace is truly marvelous. Unfortunately, it is not a frequent or common spectacle nowadays, but when we see it, it arouses admiration, sympathy and pleasure as in the time of the poet who wrote Psalm 133. One of these exceptional fraternal communities has been described in three moments by St. Luke in the Acts of the Apostles. The story of this community is also the last story about brothers and sisters that I want to present to you.

After Pentecost the small Christian community became much larger. Three thousand believers, then another two thousand, had requested Baptism.

They devoted themselves to the instruction of the apostles, they lived together and held everything in common. Those who had possessions sold them and distributed the proceeds to all, according to the needs of each one.

And each day, by common agreement, they went to the temple, and breaking the bread at home, they took food with joy and simplicity of heart, praising God. The Christians were esteemed by all the people because they formed only one heart and one soul.

They were like the model of a great family, open, enlarged, universal in spirit, capable of discovering and living a relationship of fraternity not based on the bond of blood, but on the unitive and innovative power of the spirit of Jesus Christ.

Living as Brothers and Sisters

Which of the many brothers and sisters of these six symbolic stories do we resemble most? Whom do we embody more frequently in our daily life?

Certainly none of us is always and in everything a Cain or a Jacob or a Joseph or the dissolute son of the parable or the Christian of Jerusalem. However, we are called to grow in fraternal love.

In order to act as true brothers and sisters, it is very important to be convinced that fraternity is not a utopia, an ideology, or a beautiful feeling, but is a fact, a reality, a component of human nature created and redeemed by God.

The *Declaration of the Rights of the Person*, born of the civil conscience of the people, recognizes universal fraternity in its first article: "All people are born free and equal in dignity and rights; they are gifted with reason and conscience, and must behave toward one another as brothers and sisters."

This awareness, which has increased so much in our time, becomes even more certain and operative if it is placed in the light of God's revelation in Jesus Christ.

"God...has willed that all people constitute only one family and that they treat one another as brothers and sisters. All, in fact, have been created in the image of God...and all are called to same end which is God himself." Vatican Council II teaches us this, developing the expression, full of hope and certainty, used by Jesus: "You are all brothers and sisters" (Mt 23:8).

On the idealistic and sentimental plane, everyone wants to be brothers and sisters. What then can hinder us from being so?

In every person, right from birth, there is—together with the desire and the design for fraternity—an arrogant and hostile affirmation of the ego in opposition to others. There is a disintegrating, egoistic and homicidal force that moves us to deny the others, not to recognize them as brothers and sisters. It convinces and instigates us to exclude them from our life, to marginalize them, to fight them, to exploit and sell them, even to kill them.

When we give way to our irrational and antisocial pride, which does not want us to be on the same level as others, we refuse to be equal to them, we despise and belittle them, we want the glorification of our ego and its superiority, we continually argue, we become accusers, masters and slave drivers of our brothers and sisters.

The evil of the world lies in the lack of fraternity among persons and peoples: wars break out which vanquish individuals and communities; racial and religious discrimination arise; the supremacy of political and economic interests dominate; exploitation, injustice and violence are justified; theft becomes a right; crime becomes the habitual recourse; and peace is destroyed. Even within a religious community, a parish, an association, if the truth that "each man is my brother and each woman my sister" is denied, then antagonism, rivalry, malice, envy, jealousy, and a subtle and clandestine conflict explode.

How Can We Educate Ourselves to Fraternity?

Discord is a congenital illness, the most widespread and the most difficult to care for and cure.

Now we ask: how can we recover within us the sense of universal fraternity in case we have lost it? Or how can we increase it and make it more effective?

All fraternity supposes, requires and is founded on paternity. Father and mother are the roots of any real fraternal community.

We first of all need to rediscover the Father, source of life for everyone, point of reference, model of behavior, reconciler of brothers and sisters.

When the father of the family is missing, is not recognized, is not obeyed with love, it is difficult for the children to be united to one another, to love one another, to help one another.

God became man in order to manifest his fatherhood in Jesus Christ, to communicate to us his grace which reconciles and reunites the entire human family. Our God is a Trinity in which Father, Son and Holy Spirit are persons in a perfect union and communion. His Word guides us to meet our brothers and sisters; it helps us to recognize them, accept and support them, esteem them, and live together with them.

If, like the first Christians remembered by Luke, we used more patience and intelligence in reading and meditating the Word of the Lord, how we would succeed in living together as brothers and sisters!

Those who love their father also love his children; those who love God must also love their brothers and sisters (cf 1 Jn 5). But the opposite is true: those who love the children also love the father; those who love their sisters and brothers love God (cf 1 Jn 4).

A practice that will lead us to live as sisters and brothers is that of "behaving as brothers" with everyone, in the spirit of the Gospel, whenever the occasion presents itself. Just as one who wants to learn how to paint must paint, and one who wants to learn a language must speak it, so those who want to become more and more a brother or sister to others and build fraternity, must daily live the psychology of being brother or sister and practice the rule of fraternity. To this end I am offering six simple and practical rules.

Recognize That We Are Not Very Fraternal

In fact, we expect respect and understanding from others, but we offer it rarely or only to those in whom we might have an interest. We are immediately offended when others oppose or criticize us, and yet we feel we have the right not to speak well of others and to offend them. We ask for help presumptuously and arrogantly, while we refuse to give a hand to those in need. We are expert in perceiving the defects of others, but we do not see the injustices, even serious ones, that we practice; we are always the only innocent ones, because the fault is always the other person's. We want to be pardoned without having repented; on the contrary we vindicate ourselves, and we make those who have injured us pay. We demand honor and love when we are stingy in showing esteem and goodness to our neighbor.

Don't Do to Others What You Don't Want Done to You

If this simple norm were really practiced by everyone, it could change the whole of society. Let's begin to observe it ourselves without waiting for others to begin, without expecting and demanding that everyone else put it into practice. This first rule of life affirms the principle of non-violence which is one of the greatest forces at the disposal of humanity. Non-violence is a choice of life and a rejection of death; it is the desire for peace in opposition to the diabolical instinct for war.

Any intrusiveness, aggression, injury, murder, committed against one person is an act of violence against the whole human family, because of that natural solidarity which unites us. The evil that we do to children, to young people, to the elderly, to women, to the sick, to the weak...falls back on us, on all of society.

Let us "unlearn" the art of war, whether family or civil, international or planetary. Let us stop the habit of fighting, the mentality of living in opposition. Let us break off all forms of teaching violence, even if only verbal, and learn and teach how to be non-violent, how to be builders of peace.

Non-violence is a virtue that can be practiced by everyone, rich and poor, those who command and those who obey, as long as we understand that our neighbor is like ourselves.

Let's Show Complete Availability in Listening to Others

Today people have more need of listening than of words. We have all learned how to speak, even many languages, and yet we are not more capable of listening to one another. Only when we listen to the other with attention and not distractedly, with patience and not in haste, with wonder and not annoyance, do we acquire the right and the authority to speak to his/her heart. Efficiency-minded as we have become, at times we believe that time given over to listening is time lost. In reality, if we think this way perhaps it is because we do not have time for others, but only for ourselves and our interests.

Not rarely, "speaking" expresses a will for power over others, it hides our feelings of distrust and rejection, it is a series of rationalizations and excuses for justifying ourselves, it is full of ambiguities and contradictions. "An attentive listening," instead, becomes a great and effective help offered to others.

People need to tell their problems to someone who understands them in order to minimize them, so as not to feel alone in painful situations, in order to discuss ways of solving problems or getting away from them. When one does not find someone with whom to share them, personal problems can become gigantic, frightening; they weaken the sense of life, they suffocate hope.

Let's Bear One Another's Burdens

This norm of community life, recorded by St. Paul in writing to the Galatians, is quite simple, it can almost seem a game, but it sums up the whole law of Christ. It invites us to serve others, to offer concrete help to a needy brother or sister. How many services may be asked of us in one day, often indirectly, by those who are close to us. They may be small services, apparently insignificant, but very effective in building up a fraternal community, in creating family union: serving at table, substituting for a moment for a companion at work, offering someone a cup of coffee, visiting a sick person, giving someone a bus ticket, writing to a prisoner, helping a child with his homework, answering the telephone, giving up one's seat to another, respecting the environment of the community, inviting a poor person to supper....

Jesus washed the feet of his disciples, inviting them to do as he did. Let's not turn away when we see someone in need. The "it's not up to me" attitude is often a sign of mental laziness, stinginess of heart, the negation of fraternity.

We bear one another's burdens when, in our activity, we allow them to interrupt us without becoming irritated, when we tolerate those who disturb us, annoy us, provoke us.

Bearing the burden means shouldering one another's weariness, enduring the difficulties that arise from living together, patiently agreeing to the desires of others. It also means being kind and loving with those who might not deserve it; kindly repeating an explanation to someone who did not understand; bearing with busybodies; forgiving those who repeat a mistake; humbly correcting someone who is in error. If we want to be brothers and sisters, we must become strong and untiring in bearing burdens.

The burdens we bear also include sins, ours and those of others. In this, too, Jesus Christ, he who bore the sins of the world, is our model. All our crimes were heaped on him. And he never complained. Jesus carried these burdens of ours freely, lovingly, continually.

Daily service to our sisters and brothers can give meaning to our whole life, can make it happier. And when the service becomes mutual, is reciprocal, it truly creates that union Jesus prayed for at the Last Supper; it makes us live the experience of the embrace, of charity, of real joy.

Let's Forgive One Another

Those who believe they have done nothing that requires forgiveness are proud and blind. This was why the older brother in the parable of the prodigal son was irritated by the father's forgiveness. He was convinced that he did not need to be forgiven for anything by anyone. The scribes and Pharisees, too, who were so convinced that they were just, went away when Jesus invited those who were without sin to cast the first stone (cf Jn 8:9).

In order to learn how to forgive one another we must experience Christian sorrow and repentance. Repentance requires an awareness of having done wrong, of having violated the plan of God, impoverished the community and made it suffer.

From this awareness arises a sorrowful love, an interior uneasiness, sorrow for having wounded others and ourselves, for having betrayed God's love for us. There follows the determination not to renew these wounds, to make some compensation for the injuries inflicted, and then a humble request for God's pardon.

The kindness of the divine forgiveness of our fault is what sustains our ability to forgive. Christian forgiveness must resemble that of God the Father, who forgives everything, any evil, always.

The father of the prodigal son did not tell the brother how he must forgive; he let him see it in deeds. He saw the son, was moved by the miserable state to which he was reduced, ran to meet him, embraced him, kissed him, clothed him well, completely rehabilitated him, and integrated him into the family with full rights. And then he manifested an indescribable happiness, an infinite, divine happiness, sealed by Jesus with that upsetting assertion that ninety-nine just persons count less, before God, than one sinner at the moment of his conversion!

Together Let's Work for the Common Good

If we have not yet attained the unity of love practiced by the Christians of apostolic times, let us at least aim for that degree of harmony that is indispensable for working together as a family, a community, a society, a Church. Otherwise it could happen that some tear down what others build up. With harmony, as the ancients said, even little things grow; with discord, even the most solid fall into ruin.

Concord lies in the consensus of wills in a specific decision, in a specific objective shared by everyone. In actual fact, there can be harmony even among dishonest persons.

Our harmony must be born of, root itself and have its final goal in the common good, in the interest of everyone, in the happiness of each individual person, a living member of the family to which we belong. It must not be tainted by the pursuit of individual advantages and interests, or those of a class or party.

Perhaps we must rediscover together what the common good is. In the Our Father, after the request for the saving presence of God in our history, Jesus has us ask for three common goods which, in their primary meaning, respond to the fundamental needs of each person: daily bread for everyone, and that means work, instruction, a humane environment, a dignified life for all; the peace which is born of reconciliation and true social justice, a peace capable of putting everything in its proper place; and freedom from evil, from egoism and individualism, from hatred and violence, from everything that does not allow humanity to fully develop and fulfill itself in an integral and definitive manner. If we achieve harmony concerning these goods, we will succeed in working together: in collaborating completely by recognizing, appreciating and usefully applying the intelligence, sensitivity and aptitudes of individuals; in recognizing, not just in words but in an equal share in benefits, that work truly serves to humanize our world. We will then be aware that work done in common, in the sharing of fatigue, hope and moments of joy, unites wills and hearts; by working together, we will discover ourselves to be brothers and sisters.

May the mystery of God who united himself to our humanity enlighten these essential goods of life and make us understand that through them we are called to participate in that peace and concord that never end, and which I wish for all from my heart, in a Christmas of joy.

A blessed Christmas to all!

Letter to the Diocese, Milan, December 1989

CHAPTER 12

The Gospel of Matrimony

Premise

I have greeted you with the biblical formula which says: "To you, brothers and sisters, who serve the Lord with incorruptible love, peace, charity and faith. I renew this greeting wholeheartedly and would like to add to it the beautiful words of Paul to the Philippians: "Children of God without blemish in the midst of a crooked and perverse generation, in which you shine like stars in the world...holding fast to the word of life" (2:15-16). I thank you because you want to reflect with me on this word of life which concerns the sanctity and grace of the married life, especially in its first years (I too feel that I share somewhat in this since I have not yet completed the tenth year of "marriage" to the Church of Milan).

We think, however, of all families, of those who have greater experience, of those who need to hear proclaimed once again the good and encouraging word of the Gospel, the "good news." And if this meeting is dedicated in particular to young couples, it is precisely for the purpose of pointing out that they have the right to and the need for special pastoral attention. As the Pope wrote in *Familiaris Consortio*, we need "the commitment of all the members of the local ecclesial community (in) helping the couple discover and live their new vocation and mission.... This holds true especially for young families which, finding themselves in a context of new values and responsibilities, are more vulnerable, especially in the first years of marriage, to possible difficulties, such as those created by adaptation to life together or by the birth of children" (n. 69).

Our meeting can be set under a biblical image, which I find in an icon of the Benedictine monastery of the Mount of Olives; it is the image of Jesus, Joseph and Mary in the first years of marriage. Joseph embraces Mary with his right arm while his left arm reaches toward her right arm, their hands joining with the left hand of Jesus, so that the three hands are united in the front of the icon. Thus Our Lady is embraced by Joseph and she, in turn, extends her arm to Jesus who is in the center. You cannot tell whether he is supported more by one or the other; he is supported by both, upright, secure, serene, with his hand in the act of blessing. Joseph has his gaze fixed in the distance, he needs to look to the future; Mary, instead, has her gaze turned mostly to Jesus, but the gaze of the three is united. It is an icon which expresses, with affection and color, what we would like to say this evening.

We seek first of all to answer the question: *what is the importance of the first years of marriage?* It seems an obvious question but it can be important to answer it.

As the Pope said, new problems are faced, new difficulties must be overcome for the first time. In addition, the bases are laid for what will be tomorrow. The married life that has a good beginning acts as the premise for a long future, while one that unhappily unravels right at the beginning, runs the risk of being short-lived.

These are obvious psychological reasons for the importance of the first years of marriage. I would like then to add some theological motives, explaining them more in depth, for it is precisely in the first years that the young spouses can for the first time experience what is called a mystagogia. This difficult word signifies that one is involved in mystery.

I can give a personal example of this, which concerns my "nuptial" experience as bishop of a Church. Before having had the experience of being bishop, it was a very different thing to speak of the episcopate. I knew the theological texts, I knew how to cite the biblical texts, but it is quite another matter when one begins to live the grace of the episcopacy from within, day by day, is called upon to respond to it with the strength one has, required to draw to the utmost on the grace of the sacrament so as to respond to the daily demands which life brings and which cannot be renounced. And if one lives this moment with faith he begins to draw on the riches of sacramental grace in an unheard-of manner, unexplainable to one who is outside. How many families could do much more of this work of "excavating," letting themselves be helped to draw out the grace of their marriage, which is the fundamental grace of their being, instead of seeking support outside (in friendships, in diversions, even in psychology)! Let us first of all seek the strength of the grace that dwells *within* us! Before, we did not have it and no one could explain it to us, but through the sacrament it is given to us.

It is a powerful reserve, that of being able to draw on the grace of the Holy Spirit, which is ours and no one else's, that grace which no one can explain to us or make us understand as well as each one of us can for ourselves.

I will attempt to answer *some questions.*

Where does your marriage find its roots? How did you become husband and wife?

What relationship exists between your being spouses and your being Christians?

What is the meaning of your spousal love with regard to your journey of faith?

What duties and responsibilities result from being Christian couples and families?

These are extremely simple questions. If you pose them to yourselves in a spirit of recollection and prayer, your experience will offer you marvelous answers, capable of nourishing your spirit and of sustaining it in difficulties, capable of opening up new horizons.

I will respond in a schematic way, almost as though to begin a meditation which I hope you will continue in your family groups, in your parishes, in your various encounters.

Where Did the Decision to Marry, and to Marry in Church, Stem From?

The answer may seem obvious: we married because we love one another, we married in church because we are Christians. This is not yet, however, the real answer. In reality *there is another Love* which has preceded you, has called you and has enabled you to speak and to live your love.

You are married because from all eternity *God the Father* has thought of, loved and called you in his *Son Jesus.* You married in church because Jesus was the first to say his "yes" to the Father, to the supreme act of love and obedience; and he has given you the strength to say your "yes." You married because the *Holy Spirit* whom you received in Baptism has little by little been conforming you to Jesus, according to the gift and charism of married love.

This is the deepest reality of your being and of your

life, the one from which the second question flows.

What Relationship Exists between Your Being Spouses and Your Being Christians?

The relationship between your married life and your Christian life is not purely an external juxtaposition. *Matrimony*, in which you have been constituted as a grace, is for you a *particular way of following Jesus.* Those who are married in church will be Christian in their marriage, will follow Jesus in their married life; and their holiness, their Christianity will consist in this.

I refer again to the words we have heard from the Letter to the Philippians and from Deuteronomy. "You shall love the Lord your God with all your heart, and with all your soul, and with all your might" (Dt 6:5); "be blameless and innocent, children of God without blemish in the midst of a crooked and perverse generation" (Phil 2:15). But where? How? In following Jesus. Where? How? In your married, spousal, family life.

We could then conclude: *you have married as Christians in order to love Jesus Christ more.* This is the secret of Christian marriage.

In this way, on the one hand, marriage is exalted as a means of following and imitating the Lord Jesus. On the other hand it is also made relative because, as with every other created reality, it is at the service of the kingdom of God, it is a means to live in Christ and to follow him. The absolute, ultimate good is to follow Jesus; all other goods are not ultimate but rather open and relative to the absolute which is Jesus and his kingdom.

Sometimes, when I explain these truths, I ask myself: how many understand? How many grasp the Christian power (that is, related to Christ) of matrimony? There are many, unfortunately, who try to live their married life by going to church once in a while, but without understanding the intimate bond which connects the two realities.

Here is the grace, the revelation that is given to you by means of your Christian journey. And you have a responsibility toward those numerous couples who neglect their marriage or their Christianity, living one or the other without joy.

You must therefore shine as stars in the world. *For your marriage is your specific journey of holiness* (cf GS 48).

What Is the Meaning of Your Married Love with Respect to the Journey of Faith?

We could summarize it thus: *your marriage contains a vocation to unity as a couple and as a family, a unity to be built day by day*; it is an essential and irrepressible vocation to unity. For this reason we have read the words of Jesus, and they apply to each one of your families: "I'm praying...that all may be one, just as you, Father, are in me and I in you, so they, too, may be in us" (Jn 17:21).

The experience of the first years of marriage is precisely that in which you seek in every way possible to build up this unity, with enthusiasm, with the joy of seeing that you are made for one another, but also with the difficulties that come when you discover that married life is not exactly as you pictured it, and that you therefore need to make a long journey of integration, of ascent, of pardon, of patience. Unity is not automatic. It is a miracle when two persons are able to live together for a long time without becoming tired of one another; when they are able, rather, to clearly recognize the gift of God to them; it is a gift that God gives, it is a grace. Getting along in a family is not to be taken for granted, it does not just happen by chance; in fact, the contrary is true. It is the grace of the sacrament of marriage that commits you to living together and to making the one journey together, no longer fulfilling all the actions of the day as a single individual, free to choose and to do what you want and to be respected by the other. Instead, everything, directly or indirectly, has to be done "together," or at least in view of one another. This is very hard, and there are persons who, even after years of marriage, have not understood it. They even complain about having problems, about not being understood; they have not understood this fundamental rule.

It is clear that in order to be able to live well "together," you also need some *moments of tranquillity, privacy, solitude* (because one thing helps another); not moments of closing oneself off, but of reserve, so as to be better able to rediscover the other person.

Here we come to the important topic of *sexual intimacy* as an expression and nourishment of a complete interpersonal communion—in the logic of the gift of self—that is accepted and received in the sacrament of Matrimony so as to lead toward perfect unity in Jesus. In order for this to take place, for the most profound intimacy to be truly lived as a gift, *a constant education to chastity* (a word which is rarely used today but to which I referred in *Itinerari educativi*) is important, "as a virtue which fully promotes the sexuality of the person and defends it against every kind of impoverishment and falsification." This is how the Italian bishops expressed themselves in the recent document, *Evangelizzazione e cultura della vita umana* (*Evangelization and the Culture of Human Life*, 29). And they continue: "In addition, in married life it is necessary to cultivate between spouses a relationship of mutual acceptance and self-giving, which is also fostered by recourse to natural methods of regulation of births." These methods are thus seen in relation to a progressive, well-controlled, and lived intimacy.

Certainly, as St. Paul has reminded us, you must shine as stars in a rather dark world. The society in which we live gives us no help, but let us remember that there has never been a perfect society. In Jesus' time things were much more difficult, the idea of marriage lived in this way was unheard of, and therefore chastity is the power that has conquered the world.

As I wrote in *Getting Along in the Family*, we must not become discouraged, because unity requires much effort, pardon, and patience. It means always beginning over again. It is a continual mutual education, letting oneself be formed by the other, which throughout your life together represents a goal to be kept in focus, to be refined each day.

What Duties and Responsibilities Derive from Being a Christian Couple and Family?

The response is twofold: your marriage contains the *vocation to the gift of life* (and this resource belongs especially to the first years) and it involves a *missionary vocation* (which is perhaps carried out in the early years through example, and later on more through positive action).

As the Pope said last October to young couples in Taranto: "*You collaborate with the Creator* in the multiplication and education of human life" (n. 4).

The early years of marriage are, in this sense, rich in stupendous resources, but at the same time threatened by fears and difficulties. When awaiting the birth of the first child it is easy to perceive the fullness of joy and responsibility of this service to life. However, fears and hardships, at times even serious ones, are not lacking, not only those of an economic and social nature, but even those related to physical health and psychological well-being. And fear can develop into a lack of esteem for and even the planned rejection of the child. The bishops' document *Evangelization and Culture* states: "There are young couples who tend to postpone the birth of the first child for a long time, first providing for other things believed to be essential according to today's prevalent models" (n. 9).

In a context such as ours, then, it is important to ask God for the grace *to rediscover the authentic meaning of procreation and of responsible parenthood.* We need to respond to the dominant mentality, to accept the invitation to generosity, self-giving and trust (cf *Evangelization and Culture*).

And we must *never subordinate the children to less important goals.* The child must not be sought in relation to something else; otherwise there arise forms of disappointment or domination, which later poison especially the child's adolescent years.

The primary condition for adequately facing the problem of vocations that preoccupies our diocese is this attitude of readiness to joyfully welcome even those choices which may lead a son or daughter out of the family toward broader horizons. After the initial inevitable sacrifices and detachments, these choices return as abundant grace and joy for the life of the family itself.

Missionary action. You must be *protagonists in the Church and in society* through your *married and family life lived in a Christian way.* In the face of concepts and forms of family life that are contradictory and unacceptable, those who want to live the Christian ideal serenely, simply and courageously are already missionaries.

It is up to you to offer, especially with the witness of your lives, a concept and form of family life whose foundation lies in matrimony understood as a lasting union of man and woman, a union founded on spousal love.

But then, above all after the early years of marriage, it is important that you all be collaborators and promoters of a *renewed pastoral action involving young couples like yourselves.* This can be done in many different ways: family groups, involvement in the parish, pastoral work with families, volunteer work on an international level, forms of hospitality, missionary openness. The expressions of generosity that I see in young families are extraordinary. At times I am truly amazed at seeing the courageous choices of hospitality, of adoption, or of missionary life that exist in our diocese, choices which are the more beautiful the less they are publicized.

I would like to read some words from a young Lebanese couple who belong to the Èquipe Notre Dame: "In these three years of marriage, we have formed ourselves...to be a living sacrament, open to hospitality, forming a family that is an oasis of peace. This year the war is even more devastating. But hope does not abandon us; and for Christmas of 1989 our first child will be born." This is a family that has striven to live through a painful trial, irradiating peace around itself.

I want to recall another topic which I have very much at heart, that is, *attention and closeness to the elderly*: a social pact, by which the elderly can be cared for by their children until the end of their lives.

And I also want to broaden your perspectives to a more *direct social participation*, in the world of the school, of the economy, and of politics, so that living together in society involves more respect for each person, considered within the context of his/her family life.

I conclude with an exhortation that is always needed: whatever may happen *do not lose trust. The Lord prayed for you too*: "I don't pray for you to take them out of the world, but for you to preserve them from the evil one.... Make them holy in the truth" (Jn 17: 15, 17). Jesus not only prays for you, *but he is with you.* The Council affirms: "For as God of old made himself present to his people through a covenant of love and fidelity, so now the Savior of men and the Spouse of the Church comes into the lives of married Christians through the sacrament of matrimony. He abides with them thereafter" (GS 48).

May your daily experience, even in trials, in sufferings, in difficulties, witness to this profound joy which is the joy of the Gospel, the precious pearl of the Gospel lived in the Christian family, so that this joy may spread around you and render our Church more resplendent.

Meditation for young couples, Milan, January 27, 1990

CHAPTER 13

The Future of Our Children

Good Night

It is still a custom, I believe, for parents—before retiring for the night—to enter the room of their youngest child who is already sleeping, to assure themselves that he/she is not uncovered. They might even remain a moment to listen to the child's quiet breathing, a sign of slumber.

At those moments the question arises: what will the child become? What awaits him or her? What kind of world will welcome him or her? Children make the parents think of the future, and in the succession of questions trust and fear alternate.

The consolation of parents is to perceive reasons for hope in the goodness of the child's daily actions ("after all, he is a good boy"), in their children's good attitude toward life, in their right relationship with others and with the mystery of God.

At times, as they pause to follow the regular rhythm of the child's breathing, they feel a very intense, legitimate pride in being able to say: "I have given my children as much as can be desired; this home, these toys, this security in which the future looks bright."

Often, perhaps, a worry that resembles repressed anguish marks their last thought with sadness: "Our children advance toward their future defenseless and alone.... What will become of them? In this very complex and broken world, who will protect them when we are no longer here?..."

Children make us think of the future.

But if our faith has formed us to a deeper view of life, then even the thought of the future becomes more intense and real. In fact, when a mother and father wish their sleeping children good night, they ask themselves: "What will become of these children of ours?" In reality their question means: what is God's will for them? What is their vocation?

Faith knows how to see in the story of each man and woman the grace of the new and mysterious name by which each is called. Parents who make the journey of faith pray for their children every day, that the will of God may be done. In fact, they know that God is love and wills the happiness of his children with a tenderness and fidelity that surpasses even the affection of a father and mother.

Believers know that in God's will is our peace. And after having prayed according to the teaching of Jesus, parents, too, can go to sleep with more serene trust, perhaps to dream of a world they will not see but which will continue to be loved by God.

Table Conversation

When everyone is finally seated at table to have supper together and all kinds of tidbits are placed before them, conversation soon lags. As long as there is a small child in the house, it is easy to say something; for the most part the child loves to tell stories and to ask questions, and at times surprising funny remarks come out that put everyone in good humor.

The difficult moments come when the children become adolescents and cultivate their own secret world—one that loves to escape questioning. At times they silently harbor inexplicable resentments, incomprehensible expectations, long periods of discontent, and it all comes out in harsh monosyllables and outbursts of anger and, perhaps, especially for girls, in ill-concealed tears.

Certainly everyone has times when life reveals its harshness and puts us to the test; each one must cope with these and not look for a substitute. Fortunately, these storms often end soon; it is not wise to dramatize them.

However, for parents it is wise and necessary to go beyond the caprices of a day and to practice the art of narration, the art of speaking and of bringing others to speak at table.

Part of the art of narration lies in not presuming that we always have something to teach, but rather in finding a way to recall an episode which makes others laugh, or a sad event which has caused suffering.

The art of narrating is that capacity for confidence with which the mother and father know how to describe themselves without complexes and without presumption as a man and woman who have lived and continue to live a story of love.

We can read in books that life is a vocation. However, we begin to believe it when we meet persons who, in telling us their story, know how to find the signs of grace there and know how to give praise to God. They know how to help others understand that life is something good, beautiful and even joyful. They know how to tell why they felt the need to make their honeymoon in Rome and pray a Hail Mary together in the Basilica of St. Mary Major, for the children who would come: it is a way of attesting that they want to follow God's way.

Staying at table together, you share your life while you share your bread, and you experience a reassuring harmony. These moments can disperse the oppressive clouds of misunderstanding and help overcome the fears which make the journey uncertain. It then becomes possible to arouse in the souls of the youngest children a joyful generosity that is disposed to step forward and welcome the voice of the Lord who calls.

For this reason it is important that families defend their moments of being together. It becomes essential to resist the invasion of television, the outbursts of nervous irritation which wound the persons who are most loved; to dominate the desire for revenge which generates heavy silences. In short, the art of conversing presupposes knowing how to relax and how to pardon.

The day will come when, with courtesy and discretion, we will be able to ask our young people about their future, because it will then be up to them to continue their story.

In discussing what school to attend or how to set up house, or in any case, what to do in life, it would be wonderful if, in addition to calculations and plans, the family took a moment to say the Hail Mary, asking for help to do the will of God.

The Twelfth Birthday

When they celebrate the third birthday of the first child, the parents often get a special cake and perhaps even invite the child's friends and closest relatives. They think: "It seems that she was just born and now she is already so big!..."

When the twelfth birthday is celebrated, the party is

noisier and the gifts more expensive. The parents already feel a bit like intruders in the games that the child now plays. Yet in their hearts they think: "She is still a girl."

So it happens that a birthday celebration is a time for eating pastries and accumulating sophisticated games; it is a day on which the parents give everything and ask nothing. At times it even seems legitimate to suspect that deep down the parents would like to keep their son or daughter in infancy, would like them to remain children, so beautiful, so likable, so trusting.

There is always the subtle temptation to use children: children fill our house and our life, they are a remedy for the solitude and frustration that can mar the life of the couple. The child seems safe, as long as he remains a child, from the hidden threats of a sick society.

The birthday can, instead, be an occasion for becoming aware that one's child is growing into manhood or womanhood. Perhaps when the friends have gone away and the exchange of best wishes and of "thank yous" is over, the evening of the twelfth birthday can offer a moment for a more serious conversation and for a look at the future; for prayer together that the kingdom of God may come and the will of the Father be done.

At the age of twelve Jesus prompted his mother to meditate by remaining in the temple and declaring his obedience to God. The program of his life was already decided in those disconcerting words: "Didn't you know that I have to concern myself with my Father's affairs?" (Lk 2:49)...

Many parents are careful that the children learn another language as soon as possible, so that they can use it when they are older. They believe it is also a good idea to study piano and dancing, and to go into training for soccer; some parents nourish the unspoken and improbable dream of having a champion in the home.

Instead, the invitations to listen more attentively to the Word, to reflect more seriously on the topic of vocation often meet with indifference, if not distrust. It seems, in short, that there is more trust in the coach of a football team than in the traditional care the Church has for young people.

It happens not rarely that the fruit of all the efforts to provide a young person with the means useful for facing life is disillusionment. Persons who have been given the possibility of doing everything remain inactive and do not know why they should do anything.

The world of tomorrow will continue to be inhabited and the Church will still be in our midst if we learn today to offer young people suggestions that reflect the demands of the Gospel, and if boys and girls begin early on to cultivate the desire to grow up because they have many reasons to hope that they will not be useless: the Lord who has called them to life counts on them.

Preparing the Suitcases

The preparation of one's baggage requires attention and a good amount of organizational ability. There are mothers who have acquired an amazing ability to remember everything and to arrange it all in such precise order that the mountain of indispensable things fits, as though by miracle, into the narrow confines of a suitcase.

Some, however, exaggerate and, in order to provide for any eventuality, force their children to drag along with them on mountain trails enormous knapsacks which they will not even have time to unpack. Naturally, when the young people have to re-pack they do not know how to make everything fit back in the way it was. If they do not resolve the problem by forgetting sweaters everywhere, they feel forced to recover whatever baggage they can manage.

At any rate, preparing the suitcases for a departure is

a delicate operation because an oversight can cause embarrassing setbacks. Therefore, a mother stops from time to time for a quick inventory and asks herself: "What else would my son/daughter need?"

Leaving home is an interesting moment because the departure, whether only for a school trip for a few days, or for a ski vacation, or for a period of study overseas, in some way forces one to list everything deemed indispensable. A young person will certainly not forget the music cassettes that they want to listen to during the trip or the address to which they absolutely want to send a funny postcard.

The parents reveal their formative goals even in preparing the suitcases: a mother concerned about health will provide her children with pills for colds, another will take care to add an endless list of addresses for every situation; in the choice of clothing we can see who has more at heart the impression the child will make, or who feels at ease and can stretch out wherever they want. Knowing the habits of the children, there will be parents who find room for packages of candy or pen and paper.

And is this everything? It would be sad if a father or mother were to conclude that it is enough to give a child who is going away a well-furnished wardrobe, some money for "any need," and the possibility of satisfying a wish.

Parents are happy to see that, in gathering "their things," the young people do not forget to bring along some books to read, as well as the book of the Gospels which they received at their profession of faith.

But if, in the confusion of things, the young people do not remember, parents know how best to remind them, especially if it is customary in the home to overcome reserve and inopportune discretion by sharing what counts the most.

In fact, parents are convinced that it is dangerous to

allow parentheses in the life of the young person in which they can do anything and, out of love for companionship, forget their responsibilities and indulge in vulgarity.

A book to read is an invitation not to confuse free time with laziness. It is an invitation to nourish the intellect with good taste, with thoughts, with a habit of reflection that makes young people freer.

The book of the Gospels fosters daily fidelity to the word that guides our footsteps and inspires our choices, even when we do not live under the watchful eyes of our parents or in a good, youthful Christian community.

Thus a personality matures that is capable of autonomy, and the word of Jesus, who calls his disciples the salt of the earth, comes true. Youthfulness does not exempt those who have received the grace to be Christians from feeling committed, wherever they find themselves, to witnessing to the Lord and to his Gospel.

Even by means of small choices which might cost a sarcastic remark during an outing or camping trip, a young man and woman succeed in perceiving how difficult and urgent it is to try to draw friends closer to the words of Jesus and the life of the Church.

There are those who draw back in humiliation when faced with the sad superficiality of their group, and who seek to make their friends forget that "they still go to church." There are others, instead, who are led to a more intense prayer of intercession and who even ask themselves: "Can I do something more for them in my life?"

I Am Dead Tired!

Sometimes a boy or girl can be exhausted. They have spent several hours at school amidst a dizzying succession of topics, teachers, and different methods. They have been immersed in bewildering gossip and the latest electronic games. Then, when school is over, there is the mother or the grandmother waiting to take them to their piano or Judo or dancing lessons...and fortunately the dentist is on vacation! When they arrive home they have no desire to do anything, except to throw themselves onto the sofa and follow the absurd adventures of some hero or heroine on a soap opera.

While waiting to pick up their children at school, mothers love to boast about their youngsters' accomplishments. "My children's foreign language teacher says that they are learning very quickly" or "My sons will be going to .... next Saturday for the regional games...they're the best players on their team." Parents boast of their children's successes and willingly take the time to run here and there so as to bring them to their lessons or games on time. Of course they think: we are doing it for our children so that they don't miss anything.

It can, in fact, be constructive to dedicate some time to studies and sports that the school cannot offer and that are truly interesting. However, I sometimes have the impression that a sense of balance is lacking, and that this anxiety to take advantage of all the possibilities available ends in being a servitude to the demands of trends rather than a service to the growth of the children. We frequently meet priests who do not know when to schedule the classes of religious instruction because there is no evening when the children are free.

It seems to me necessary to regain a wiser balance and to give the children time to be children: to let them have time to play without needing to prove themselves champions; to let them walk in a garden and gather dry leaves just for the fun of exploring autumn, without having to make catalogs for scholastic research; to let them go to collect chestnuts with their grandparents and listen to their stories, without having to record them for a composition.

The experience of selflessness, the occasions for

tranquil contemplation of nature, the freedom to imagine fairy tales that are not just replicas of television programs, are precious moments. Such moments favor that psychological balance, those times of clarification in which the overabundance of news and stimuli is put into perspective. They help children to think calmly and to better assimilate the values that are decisive for important choices.

I would like everyone to be able to walk alone sometimes where there are no display windows to arouse curiosity and desires: to walk alone and enjoy the peace; to distance themselves from the present reality and face the big questions: "Why all this beauty? Why so much suffering? And my life?... Why? What can I do with my future?"

These are moments of grace in which we learn the words of gratitude and the heart is prepared for listening. Blessed be those parents and educators who have the freedom of boys and girls so much at heart that they introduce them to the difficult art of admiration, to the habit of gratitude, to readiness to listen.

No one will be surprised if I count on young men and women who have followed these paths. They make me hope that tomorrow many more will know how to understand life as a vocation. In fact, the first step of obedience to a call is the gratitude that recognizes and welcomes the works of God.

I am, instead, afraid that those who follow all the trends, satisfy all their caprices and are attracted by every advertisement, end up being satiated to the point of boredom. While they have everything and can do everything, they reach the point of not wanting to do anything. How much energy is thrown away, and how much frustration is experienced by the parents!

What Should I Wear Today?

There are girls who spend more time deciding which dress to wear than in saying their morning prayers.

Their closets overflow with so many possibilities as to make the choice truly embarrassing. Then they have to look for the right color combination between shoes, shades of make-up and purse. They can't neglect the search for variety either; they don't want their companions to think they have only one sweater. Finally, the label becomes more and more important, attesting to the good quality, stylishness, and high price of the clothing.

At that same moment, everywhere in cities and throughout the world, millions of people who awaken to the new day will wear the same clothes as always. Some have even slept in the same clothes. The young woman dressed like a model will carefully avoid getting too close to these people, perhaps from distrust, perhaps to show good taste.

I ask myself whether this scandalous difference should not, at a certain point, become a question that disturbs the consciences of those who live in abundance. It is, in fact, impossible to maintain that the simple fact of being born in a well-to-do family gives one the indisputable right to have everything and even to squander the goods and resources that God has created for everyone.

How then can we still tolerate the fact that even Christians celebrate their feasts according to rituals imposed by consumerism, instead of expressing their joy in a more generous solidarity?

I am aware that in this context it is not possible to treat of topics that are too complex. But to the young women who find the choice of clothing bewildering because their wardrobe is too abundant, and to all those who live in similar conditions, I would like to address the invitation to open their eyes and let their hearts be touched by the poverty of so many brothers and sisters.

Someone might say: what can a girl or boy of fifteen do in the face of problems of worldwide dimension? The answer is simple and at the same time difficult. This is what you can do: change your life.

It is possible to learn a different way of looking at others, at the poor especially: a look capable of making every unnatural gap disappear and of eliminating alienation.

We must not be naive, nor let ourselves be led by unsuitable enthusiasm; however, I have to add that indifference is not a Christian virtue. Therefore when one's gaze is opened to the light of fraternity it can always find balanced actions for expressing solidarity.

Spending a few days of one's vacation in simple acts of service turns out to be a gift received, for these suggest a style of life free from the idolatry of "good living."

But it is possible to go further. The lives of many saints, from St. Francis to St. Vincent de Paul, to St. Joseph Cottolengo and Mother Teresa, teach us that the meeting with a poor person can become the call which marks one's life because, in some mysterious manner, it draws us close to Jesus and convinces us to live for him. The poverty of our brothers and sisters is a vocation with which Jesus calls.

It isn't possible to love the Lord and remain inactive in the presence of the poorest of our brothers and sisters, for whom Jesus came to announce the Good News. Many of today's young people can still travel the way of the saints and transform generous impulses into a dedication that lasts a lifetime.

Doing Good

The human soul has an original vocation to solidarity. It is so strong that the many demands of the ego cannot eradicate it. For each of us, the act of charity and patience that led us to spend an hour with an elderly neighbor who wanted company, or to stop and accompany a blind person across the street, or to help a young person in a wheelchair ascend the stairs in order to visit a museum, is written in the book of God.

But there are young persons gifted with a particular sensitivity or touched more deeply by the suffering of others; for them an occasional action is not enough. They spend large amounts of their free time and buoyant energy, willingly dedicating entire evenings and vacation days to keeping lonely persons company and offering help to those in need.

When spontaneous generosity is transformed into a choice of self-giving, one is granted the privilege of being admitted into a world unknown to many, a world in which daily miracles of charity take place. In fact, in this world one meets sick and elderly persons who live in resigned patience, young invalids who know how to radiate an indomitable joy, suffering people who have learned unlimited sensitivity in accepting themselves so as to avoid disturbing others.

Young persons discover age-old institutions which do not tire of being in the lead along the frontiers of charity and which continue to prepare persons who know how to unite competence with a smile, who do not count the hours of work and ask only to spend their whole life in the name of Jesus.

I find it strange that the encounter with men and women religious animated by this spirit can leave us indifferent. They are, in fact, a provocative presence which points out to many young men and women the way of total dedication as a way that is possible, a way traveled by many in an exemplary manner, without attracting attention, without motives of profit or prestige.

Their lives thus pose the question: Why are they giving this kind of service? Why can't I do the same?

We could go further and discover the source of their dedication. If you visit a community of sisters anywhere, they will show you a chapel, kept as the most precious area, small perhaps, but full of light and decorated with fresh flowers. You can imagine that in that chapel the sisters pray long before the sun rises and draw strength and inspiration for the many acts of charity that brighten their day.

When led to this discovery, young men and women of today may perceive that their journey of faith is called to become one of charity. I know many young persons who spend some hours of their free time serving supper to the poor. I know others who have postponed beginning their own careers so as to travel to some corner of the earth where the need is greatest, convinced that it is impossible and unjust to be happy by themselves. I truly hope that out of the many who do this, some will be convinced to remain there forever, in the name of Jesus.

Priests and Sisters

As varied as our experiences and histories are, almost everyone has a memory of a priest and a sister.

It may have happened that, since our first encounter with this priest or sister, some of us have traveled other roads, very different roads; life has led us far away from such contacts. It could also be that a rude answer or a mistake has contributed to alienating us from the Christian community.

More often—I think—the reason lies in an indifference which the environment has fostered, a change of habits, the strenuous pace imposed by work and commitments to family and society.... These have limited our presence in church to certain special occasions.

The word of the Gospel has been reduced to fragments that have become proverbs; preaching has become synonymous with a rather annoying discourse. Priests and sisters seen from afar are perhaps considered merely as employees in an undertaking which, under certain aspects, deserves more trust than others, but nothing more.

However, days come that favor a more attentive consideration of the grace that the presence of such persons in the Church is. At times the occasion may be a loss or a tragedy in the family which leads one to discover the truth of the ancient words of hope or the comfort of disinterested concern. Sometimes it is the faith journey of the children: their way of preparing for First Communion, for Confirmation; the joy they show in feeling pardoned, the inclination to entrust themselves to the Lord in prayer....

Then even the adults and older sisters and brothers recall emotions almost forgotten and address a grateful thought to the sister who taught them their first prayers and Christmas hymns; to the priest who knew how to say the right word to release them from an inferiority complex, to help them overcome timidity, to free them from remorse.

It also happens that children hold disconcerting surprises. Their journey of faith is directed well beyond the foreseen limits and looks to the distance. It becomes a task that requires time and dedication and promises much more.

The mother and father return to church after many years in order to see the son who serves as altar boy or to listen to the choir in which their daughter is singing. Or they return to assist at a recital or a game.

But one day when young people ask their father to get up a little earlier on Sunday and bring them to a vocational retreat, some perplexity begins to surface. It seems improbable, and yet, who knows?...

Then, when more specific plans are in progress, it is easy to be skeptical of a boy who desires to enter the seminary. It is easy to be incredulous toward a girl who dreams of becoming a sister. It is easy to pile up arguments to show the improbability of these youthful longings: their age, the renunciations required, the suspicion of hidden pressures....

I ask myself whether it would not be more correct to consider with greater care those signs which at times enter unexpectedly into the family's life.

In the name of that sister who taught Christmas hymns and of that priest who absolved the sins of childhood, I ask the parents, even those who nourish profound skepticism, whether a vocational plan of this type should not be considered a grace rather than an uncertainty.

The journey of discernment which a seminary or novitiate has the young person make is so long and so attentive to their freedom that it alone is sufficient to put false hopes into perspective and to form a more realistic picture of the priestly ministry and of the religious life.

The good which almost all of us have received and do receive from sisters and priests, the disinterested good work that characterizes the surroundings in which they work, the nostalgia that lingers in the places they have left, can be arguments which convince parents not to be too prejudiced on the day on which a young man announces at home: "I want to enter a seminary or a novitiate," and a young woman says: "I want to become a sister."

Falling in Love?

While a daughter is at school, her mother sometimes dares to venture into her room and attempt the arduous undertaking of putting her things in order. The mother knows that it would contribute more to the daughter's formation if she expected the girl, who is no longer a child, to take care of putting away her own sweaters and shoes, souvenirs of the summer and school books, music cassettes and posters. But in these "raids" there is all the tenderness of the mother who always hesitates somewhat to accept that her daughter is no longer a child; and, we have to admit, there is also some curiosity.

In fact, while she arranges the knickknacks and cards on the shelves, the mother can't help glancing at the notes and post cards with which a young man has sent his greetings. If the daughter forgets to put away her diary, it is impossible for the mother to resist the temptation to leaf through the adolescent confidences recorded there.

The mother continues to read. She is a bit uneasy because she feels she is being indiscreet, and yet she desires to come to know the secret face of a daughter who is becoming a mystery to her.

Among the commonplace phrases and coded messages, famous quotes and clippings from magazines, the mother tries to discover the companions whom her daughter spends time with, her tastes, the reasons for her bad moods and for her enthusiasm. And naturally she traces the most faithful friendships and the entries that speak of love.

It is somewhat inevitable that a mother find her own self in these pages, that they lead her to recall faces and words that have left a more lasting mark in her life and perhaps even a deeper wound.

I think that a mother must smile at the obstinacy and jealousy which adolescent friendships speak of, but I also imagine a tinge of sadness in this smile. In fact there comes to mind the tumultuous intensity of falling in love and the thousand promises of months lived in a dream; there comes the nostalgia for the words of tenderness, of laughter over nothing, of holding hands, all of which made it wonderful to be together.

Then came life, and in too many love stories daily living together has colored the dreams gray: arguing over nothing, picking up on annoying words and finding certain small obsessions of one's spouse unbearable, being humiliated by the impression of having to satisfy exaggerated expectations, using vulgar language and indulging in sulky silence.

Life with its burden, the work, the daughter, the house, a death in the family...there is a reason for smiling at adolescent love. However, perhaps a mother can ask herself if it is really destined to end this way. Isn't there a way to help the daughter not to build up too many fond hopes and not to grow old too quickly? Is it really impossible to learn an art of loving that stands up to life and its burden?

There are mothers inclined to renunciation, because, while growing up, they saw a lot of renunciation at home and in the homes of their neighbors. However, the longing that remains for a more genuine love, for easier communication, and the eagerness with which they begin dreaming because of unexpected attention and sensitivity shown by another, encourage them to think that we are not made to pay for the infatuations of youth with an unhappy marriage. We are made to be loved and to love all the days of our life.

While the daughter is away at school, the mother could think of a discreet way of introducing her to the art of real love.

There is, in fact, an interior freedom, a watchfulness over the senses and the heart which are conditions that prevent love from being merely an instinct that suddenly blazes up and just as suddenly dies out.

I would like to recall that the words of Jesus shed

light on the reality of love. They help us see as a vocation from God what shortsighted people interpret as casual coincidence and unavoidable fate.

When at the well of Sychar Jesus meets a woman who has led a disordered life and who tries not to think of her sentimental failures, he leads her to perceive the existence of a water that truly quenches the thirst. He presents himself to her as the one who can bring to birth a new heart able to encounter the mystery of God.

I would like to repeat to all men and women today the encouragement and consolation that come from these words of Jesus. There is living water, it is possible to nourish in the human heart the love which comes from God, and it is possible to help those being introduced to life to live love as a vocation directed to the freedom of persons so that they might find joy and peace.

Will There Be Priests Tomorrow?

Priests always seem to be under pressure, absorbed by a thousand thoughts, pulled everywhere by a thousand expectations. There are days in which, like the first disciples of Jesus, they do not even have the time to eat in peace, because there are so many people coming and going (cf Mk 6:31). They give the impression of having so many things to do that they always forget something. They seem to spend their days running to keep up with numberless demands.

It is surprising, however, what a penetrating understanding of people's spiritual lives many priests develop while they are leading a life filled with so many obligations. I am certain that the secret of this spiritual gift lies in the silent prayer that people do not see, the prayer in which many encounters of the day become reasons for gratitude and supplication. In this way priests learn to look at persons with the kindness and wisdom that the

Holy Spirit suggests to them. They know how to share joys and sorrows, they know how to interpret reserve, they find words of consolation, they receive extraordinary confidences, they propose paths for Christian living.

Sometimes, after many prayers and much thought, priests invite a boy, a teenager, a young man, to more specific questions. They have recognized in a boy an especially clear gaze, they have seen an immediate response, even an enthusiasm, to the most demanding words of the Gospel. They have noted love for prolonged prayer and acts of charity, repentance and unusual sensitivity. They have been surprised by the young person's freedom with regard to the "idols" of the moment and by his great aspirations. They have noticed an ability to forget self that could be a good commentary on the Gospel, which exhorts us to seek first the kingdom of God and his justice.

While tracing some signs they waited for an appropriate opportunity to make an explicit proposal: "Perhaps the Lord is calling you to become a priest; have you ever thought about it?"

The answers are varied, but, not rarely, together with the amazement comes gratitude for a word that has finally deciphered confused desires to do good and dreams thought improbable because of timidity, humility, or a tendency to delay.

However, when the circle of discussion is enlarged and the search for God's will begins to involve the parents, it often—and surprisingly—happens that with complicated arguments or critical attitudes the parents manifest suspicion of undue pressure and claim that their prerogatives have been violated.

The priest who has made a proposal to the boy with the intention of helping him give a Christian face to his freedom, has the impression that he is being judged as an imprudent intruder. The very idea that a boy could enter the seminary at such a young age is taken as an offense to the family's ability to educate.

It is easy to agree that there should be careful reflection and that all elements be considered. But at the root of much of the hesitation and resistance to a priestly vocation, I seem to see at times a kind of suspicion of the itinerary that the seminary offers—almost as though it is not suited to a harmonious growth of the boy's personality and his free determination.

Perhaps there is even suspicion about what the Providence of God is preparing for the future of his Church and his priests, almost as if he is preparing a future of solitude and insignificance for those who accept the invitation to commit themselves to the proclamation of the Gospel. Some parents equate defending a boy from the demands of the Gospel with furthering his hopes for happiness.

We cannot omit mentioning that these parental reactions are often inspired by the fear of having the house empty and of not being able to bear the separation, even though intermittent, of a boy who with his lively youthfulness, his wonder and his gratitude imparts a sense of the joy of living.

For all these reasons, the vocational proposal of a priest who believes he has seen promising signs in a boy can be a motive of distress and even of resentment for the parents.

But the truth is that such a proposal is above all an invitation to a spiritual journey that the parents, too, are called to make. On some occasions, in fact, I have seen pleasure taken in a dialogue between husband and wife that puts aside the daily preoccupations in order to take time to examine in depth the personality traits of their son, the formative proposals for a precise plan for accompanying him, and the foreseeable difficulties and advantages. I have seen them engaged in more extended prayer to ask light and courage. And the Spirit of God knows how to multiply joy and increase hope, so that those parents who decide, out of an act of intelligent trust, to support their son's choice of the priesthood, are finally persuaded that they have received a grace.

Milan, November 1990

CHAPTER 14

Witness to the Fact that Love for Life Is a Choice of Freedom

Introduction

1. Dearest brothers and sisters, after having listened to the Word of God, to the words of the bishops and of two witnesses—for which I heartily thank those who have offered them, beginning as they did from their profound experience of daily life—I desire to *greet you one by one*, and to greet with you and through you the parishes, associations, and groups, the situations from which you come and in which you are inserted.

I express to you my *gratitude* for having responded to my invitation by coming together here to pray and reflect on the theme of life. Our encounter—as you know—had been set for February 2, vigil of the Twelfth Day for Life, for which the Italian bishops had written a message on the topic: *Love for life, a choice of freedom.* At that time, because of the additional *ad limina* visit of the bishops of Lombardy, I was unable to be present. However, I wanted another meeting to be scheduled at once, because I did not intend to miss a precious occasion for reflecting on a topic of such great importance, important not only in itself but also socially and politically.

Among other things, upon close examination all this can be seen as providential. It tells us, in fact, that love for the life of the human person cannot and must not be the commitment or the sentiment of only one day of the year. It is rather a perpetual, daily question, even for a Saturday evening such as this, which for many is a time of relaxation and entertainment.

In the meantime our reflection on the theme of life has been deepened since the moment, immediately after Easter, when I, together with all the Cardinals of the world, was again called to Rome by the Pope for the precise purpose of speaking about the threats to life present in the modern world. It is not unlikely that the Holy Father will publish a document on this issue. And so, we want to unite ourselves to him in prayer and gratitude, in expectation of this pronouncement.

Two Roads: For Life, Against Life

2. Our presence today in this cathedral is also *a sign of love for life*, which becomes a daily lived experience and which we together, humbly but boldly, want to witness to.

Among us, in fact, there are *men and women* who, in giving themselves to one another according to the demands of married love, have transmitted the gift of life to their children and continue to transmit it through a convinced work of formation and education. Together with them there are *doctors, pharmacists, nurses and health care workers*, whose profession calls them each day to guard and serve human life. There are also *representatives of the various associations of volunteer health workers* who, by means of a generous, selfless, competent and qualified commitment, remind each and every person of those ideals of service to life which they themselves, first of all, seek to cultivate.

I cannot forget *those who teach the natural methods for*

the regulation of births. With their personal witness and competence, they help married couples live their gift of love in genuine openness to life. *Those who act as consultants to families*, by adopting the teaching of the Magisterium regarding the promotion and safeguard of family values, of marriage, of life, of sexuality and of love, carry out a precious task that enables the family to truly be the first environment where life is loved and respected.

We have present here *teachers* and *educators*. These represent a broader and more complex concern with education and incarnate it, often with genuine passion. In this way they offer their contribution so that children, adolescents, and young adults may grow in life, love and liberty. By means of their concrete help to those who are most needy, *the persons who are in charge of or who work in centers for the promotion of life or in various homes and communities that offer hospitality, shelter and assistance* show us that when we truly love we feel the need to give a bit of life to one who does not love it or who is tempted not to love it. In so doing we experience and receive in exchange the joy of seeing life loved once again. Finally, those who belong to the *pro-life movement* remind us of the presence in our society of persons who make the defense of life a specific plan of action and of participation in cultural and social life.

The *two testimonies* we have heard also lead us to recognize the presence in our world and in our cities of persons—and they are not few!—who are aware of their serious responsibility. Despite difficult moments, even possible failure, they know how to see their profession as a choice which "forces them" to prove their ability to love. These persons daily seek to live their profession in love. We are also told that there are those who choose to witness to love for the poorest, the most abandoned, adults and adolescents in serious trouble. These experience the fact that without our personal and communitarian love for life, there is no choice of freedom.

Finally, the remembrance of the moving incident of Lucia—which was recounted to us with deeply-felt, attentive and discreet words by Professor Zampetti[*]—tells us that even today persons capable of genuine heroism are not lacking. A similar case is that of Gianna Beretta Molla, whom we hope soon to venerate as blessed and to point out as an example and model of true freedom and of love for life until the end.

The presence of all of you, therefore, and episodes such as these are motives for great comfort because they witness to the fact that in our society, so troubled in many ways, there are still concrete and tangible signs of love for human life, of care and respect for the dignity of the person, of the search for the good of the person, of true, profound freedom.

3. But we know that it is not always this way and is not this way for everyone. "Without doubt there is a growing *esteem for the value of human life* and awareness that its defense and promotion demand greater commitment and solidarity on everyone's part, at every level" (CEI, *Evangelizzazione e cultura della vita umana*, 5). But at the same time it is true that "multiple forms of *threat to, violence against, and rejection of life persist,* even increase. These are the more insidious the more they mask themselves behind false appearances of civilized behavior" (*Evangelizzazione*, 6). Among other things, in addition to abortion and euthanasia we can think of drugs, alcoholism, sexual violence, abuse of minors and especially of children, kidnapping, suicides....

In grave and concerned accents the recent extraordinary Consistory—convoked from April 4 to 7 and to which I alluded earlier—offered us a picture which un-

---

(*Translator's note: for the story of Lucia, see p. 241)

doubtedly leads us to serious reflection. The interventions of the Cardinals coming from Europe, Africa, Asia, Latin America, and Oceania have disconcerted us, by listing the many realities which seem to be running blindly down the road of death.

Thus the final bulletin points out: "the enormous growth in the number of abortions, which legalization has promoted rather than curbed; the most recent attempts to legalize euthanasia; the exploitation of children and adolescents; the abuses of prenatal life connected with experimentation on embryos and the practices of artificial procreation; these abuses are often programmed and sometimes even justified by motivations of various types. These motivations constitute other forms of attempts on life, which add to the painful loss of human life due to underdevelopment, to hunger, to various forms of violence as well as to war" (*L'Osservatore Romano*, April 8-9, 1991).

In his intervention, Cardinal Ratzinger spoke of "a real war of the strong against the weak, a war which aims at the elimination of the handicapped, of those who are a burden, and even simply those who are poor and 'useless,' in every moment of their existence." And he added: "With the help of the States, colossal means are employed against persons, from the dawn of their life, or when their life is made vulnerable by an accident or sickness, and when it is close to the end" (*L'Osservatore Romano*, April 5, 1991).

The Italian bishops too, in the message of their Permanent Council last February, refer to this picture and emphasize that many forms of violence against life "are often invoked and justified as affirmations of freedom," a freedom "invoked in the name of the quality of human life" (CEI, *Message for the Thirteenth Day for Life*). But we need to ask: What is freedom? What is quality of life?

As it is, we find ourselves faced with *two concrete and opposite modes of looking at the life of man*: one is for life and the other is against life. The alternative lies between a culture of death and a culture of life or, more profoundly, between a real culture of life and a pseudo-culture of the quality of life (cf. *CEI, Evangelizzazione,* 4).

Need for a Moral Choice-decision

4. Faced with the two roads with their alternatives and opposites, *we must choose*; we cannot remain indifferent. This is the specific invitation that rang out for us a while ago in the word of God: "See, I have set before you today life and prosperity, death and adversity.... I have set before you life and death, blessings and curses. Choose life so that you and your descendants may live" (Dt 30: 15, 19).

The passage from Deuteronomy does not only record what happened to Israel at that time, but that reality which every civilization, every culture, every group, every person faces. It would thus seem to be an invitation purposely thought of for a situation such as the one we have described. It could seem to be the invitation to choose between life and death, between a culture of life and a culture of death, for life or against life.

But the appeal of Deuteronomy is even more profound. Yes, it is an invitation to choose life over death, but life is perceived as a gift and a task, as a responsibility. It is truly life when it is lived within the ethical and religious experience. *The invitation,* then, is precisely to *make a moral choice-decision.* We therefore want to reflect on the seriousness of the moral decision which is incumbent upon each human person.

This decision is, in fact, a matter of giving a fundamental orientation to one's own life and, consequently, of acting in ways that are full of meaning. Only these conscious moral choices lead to life; choices of immoral behavior lead to death. The first give meaning and fullness to existence, the latter negate or annul this fullness and prevent persons from discovering any meaning in life. Correct moral choices help us fulfill our humanity, choices of immoral behavior destroy the dignity of each of us and of every other person. In this light we understand the statements of Deuteronomy: "If you obey the command-ments of the Lord your God that I am commanding you today, by loving the Lord your God, walking in his ways, and observing his commandments, decrees and ordinances, then you shall live and become numerous, and the Lord your God will bless you in the land that you are entering to possess. But if your heart turns away and you do not hear, but are led astray to bow down to other gods and serve them, I declare to you today that you shall perish; you shall not live long in the land that you are crossing the Jordan to enter and possess.... Choose life so that you and your descendants may live, loving the Lord your God, obeying him, and holding fast to him; for that means life to you and length of days, so that you may live in the land that the Lord swore to give to your ancestors, to Abraham, to Isaac, and to Jacob" (Dt 30:16-18, 19b-20).

In short, we are asked to make decisions in favor of life, so as to truly live our humanity to the fullest. Other-wise we are destined to perish, that is, not to achieve the moral quality of our existence. Among other things, in reference to the themes of human life and its defense and promotion, death—besides its profound moral dimen-sion—can also be brought about physically both for our-selves and for others!

For an Authentic Cultural Change:
What Is the Relationship between Life,
Freedom and the Gift of Self?

5. Faced with the two ways that we have described, we must decide and choose life.

Such a choice, and the consequent service to which

it commits us, is serious and demanding for the whole ecclesial as well as civil community. It includes the duty to *denounce* any disregard of and every attempt on the life of the person and to *recall and proclaim* that life "must always be served in its entirety and in every step of its development, whatever its condition" (CEI, *Evangelizzazione*, 44).

In particular, we cannot tire of clearly reaffirming the moral gravity of each procured abortion, even if it is carried out by means of drugs, just as we cannot desist from rejecting and condemning euthanasia. With similar firmness we are called to reject the abuses of genetics and of the techniques of artificial insemination, remembering that the embryo must be respected and treated as a person. At the same time we also reject other forms of the violation of life, such as child abuse, the abuse of minors, sexual violence, pornography, prostitution, behavior which facilitates the spread of AIDS, the sale and use of drugs, kidnapping, suicide, the lack of adequate security systems in the workplace and in meeting places, the pollution of the environment, war and any kind of unjust aggression (cf *Evangelizzazione*, 23).

6. However, these denunciations and these proclamations—though without a doubt necessary and binding—are not sufficient. They must be part of a wider picture and urgently require a renewed commitment that is fuller and better articulated. As has been emphasized many times, it is a matter of *realizing a genuine cultural change* and of bringing about a reverse in direction, capable of leading our society to discover and to live the entire truth about the person and about his life.

Even the pastoral directives of the Italian episcopate for the 1990's refer to these urgent needs, specifying that the protection and promotion of the right of each person to live, from the moment of conception to the end of earthly existence, and in conditions of real personal and social dignity, is an inalienable value on which to focus the work of evangelization, of charity and of civil obligation (CEI, *Evangelizzazione*, 30).

But how can we lead the whole of society to a change of direction? How can we promote a cultural change? We must first of all *"form a mature moral conscience regarding the immeasurable and inviolable value of every human life"* (CEI, *Evangelizzazione*, 43).

7. Now we want to pause a moment to illustrate an *initial fundamental step* to be taken toward this formation of conscience and for the realization of the necessary cultural change. This step *concerns the relationship between life and freedom*. In fact, as I recalled earlier, different attitudes and behavior contrary to life are lived in the name and as the affirmation of freedom, as well as in the name of the quality of life. We therefore need to ask ourselves about the meaning of freedom, of life and of its quality, and of the relationship between life and freedom.

In their message for the last Day for Life, the bishops affirmed that "life and freedom are not two inseparable realities. They are indivisible: where one is violated the other is violated also. *There is no real freedom wherever life, every human life, is not welcomed and loved*" (CEI, *Message*, 1).

Even when we understand freedom only as freedom from conditioning and coercion, there are still *experiences and situations that verify the existence of this indissoluble and mutual connection between life and freedom.* Suffice it to consider, for example, the situation in many areas of Europe, where—similar to what has happened and does happen in other totalitarian regimes—social and political systems that deny the freedom of their citizens have often brought with them serious forms of violence and even the taking of life: from prisons to torture, to forced labor, to the physical elimination of undesirable adversaries.

On the other side—that of the negation of freedom when there is no authentic respect for the life of each person—I wish to recall, again as an example, the serious plague of kidnapping, which still keeps persons and their families in anguish.

8. But these observations are neither sufficient nor decisive for establishing the indissoluble connection between life and freedom. We need to *seek a deeper and sounder reason*, one capable of serving as foundation to this indivisible bond. And it is here that we need a serious and genuine cultural change!

Our culture finds it difficult to establish a full relationship between life and freedom. To the degree that it has its roots in theories from the Enlightenment and in those of the social contract, our culture will not only be unable to establish this relationship, but it in fact will lead to its negation, giving an absolute and unquestionable role to freedom, understood as self-determination, self-affirmation, the absence of any restrictions in following one's own reason, emancipation from any reference to the good and to truth.

As Cardinal Ratzinger emphasized in his already cited intervention at the extraordinary Consistory in April, since the Enlightenment, "freedom is no longer seen positively as a tendency toward the good, as reason—aided by the community and by tradition—reveals it to be." Further on, concerning the theories of the social contract, "from the affirmation of the rights of freedom, detached from any objective reference to a common truth, we pass to the destruction of the very foundations of such freedom. The 'enlightened despot' of the theories about social contract has become the tyrannical, totalitarian State, which disposes of life and of the weakest members, of the unborn child, of the elderly, in the name of a public utility which in reality is nothing more than the interests of a few" (*L'Osservatore Romano*, April 5, 1991). In other words, freedom is not always seen as a tendency toward the good, but rather as a pure generic affirmation of rights, without taking into account their ultimate meaning for the person.

It will be possible to outline the deepest reason that explains how life and freedom are two indivisible goods only *by identifying a native and original reference point common to both realities and present in each of them.*

9. If we consider *life* and its *quality*, we must first of all point out that real quality of life does not consist simply in the absence of discomfort, poverty and suffering, but rather in that which permits life to be lived according to its intrinsic ethical value. It is also obvious, on the other hand, that physical life is a point of departure and a fundamental presupposition for the person to lead an existence charged with meaning. From this viewpoint it is a question of rediscovering the fact that *the truest meaning of human life lies in love,* and that it is precisely the ability to love in self-giving that gives life its meaning and makes it a reality with moral significance. In fact, as human experience itself reveals, "only the gift of self truly elevates the gift of life. Persons feel mature and truly fulfilled when, overcoming the tendency to turn in on self, they are able to be open to others, to give, to give themselves" (CEI, *Evangelizzazione*, 24).

We find here a reference to the Trinitarian mystery of communion and of gift, a mystery which we have placed at the center of our contemplation in the pastoral program, *Ephphatha, Be Opened.* The community of the Divine Trinity, of which man is a reflection in the world, is communication and divine communication is first of all the communication of life. Life therefore has meaning when it is a communicated and communicating gift, when it enters into the communication of gift. Then life assumes its fullness and its true quality, which consists in the very essence of life: a gift given so as to be given back, just as it is in God, from the Father to the Son in the circulation of love of the Holy Spirit. This is the culminating point, the heart of cultural change, which must begin from the mystery of the Cross as the revelation of Trinitarian love. We must, then, conclude that, in reference to the Trinitarian mystery and in light of the words and the cross of Jesus, it is possible to grasp without a shadow of a doubt that "only in the unconditional gift of self does the human person find the taste for living, conquer the meaning of his existence and free it from inevitable decay" (*Evangelizzazione*, 25).

10. The same must be said of *freedom*. However, it is a question of giving it *an adequate and genuine interpretation*. Clarification of the concept of freedom will enable us to grasp the unbreakable tie between life and freedom. By reflecting on our original experience of freedom, we are enabled to grasp the fact that freedom is a profoundly human and humanizing reality. It is a good that belongs to the person and makes him grow as a person, according to his integral truth as "gift fulfilled as gift." The human person, in fact, is "gift," because he/she is the fruit of the love of God who creates each individual person. At the same time the meaning of the person's existence lies precisely in self-giving. As I have already recalled, the human person is made to give of him/herself and "finds himself" only to the degree that he gives himself (cf *Gaudium et Spes*, 24). It follows that *human freedom is fully realized in this gift of self*. As the bishops wrote in their message, "man is truly free when, as master of himself, he knows how to give himself to others" (CEI, *Message*, 4). If we reflect on our experience we become aware that we are really free, not conditioned, not constrained by habits or fears, only when we perform a totally selfless action.

Revelation confirms all this for us and tells us that growth in freedom is connected to growth in charity. In particular St. Paul emphasizes this as soon as he presents freedom as a possibility offered to human persons to live according to the demands of the Spirit, that is, according to the demands of charity, which appears to us as the one law with which the freedom of the children of God must be concerned. But it is especially the experience of Jesus that reveals this truth to us. In fact, he "freely" hands himself over to his passion and death, in this way telling us that in the gift of oneself to the very end, one's freedom is fully realized.

11. In synthesis, we can and must state that it is precisely in the *sincere gift of self* that it is possible to give real meaning to life and to fully live and actualize one's freedom. This is the first fundamental aspect of the cultural change we are called to bring about and to awaken so that the life of human persons may be respected and served.

The pastoral journey in "communicating" which we are making in our diocese can offer us further points for reflection which I can neither take up nor develop here. It is, then, a step toward the cultural change that we must realize. Every task of ours that is imbued with this communication, which is a free and gratuitous gift of self, contributes to this clearing up and this opening of horizons; it serves life and serves freedom.

Therefore, while I invite you to reread the letter *Ephphatha, Be Opened*, from this perspective, I would only like to point out that communication, to which we are called and which the gift of the Spirit makes us capable of and participants in, is identified with the gift of self, because it finds its origins in the mystery of the Trinity and of God who communicates himself by loving and giving himself.

It is also important to reflect on the fact that this very

communication, to the degree that it is a gift of self, while letting ourselves be questioned by the other and by their existence and questioning the other, always respects the mystery of the person before me and requires that my freedom never be transformed into possession and domination of others.

An Obligation and a Responsibility for Everyone

12. The responsibility to contribute to the realization of this cultural change weighs on each and every person. In this last part of my reflection I intend simply to indicate some obligations that especially concern some of us.

First of all it is a responsibility that concerns *married couples, parents, families.* It "arises from the very nature and mission of the family willed by God as a community of life and love" (CEI, *Evangelizzazione*, 55). In the picture we have been describing, the *repossession of the moral character proper to the procreative act* takes on a particular significance, even as a reality emblematic of a whole way of perceiving life, freedom and their respective meanings. In this regard it would be interesting to look again at the rich reflections of last February's session of our diocesan priest's senate on "Birth and Death in the West." Obviously I cannot do this here at length; I can only make some quick allusions.

Today the act of procreation seems to be easily authorized by a generic desire or even a somewhat narcissistic will for a child, which reaches the point of the "child at any cost" syndrome.

All this leads to seeing in the child that is desired, and in the one already born, the fulfillment of all one's own expectations, and to project on the child one's own need for recognition and existential affirmation. In this way, the act of procreation is understood as the fulfillment and affirmation of self.

In reality, instead, the act of procreation—even beyond the specific and explicit awareness of the parents—is something that surpasses a project and a need for self-affirmation. "Procreation," write the Italian bishops, "is the privileged event in which is clearly manifested the fact that human life is a gift that is received in order to be given.... The parents themselves feel that the child is a reality greater than their gift of love: 'if it is the fruit of their mutual gift of love, it is, in turn, a gift for both, a gift that arises from the gift'" (*Evangelizzazione*, 30).

In this sense, you parents are asked to see your child—according to biblical tradition—as a gift, a promise, and a duty. Rather than planning the child, you can invoke the child as a gift that you are not able to guarantee, and you can welcome the child as the one who confronts your freedom, so that you may know and "serve" him or her with a love which, day after day, becomes an education and a fostering of God's plan for the child.

For you, then, the child is not only a precious gift but is a "reason for life." Thinking of and looking at him or her, may you be able to fully recognize that your life would not have hope, that it would be dull and useless if you did not find someone to give yourselves to. Instead, your life will appear full of meaning when you have someone to whom you can make a gift of life. This is your real self-fulfillment. This is how you rediscover your authentic freedom. And it is in this way, with your concrete experience as parents, that you will witness how true it is that love for life is a choice of freedom.

13. I intend to address a special word also to *doctors* and *health care workers*, to emphasize their responsibility which stems from the fact that all health care activity is in the service of life, for its protection, for its care, for its promotion. I therefore invite you to continue to *live your natural mission as custodians and servants of human life*, be-

cause in this lies the dignity of your profession. You, then, according to the ancient yet always relevant Hippocratic Oath, are asked to bear witness with your profession to respect for human life and for its sacredness, founded on the dignity of the human person as the image of God. It is precisely this dignity of each individual person and of each sick person, in whom we are invited to see the presence of Jesus Christ, that requires on your part adequate and proportionate care, in the certainty that to "cause someone to die" can never be an answer, not even when it means acceding to a request from the patient.

But you know very well that the *relationship with the sick person* is always a relationship of person to person, because the sick person is always first of all a person and can never be reduced to a mere clinical case. Your service to life directly involves your freedom, challenging you to give yourselves through a style of *communication that always knows how to respect the mystery of the person* present in every patient of yours. You are thus called to become involved as persons, calling into play not only your knowledge and your skill but your very selves.

One of you, in the testimony to which we listened earlier, underlined, among other things, the fact that some serious decisions which persons consider or eventually make are often due to the fact these persons have not found others who can be close to them with help, with counsel, or even only with an act of love. You are also asked to assist the sick in these ways.

Your care for the sick also includes a capacity for donation and communication that knows how to be attentive to their story. You are not asked simply to be at their side but, in some way, to "enter into their story," with that discretion and love that make you aware of all the nuances and all the conditions. From the same viewpoint, respect for the sick is also the capacity for progressive and delicate communication with them, especially when it is a matter of presenting a demanding form of therapy, of giving information so as to obtain a knowledgeable and free consent, of communicating an unfavorable diagnosis. Your ability to give yourselves will also be measured by your availability in establishing with the sick a rapport that infuses joy and hope, not only when you see the possibility for a cure but also when a cure is not possible. Even in these latter cases it is possible to continue to "take care" of them, transmitting important values such as the assurance that they are still loved, and helping them to perceive life as a "mystery" entrusted to the love of God.

14. The profession of *pharmacist*, too, possesses a dignity that cannot and must not be obscured. The work of pharmacists, in fact, daily brings them close to the sick to help them recover their health and to defend the inestimable gift of life. For them, too, the love and service of life continually require growth in a freedom that is an authentic gift of self.

As John Paul II pointed out in his discourse to members of the International Federation of Catholic Pharmacists, on November 3, 1990, for such self-giving to be realized, the *relationship between pharmacists and those who seek their aid must go well beyond the simple commercial aspects.* The profession of pharmacist, in fact, cannot be reduced to that of a salesclerk or of a distributor of ready-made drugs. Pharmacists "have the duty to be attentive counselors to those who obtain remedies for themselves, not to mention the moral assistance they can give to whomever comes to purchase a product and awaits the pharmacists' advice, a reason for hope, a path to follow" (*L'Osservatore Romano*, November 4, 1990).

From this perspective pharmacists who sincerely want to love those who turn to them must concern themselves not so much with filling immediate requests as with helping others recognize the true and the good. In doing this, pharmacists, because of the dignity of their vocation, will be unable to consent to the distribution of products that have "non-therapeutic purposes, capable of contravening the laws of nature, to the detriment of the dignity of the person" (*L'Osservatore*). From this viewpoint, in the distribution of medicine pharmacists are required to adhere to a strict moral code, formulating a conscientious objection. My wish is that the group of Catholic pharmacists recently constituted in Milan may be a valuable center for deeper study of these topics and for supporting pharmacists' choices in the service of human life.

15. I have already had occasion for speaking about *nurses* and their role in love for life and about the conditions needed so that their profession may be fulfilled in a suitable way. I would simply like to emphasize once more that, precisely because illness is an experience that proposes to the conscience and the freedom of the individual problems about the global meaning of life, the sick must not be left to face such problems alone, must not be condemned to secrecy, but be able to enjoy the presence of persons close to them and supportive. The nursing *profession*—provided that it is presented, matured and lived with an explicit and constant attention to ethical values and dimensions—of its nature *is animated and permeated by solid ideals and fruitful humanitarian attitudes.*

It follows that the Christian vocation of the laity can today find one of its most demanding paths, one that is full of meaning, in the nursing profession. Let it then be suggested decisively and continually to the young, with the awareness that "the task of nursing certainly demands an additional supply of austerity and a spirit of sacrifice, but at the same time offers a serious opportunity for carrying out in a concrete way the human and Christian ideals of sharing, of solidarity, and of self-giving" (Lombard Conference for the Pastoral Program for Health Care, *Una professione per aiutare il prossimo*, May, 1989).

16. I would also like to address a word to the *educators* who are present: from the religion teachers to the catechists, from teachers in nursery schools to others in Catholic and non-Catholic schools. As the Italian bishops wrote, they "are called to fulfill a formative task that is able to promote the human person in the wholeness and the unity of his values and needs."

As a consequence, an appeal is addressed to them that they "not tire of depicting the meaning of each human life and the real reasons for which it is to be interpreted in terms of a vocation and of a mission to the giving of self" (CEI, *Evangelizzazione*, 56). Let us think how many crises, how many slips, how much desperation— even to the point of suicides attempted by teenagers— could be prevented if educators knew how to recognize the problems and sufferings of many young people, the meaning of their silence and their withdrawal.

Against this background the task of teachers and educators is truly valuable in attaining the formation of consciences and bringing about that cultural change that is seen to be urgent. It is true that this task of theirs is not always accepted and recognized; occasions for discouragement and temptations to abandon the field are not lacking, especially when we encounter a series of bureaucratic and administrative difficulties, as seems to happen even in Catholic nursery schools. But it is the clear, renewed awareness of the irreplaceable role of this education that moves us to face and overcome every problem. It is the same awareness that causes us to send out a message to those who contribute to augmenting these problems, that they may not be held responsible for hindering an adequate formation to life and freedom, a formation that cannot but be to the advantage of the whole of society.

Again in the field of education, I would like to say a special word about "putting into effect all the initiatives that can help [young persons] to understand and live sexuality, love and life according to their deep inner meaning and in their intrinsic co-relationship" (*Evangelizzazione*, 45). I am thinking, among other things, of an organic and systematic proposal for *education in sexuality, life and love,* to which our Family Advisory Bureaus can offer a qualified contribution. I am also thinking of the valuable work that suitable teachers can carry out for a correct and adequate *education in the natural methods of regulation of births.* In both cases, in fact, we find initiatives that are completely consistent with the values of freedom, life and the gift of self, on which we have reflected during this encounter.

Conclusion

17. Let us once again reflect on the word of God: "See, I have set before you today life and prosperity, death and adversity.... Choose life so that you and your descendants may live" (Dt 30:15,19).

Today, O Lord, we hear your word resound in our hearts. We sincerely want to listen to your invitation, and renew our commitment and will to love every brother and sister, to respect their dignity, to defend and promote their life.

But we must also recognize that we are very fragile and indecisive. Locked up in our pettiness and egoism, we do not always know how to make the decision to love, of which you are the source.

Grant that our freedom may let itself be questioned by the face of every man and woman—especially those who are more lonely, poor, defenseless, sick, small, suffering, needy—and may thus be open to the sincere gift of self.

Purify our heart and our life from every form of

narrow-mindedness and from the recurring temptation to affirm ourselves, even at the cost of not recognizing and respecting the dignity and life of others. With the gift of your Spirit, open our freedom to the love that knows how to foster interpersonal communication and selflessness without reserve. Transform us into the image of Jesus, who on the cross freely gave himself so as to give life to his brothers and sisters.

Enlightened by you, Lord, who are the light of the world, may we know how to discern the reflection of the splendor of your face on the face of every person: on the small face, just being formed, of the unborn baby; on the sad face of those touched by illness and sorrow, solitude and marginalization; and on the tired face of the elderly and those about to die.

O God, lover of life, infuse your grace, your strength and your consolation in all those—doctors, nurses, pharmacists, volunteer workers, parents, teachers, educators—who each day spend the best of their energies in loving service to their brothers and sisters.

May we, in this way too, bear witness in the world to the joyful truth that love for life is a choice of freedom. Amen.

Appendix: Biblical Text

"See, I have set before you today life and prosperity, death and adversity. If you obey the commandments of the Lord your God that I am commanding you today, by loving the Lord your God, walking in his ways and observing his commandments, decrees, and ordinances, then you shall live and become numerous, and the Lord your God will bless you in the land that you are entering to possess. But if your heart turns away and you do not hear, but are led astray to bow down to other gods and serve them, I declare to you today that you shall perish; you shall not live long in the land that you are crossing the

Jordan to enter and possess. I call heaven and earth to witness against you today that I have set before you life and death, blessings and curses. Choose life so that you and your descendants may live, loving the Lord your God, obeying him, and holding fast to him; for that means life to you and length of days, so that you may live in the land that the Lord swore to give to your ancestors, to Abraham, to Isaac, and to Jacob" (Dt 30:15-20).

Message of the Permanent Council of the Italian Episcopal Conference for the Thirteenth Day for Life

1. *Love for life as a choice of freedom.* Life and freedom are not two separable realities. They are indivisible goods: where one is violated, the other is violated. *There is no freedom wherever life, each human life, is not welcomed and loved.*

This is the truth that the Italian bishops, on the Day for Life, February 3, 1991, intend to proclaim, to bring to the intention of the men and women of our country, and to entrust in a special way to young people, who are the future builders of the new Europe and of the world.

2. Not only abortion and euthanasia but many other forms of violence against life, such as suicide and drugs, are invoked and justified as affirmations of freedom.

Experience, instead, attests dramatically to the fact that the refusal to live and to let live goes hand in hand with the end of freedom.

Cut off from its original and essential bond with the inviolable dignity of the person, human life becomes an object to be used, sought or rejected by the violence of the individual or of society.

3. The freedom of decision and action inherent in all that concerns life is today invoked in the name of the

quality of human life. But we must ask whether freedom and the quality of life are understood according to the truth. As we have written in a recent pastoral document, "we must ask ourselves whether human life is worthy of being lived because of its presumed quality, which would consist of the absence of discomfort, poverty and suffering, or rather for itself, insofar as it is the life of the person" (cf *Evangelizzazione*, 7).

In truth, every human life merits and demands the wisdom and courage to be lived with gratitude. The dignity of the person requires that life always be welcomed, defended, and sustained in every human creature, from the moment of conception until natural death, and should be supported in its integral, physical and spiritual development.

4. Faced with a widespread conception of life which does violence to life itself, *it is absolutely necessary to bring about a cultural change*, a change of direction.

This is possible on the condition that personal freedom is cultivated in the "sincere gift of self" (*Gaudium et Spes*, 24), and that the immutable, universal commandment: "You shall not kill," is observed always and by everyone, in defense both of every human life and of all freedom. Freedom, in fact, welcomes life. The person is truly free when, as master of himself, he knows how to give himself to others.

Civilization is in question here, that is, the human good not only of individuals but of peoples. Only unconditional respect for the right to life of each person can be the foundation for respect for all the rights of the person and therefore of the democratic freedoms themselves.

The serious problem of widespread violence, the abuse of minors, kidnapping, and organized crime in general, tell us with extreme clarity that only the recovery, in the awareness of everyone, of the value of every life, beginning from the most defenseless, can offer a radical and effective response.

5. This change of direction is urgent even *in view of the unity of Europe* and of the processes of progressive integration of the various democratic institutions and the different life models.

The sources of the law and the documents of the ancient civilization of Europe are permeated by the message of the Gospel, which provides a secure foundation for the highest principles of the inviolability, the dignity and the freedom of the person. Faced with the impressive influx of immigrants, it becomes even more urgent to cultivate the most profound Christian soul and root of our history.

6. We are confident that a mature reflection on the relationship between human life and freedom will lead believers and persons of good will to welcome our appeal.

May the *Christian communities* be aware of their mission to render witness to Christ, the Truth who makes us free, by announcing the Gospel of life and serving persons with love. May parishes, associations and movements feel called to develop the mentality and initiatives that welcome new life, that give more ample and concrete attention to the rights of minors and of the elderly, and solidarity with families in situations of suffering. In particular, may they offer to young people strong ideals and commitment to life.

We ask of *Christian families* the courage of a more generous and responsible openness to life in procreation, and of a clear and solid formation to authentic freedom, as a conscious and responsible "yes" to a life understood as vocation and mission to love.

We ask *politicians, administrators, and those engaged in social work and health care services* to recognize love for life as the fundamental presupposition and content for the promotion of the common good. May they leave nothing untried in assuring the necessary economic, social and cultural conditions for the promotion of an effective freedom as a choice of life: the freedom of young people to have a home and to marry, not only live together; the freedom of women to give expression to their social and professional aptitudes, without having to renounce the rights and duties which form part of being spouse and mother; the freedom of spouses to conceive the children they desire and to give them birth; the freedom of families to directly assist the elderly.

Rome, November 1, 1990, Feast of All Saints

Testimonies

Professor Alfonso Zampetti Chief gynecologist at the Hospital of Niguarda

If in recent times we have found the seed of a reawakening, of esteem for, of defense of, and of increased value given to the existence of the human person, nonetheless the hold of the dominant culture is still strong. This culture obscures, at times suffocates, the great value of life, giving first place to an exaggerated search for the satisfaction of the ego, of contingent well-being, freeing persons from the responsibility for subjective acts that imply renunciation, dedication and altruism.

And in the wake of these orientations life itself, the primary value of the human being is questioned, is at times sacrificed, subordinated to individual and social interests, despised even by the laws of the State.

We can verify this state of affairs with sadness from the privileged observation point of an obstetrics department in a large hospital, in which daily the voluntary termination of many new lives takes place.

Here, the health care worker, the nurse, the doctor, the true doctor, whether believer or not, who have made the safeguarding of life a reason for their profession, suffer, often helplessly, in the depths of their conscience at the tragedy of this sad reality. They suffer for the situation incumbent on so many small victims, but even more because they foresee that the motives which have broken down the defense of the life of so many innocent babies can also be considered sufficient for justifying a similar treatment for the weakest, those suffering from illnesses without a cure, and perhaps even for the disabled and the most underprivileged, the elderly.

This position is for you, doctor or health care worker, a source of grave responsibilities which oblige you to evaluate, within the limits of your possibilities and with the help of those who share your same anxieties, some of the serious motivations that involve you on the professional and human level, motivations which you have not, perhaps, yet made your own.

Thank the Lord for having guided you to the choice of a profession which forces you to prove your ability to love your neighbor. Ask him for the strength to overcome the moments of confusion which can arise from witnessing firsthand how so many persons face—with a superficiality equal to their lack of preparation—the voluntary interruption of a life in its initial development. Such an interruption is considered to be an occasional incident in the course of existence and, following the cultural mentality of the time, is no longer considered as an attack against the most important ethical value.

And then you ask yourself: is the woman truly free who in a moment of grave decision, alone, terribly alone, does not receive the truth from those who could give it, nor find selflessness in the actions of those who should help her, nor solidarity in the behavior of those who are near her?

It is the answer to this question that upsets us in the depths of our consciences.

And you, doctor, health care worker, nurse, who have received from God the grace of education, good health, learning, perhaps even for this reason you can consider your lives as a gift that your parents have transmitted to you in an act of love. How can you ignore, how can you be indifferent to that creature, the victim of non-willful ignorance, who is oppressed by need in an egoistic, impersonal and at times inhuman society that is deaf to her modest needs, and who consequently considers the new life that is developing within her as a burden, one more burden that weighs heavily on her already burdened existence?

Haven't you considered that many of these serious decisions can mature because that person has not found in those who are close to her, perhaps not even in you, help and counsel, or even only an act of love that allows her to understand that in life there is such a thing as pure, disinterested love, which helps one to live and to let live; and that, next to your love, there is the love of God who lives in every creature right from its conception?

I do not want to conclude this brief testimony without remembering Lucia, a journalist hospitalized some time ago in our department. In the fifth month of her first long-awaited pregnancy, she was found to be suffering from an acute form of leukemia. As Lucia thought about the diagnosis and especially the prognosis, the joy that filled her heart at the thought of her baby seemed to fade for a time. Then she rallied: with courage and firmness she wanted to know the truth, the whole truth, and the prognosis that soon became unfavorable.

She decidedly refused the suggestion made by the hematologists to terminate the pregnancy so as to better her chances for a cure. She also refused the medication which is used in the treatment of such advanced forms of leukemia, but which is certainly fatal to the unborn child. She spent two months, from the fifth to the seventh, intimately enjoying every little perception of the smallest sign of life coming from the child growing within her, the child whom she eventually would have to leave.

By the time the seventh month was completed, the illness had worsened. Now that the child was able to live on its own, the mother wanted to undergo cesarean section. She wanted to be conscious so as to be better able to impress on her memory—the memory of a mother about to die—the first cry coming from that new life, the life of her child, and to rejoice in this memory for the seven days that she remained alive.

This heroic witness of an absolute act of love, of self-giving that led to the greatest sacrifice, should not be touched by any comment, but is offered as a starting point for confrontation and meditation.

Mother Teresa Gaspar, Directress of the formative Community "Villa Luce" of Milan

On this day dedicated to life, I don't know how else to begin except with my personal experience of life. It is the experience of a woman who has chosen consecrated virginity as the way for a journey toward Love: the love for the Father and for her own sisters and brothers, which Jesus proclaimed and witnessed to.

Jesus said: "I am the way, and the truth, and the life." In order to place ourselves on this way of truth, my sisters and I—the Missionary Sisters of Jesus the Redeemer—have chosen to witness love for the least, for the most abandoned, in the person of adolescents in serious difficulty. These adolescents have often suffered violence and privation, privation which, if for some meant also the privation of material goods, for almost all has meant the tragic lack of affective relationships.

In our formative Community, "Villa Luce," in which we religious—according to our Constitutions—must each realize our ascent by means of service to these young people, the function of maternity has become central; I would add: the function of maternity and paternity. In fact, it is this very function of the married couple that our adolescents have felt the lack of. They have never known or been able to experience family life. If they had tasted the sweetness and security that dependence on adults gives—adults who are prepared to respond to the needs of their children—they would have been formed to making responsible choices.

I wanted to point out that the life of the girls and our life as religious are strongly connected by a bond of thoughts, affection and sharing. Such a bond guides us religious (by means of a professional apostolate) in our search for God, who is Truth in the freedom of love, and provides for the adolescents the indispensable structure of that "human person," which the Church, the Pope and our Archbishop have emphasized is the basis of the Christian person.

"Love for life as a choice of freedom": this is the theme on which we are meditating today and the intention for which we are praying. If our Archbishop has invited us to this assembly of reflection and prayer, it seems to me that this signifies that for all people the choices of freedom are not an easy undertaking, even though God the Creator has placed in each one of us a spark of that "love" which is his "Life."

Yes, God sustains us, but he also wills that we sustain one another: that we human beings bear one another's burdens—as St. Paul reminds us—that we feel ourselves to be neighbors, without judging one another, but assisting one another according to our needs.

The evangelical truths, the biblical truth of love, which succors even when there is only one just person who invokes the love that saves, are the daily experience of our profession as women religious, they are the daily experience of our profession as educators.

We experience—both in ourselves and in our adolescents, who are entrusted to us by the juvenile court—that without our personal and communitarian "love for life" there is no choice of freedom. If for no other reason, it is because freedom of choice is not possible when the person is not in a position to have the ability to choose. This means that the person cannot exercise an autonomy that leaves them room for making free choices when faced with urgent material and spiritual needs. One cannot make free choices when faced with the urgent need for someone to share his or her difficulties, for someone to help resolve their problems without condemning them for their inadequacies.

What happens, however, when a person is unprepared to make choices of freedom, even though God has preordained them in his plan of love, a plan which people have not yet known how to carry out?

As educators we find ourselves confronted with this problem every day. Our adolescents have love for life, in fact it is this love which keeps them alive, so that when it lessens, they have to face truly dramatic situations, at times made tragic because they despair of being able to continue to live.

However, what an adolescent is still lacking is precisely the freedom of choice, that is, the lack of choices of freedom: of that freedom which for us as Christians is the realization of the divine plan in which true freedom flourishes.

Too often in our adolescents the choices connected

with love for life, even on the biological level—the use of sexuality—are not accompanied by a mature love for the other, that is, a responsible and conscious love, which is expressed in behavior suited to the choice of love for life.

Then comes the drama for us and for them. The civil code of our country sanctions some laws, while the law of life, according to a plan of love, binds us to other directions.

We must not believe that the feeling of being bound by a plan of love is exclusive to us as religious and educators. Often, even consciously, this is a specific perception of many adolescents who have sought love with childlike longing, even if they did so through means and actions that belong to a conscious adult life. Despite this awareness, because some of our adolescents are familiar with the sadness and privation of the public institutions charged with the care of children, they reject a similar destiny for their child. They see no other choice than that of legalized abortion.

I believe that this fact should cause us all to reflect very much, as human beings and as Christians. I believe that this cannot help but force us to ask ourselves an unavoidable question: how can I contribute to the realization of God's plan of love when my brother or sister does not have the adequate strength? When these sisters or brothers have not had the possibility for choices of freedom which would bring about love for life, even the life of an innocent third person?

I am aware that, unavoidably, my presentation is ending up to be a provocation rather than a testimony. I see the only response possible to all this as coming from the Gospel, the Gospel which asks us to share with our brothers and sisters what we have on our table, on the table of our family.

Thus my conclusion is also an appeal.

When children come into the world, they must find minds and hearts that welcome them, persons who know how to welcome the children even if they have not physically conceived them!

This is a genuine way of bringing about, even today, that sharing of goods which the first Christians practiced, not only in the concreteness of material goods, but in that spiritual and mental communion which in Christ Jesus made them "one."

For us this word is certain: it is love that saves!

Reflection on the theme of life, Milan, April 27, 1991

CHAPTER 15

Let's Speak of Television in the Family

Letter to a Mother and Father

Dearest Carl and Laura,

The pastor rings your doorbell after supper. You have expressed the desire that the Christmas blessing find you gathered as a family. Michael is proud and excited because he wants to show the crib he has prepared all by himself. Jack has his guitar ready and will accompany the Christmas hymn, as he is used to doing to introduce his friends to the group meeting. Sylvia will willingly put aside her books, even though she has a lot to study. Without complaining Frank will miss the first half of the game with his favorite team.

Everyone contributes to creating an atmosphere of excitement and peace, of that strong, intense love for one another that calms uncertainties and encourages children to grow without being afraid of life.

You are aware that you need evenings like that, evenings filled with the simple joy that reigns in a home when everyone willingly comes together to pray. This joy repays every sacrifice and permits a more serene consideration of the many unknown elements that surround the future of your children. You experience very clearly that you are being cared for by the hand of God.

You need evenings like this, but it becomes more and more difficult to stay together. The children grow up, they have their commitments, they have their mysterious unalterable appointments, they also have many whims and want to "stay out."

Then, the one time you are all at home, with an automatic reflex that seems uncontrollable, supper is not yet finished and the television is already turned on. Every suggestion or resolution to prolong the conversation or to introduce a prayer together dies even before being put into words because of a mixture of reserve, laziness and a mortifying sense of powerlessness.

And then, the heated discussion over the choice of programs, the whims of the youngest who never wants to go to bed, the unreal and somewhat oppressive light that is diffused when the other lights are lowered, the embarrassment at scenes in which the intimacy between man and woman is violated and vulgarity is carelessly exhibited: all these have become a habit.

Now you are almost used to it: "Every evening it's the same story!" But you're left with a sense of bitterness and uneasiness, as though a hostile force were sowing weeds where you wanted only good grain to grow.

When the pastor comes to visit you and bring you the Christmas blessing, you confide your concerns: "What can good words and example do in the face of aggressive and cunning suggestions that confuse bad with good, whim with freedom, pleasure with happiness? The *mass media*, their friends, their schoolmates, advertising, all seem to speak a language that is much more persuasive than that of mom and dad!" For this reason I am addressing you parents first of all, to encourage you to have trust and fortitude.

I am, in fact, convinced that, beyond immediate impressions, the truth and the good are more persuasive than the deceptions of advertising. This fact involves responsibility for an exemplary consistency and the patience to await the fruits.

If you want to teach respect for the dignity of man and woman and therefore the rejection of violence, vulgarity and stupidity, you parents must also resist the temptation to stay up in the evening so as to secretly watch scenes that are condemned and which exercise a depraved attraction over viewers. Fortitude together with love will finally find the courage to propose occasional days of silence, as I suggested in my pastoral letter (cf *Il lembo del mantello: The Hem of His Garment*, 30), as well as the discipline of the eyes and a wise use of time. There will be other occasions when it will be necessary to arouse a renewed interest in world problems and to invite your children to attentively watch a televised debate or to carefully read a page of the newspaper. We need to help the young people of today open their eyes to the world without becoming afraid of the complexity of problems and without agreeing with widespread prejudices and clichés. This is why I have addressed them directly in the following Letters.

But I feel certain that the coherence of your choices and the determination with which you sustain the quality of your communication will speak more effectively to your children. In fact, it is up to you, first of all, to offer proposals for the Christian education of your children. You do not perform a service to the children whom you love if you accommodate the foolish way of understanding life, freedom and love that is often promoted by the means of communication; by remaining silent about the radical nature of the invitation to follow Jesus. It is not prudent to ignore the fact that the meaning of life lies in the vocation to lofty and difficult things, even if many television programs and advertising offers insist on assuring happiness at guaranteed prices.

The pastor who prays with you about the conditions in which your children are growing up will be happy to bring, on my behalf, the blessing of the Lord on a family that wants to make a journey of freedom, intelligence, and frank and constructive dialogue.

I assure you of my prayers and I wish you a heartfelt Merry Christmas.

Letter to a Young Boy Preparing for Confirmation

Dear Michael,

Perhaps the moment of your Confirmation is still far off because it will be in the spring or next fall. However, you are still preparing yourself through your presence at religion classes and through the enthusiasm with which you follow the suggestions of your pastor and catechists.

I recognized your signature on the back of the great photo that you gave me when I visited your parish and—if I remember correctly—I saw you perform your service as altar boy. While you served, you prayed and sang.

Since I know that you are ready and willing to be accompanied on the way to your encounter with Jesus, I would like to be of help to you with some advice and thoughts.

Confirmation is the moment in which you complete your journey of "Christian initiation," as the early Christians said. The gift of the Spirit makes you a living stone in the Church, where God dwells in the midst of his people.

The Church counts on you for its life and growth. Even though you are very young, you are already able and ready to be, like Jesus, one who serves. So you receive a gift, but it is a demanding gift, I would say rather, a seed that can bear marvelous fruits.

To be truly ready to serve you must be free. In fact, those who are imprisoned in laziness never have the will to step forward when there is a need. Those who are too concerned with themselves and spend a lot of time on hobbies, never have time to think of others. Those who are afraid of disappointments and of what others will think, are not selfless enough to serve.

You, too, are invited to a journey of freedom. I would especially like to invite you to freedom with regard to some habits which can become idols and to which we sacrifice the best things.

For example, some television shows lure you almost violently: a certain series or an animated cartoon, a game show or even all of these together. Even your catechist notices at once when you are impatient to go home and watch TV. Though you usually participate in your religion lessons with interest and offer a contribution that helps everyone, now you suddenly become nervous, and you can't wait until class is over because your favorite program is about to start. So you risk sacrificing your time of religious instruction for a television program.

If, once you arrive home, the TV is already occupied because your sister is watching "her stupid movies," endless arguments arise, complicated defenses of your rights and ridiculous demands. Often it all ends in long faces and resentful tears. And on those occasions when an exasperated sister gives in to you, you have to admit that you sacrificed the serenity of the evening for a program that is already forgotten.

At times it has happened that you envy your friends who have a TV set in their own room and can watch what they want. But in feeling this way, you risk sacrificing your sensitivity to the poor to the petty desire to be able to watch your favorite programs.

This is what I mean when I talk about the risk that

television become an idol to which many persons sacrifice even their souls. We call the television an instrument of social communication, but these words may seem rather abstract to you. The use you make of television demonstrates that for you it's more of a toy that serves only as a pastime.

It may seem strange to you that I am paying attention to the use you make or would like to make of the television; from a bishop you expect discussions on more important topics. However, I have become aware that at times the greatest discussions and the most important values that I have at heart, are threatened precisely by the daily slavery that fills the mind and occupies the time of bright young people like you, leaving space for nothing else.

I therefore encourage you to make this journey of freedom. With your priest decide on a program of life in which you also include how and for how long you will watch the TV and how and when you'll turn it off. Sometimes have the courage not to watch it at all. Then you can put the free time that you gain at the disposal of your pastor and your parents or a friend who needs help. I assure you, you will not find it difficult to discover better ways of using your time, your imagination and your intelligence.

From the dedication you are then able give to good works, the important question of your future will begin to arise. You may feel annoyance at useless activity and satisfaction when you do good, you may enjoy intense moments of silence in which you are able to shut out everything, including the television. Then you will begin to ask yourself whether in all this there might be a sign of a particular invitation from God, what we usually call a vocation. In my time there was no television, but I remember that my vocation matured when, at your age, I decided to give up going to the theater.

I pray for you, so that when the hands are laid upon

you to invoke the gift of the Holy Spirit, you may feel freer and more ready for the great works the Lord expects from you. I greet you with affection. I count on meeting you soon, and I repeat that I expect a lot from you. If you welcome Jesus this Christmas with an attentive and free heart, you will be able to do wonders. Best wishes.

Letter to a Conscientious Student

Dear Sylvia,

Even though study takes up much of your time and deadlines make you a little nervous, I am certain that you will willingly read these few lines.

Your scholastic achievements for the first part of this year are very promising and confirm your gifts of a good intelligence and willing application. Your parents are pleased with you and I can picture your mother confiding to her friends, with an air of satisfaction, the praise of your English teacher. Perhaps the mathematics teacher (so difficult to please!) insists on saying that you lack a bit of intuition and quickness in solving problems, but I am certain that in her heart she says: "If only all the students were like her!"

Considering the brilliant results of your work, I am surprised at the low degree of interest you show toward various initiatives which have been proposed at your school. When the student assembly was called, you took the opportunity to go over the chapter in your history book which you expected to be questioned on and which you already knew, almost by heart. Many of the other dedicated students did the same thing. They justified themselves by saying: "It's all politics" and "we lose a lot of time."

Even the religion teacher met with annoyance and lack of interest when he suggested a survey of the last address of the Pope. Perhaps for you, as for many others, the newspapers are only a means for satisfying a bit of curiosity about a certain "hot" event or a source of information on the latest styles or on sports?

It is disturbing to think that the reading of the newspaper or participation in a student assembly or in a debate on current events are put up with as "a waste of time."

I know that you participate with intense emotion in the tragic events that too often shake some area of the world. These are events which the television makes us witness in a way that is at times so violent as to overcome our habitual indifference and to move us—I hope—to prayer and acts of solidarity. However, news becomes old quickly and you tire easily of the newscasts.

It seems to me the time has come to recall good young people and diligent students to their duty of breaking out from horizons that are too narrow, from an inclination to withdraw into their own little world, into the successes and fears that are a real part of adolescent growth.

To call things by their right name, it seems to me that egoism and fear of responsibility are at the origin of withdrawal from a real interest in the world in which we live. A girl like you has the duty to open her window to the world, to become used to serious but attentive use of the means of social communication. You have the right to expect teachers to supply you with elements that will give you direction in the midst of today's complicated events and will help you exercise a vigilant critical sense over the information you receive.

I count on you, that the desire to understand our times may form part of your conversations with friends, may animate debates in your classes, and furnish convincing motives for more demanding reading. You will never have the right to complain that things do not go well and to describe the future as a nightmare. Rather you have the duty to read, to study, to discuss so as to prepare yourself to contribute to making a better world.

If you make good use of the information you receive, if you pay attention to the reflections of wise persons, to history narrated in precise reports, you will be able to discover how useful it is to read a newspaper, to be informed by television reports, to subscribe to a missionary magazine. I assure you that your parents do not fear that time dedicated to opening your eyes to the world is time lost from study. And your teachers will notice immediately in your papers—if you still do them—and in your discussion the steps taken toward a more integrated maturity.

Everyone must contribute to bettering the world, but we are right in expecting this contribution from a Christian girl. If you, dear Sylvia, stand aside, those who only want to lose time and make their subversive interpretations prevail will end up lording it over the others. So I expect to see the overthrow of the stereotype of a studious girl who thinks only about school and grades, and to find a free person, one who is able to keep informed, to have her own ideas and to speak out fearlessly: in short, a person who can become a leader.

In view of the problems that you are coming to know, you will not be able to escape that essential question of youth: what is my place in this world? What contribution am I asked to make for the building up of a better world? An intelligent girl like you does not study just for love of good grades; she studies and thinks and prays because she wants to know and live her vocation.

I count a lot on you. I greet you with warmest best wishes.

Letter to a Very Sports-minded Young Man

Dear Frank,

Even when competition for the football championship is given a break at Christmas time, the sports pages and televised programs find a way of filling hours and hours, pages and pages, so much so that I don't know if you will find the time to read these thoughts that I am addressing to you.

I believe that everyone ought to be active in some sport, if their health allows them to. It is a way of taking care of your health. The movement and physical effort promote relaxation and allow you to recover interior balance so as to face the tasks and daily difficulties with greater serenity.

The endless games for boys are often the occasion for lasting friendships and the effort exerted on mountain paths is always rewarded by some natural beauty to contemplate and an unmatched opportunity for reflection, confidence and peace. The educational wisdom of the Christian community invested many resources in structures that favor sports activities, even long before public institutions did so.

However, when I hear that restrictions are placed on programming evening activities for youth groups because of televised sports events, I am perplexed. Considering the crowd that fills the stadiums and the sports halls and that often uses violent forms and vulgar expressions to "act as fans," I ask myself whether these sports shows really help young people spend their free time in a worthwhile and happy way.

The reflection can be extended to the exasperating line of automobiles that besiege ski areas in wintertime or to the inextricable traffic jams that accompany sports events to which the *mass media* give an importance that to me, frankly, seems exaggerated.

I often think of you, Frank, and of others your age. You told me, half-jokingly, half-seriously, that the only page of the newspaper that interests you is the sports page.

I am not concerned now about analyzing the reasons why sports occupy such a large space in the papers and on television; this is not the place to evaluate this phenomenon. What I now have at heart is to invite you to consider this intrusive interest with a critical sense. If you dedicate so much time to sports, talked about, commented on, interviewed, and analyzed, you run the risk of narrowing your horizons and reducing your interests to the point of impoverishing your personality, language and relationships.

Your catechist attributed to timidity the infrequency of your participation in the group; your contribution was often limited to monosyllables. I think that it is more realistic to admit that for the most part you did not speak for the simple reason that you had nothing to say.

As you grow older, you will run the risk of annoying the girl who likes you and of limiting your circle of friends to those who, like you, have endless discussions about sports. Don't lay too much blame on the newspapers and television: they are instruments that you can make better use of. Begin, instead, to broaden your interests, to choose your reading and television programs with intelligence, make the effort to take some prolonged periods of silence to think. It will then be easy to restore everything to its right proportion.

I am certain that you will discover within yourself unexpected sensitivity, and to all those whom you meet each day you will show yourself to be a more interesting person.

There is a great need for thoughtful young people, attentive to the signs with which our times ask for hope, freedom and acts of solidarity. These are things you can read in the newspapers and see on television, if you know how to choose your programs well. I encourage you to a discipline that will allow you to emerge in the deep truth of your being, and I await the fruits.

The birth of Jesus is the revelation that man and his salvation are the desire of God. The wish that I offer you is to be close to Jesus this Christmas in such a way as to truly take to heart the widest horizons of human reality.

Letter to a Catechist

Dear Jack,

I have a great desire to express to you my gratitude and appreciation for the commitment you have made to be a catechist for the junior high students this year. I cannot hide my admiration for the generosity and seriousness with which you have accepted the proposal of your pastor, for the perseverance with which you punctually appear, well-prepared for the lesson. You have to find the time for this amidst the deadlines of your university studies and the other interests and appointments that fill your week.

When I think that in our diocese there are thousands of young people and adults who, like you, so simply, without asking for anything in return and without putting on airs, dedicate themselves to educating children and teenagers in the faith, I spontaneously offer a prayer of amazement and gratitude for the splendid gifts which the Spirit of God has given to his Church.

These first months have been enough for you to experience the consolations that the children know how to spontaneously give with their friendship. You have also experienced the nervousness and bitterness of moments in which it seems that no one wants to do anything. The group is reduced to a few distracted children, and the lesson you have prepared does not find any listeners. They laugh, they interrupt at the wrong time, they respond with vulgarity, they are anxious to finish. Then they spend the rest of the afternoon in game halls; what you wanted to tell them didn't seem to interest them at all!

You have also discovered some tricks for getting your students' attention and inviting them to reflect. In fact, you feel more at ease when the topic scheduled is presented with the viewing of a videocassette. You have asked the priest many times to provide you with a film suitable for introducing the discussion. You have noted how the visual image captures the children's attention and how incisive its message is in some scenes.

Perhaps at one time the frescoes on the walls of the church or the words of the preachers were particularly effective for communicating the gospel message. Today audiovisuals offer new possibilities. To me, however, it seems a bit naive to think that we have resolved the problem of announcing the Gospel simply because we have found a means that captures the attention of our listeners.

Nothing can take the place of personal witness, and nothing can exempt us from the journey of conversion we all must make. The message of the Gospel is not a lesson to learn or a show to see, but it is the invitation and the grace to live according to the Spirit of Jesus.

I therefore believe that you do well to use all the means at your disposal, but not so as to avoid the effort of stimulating a personal dialogue, of offering a living witness, even amidst lights and shadows and weaknesses, at any rate, in flesh and blood.

Perhaps you will not find words as exact or images as incisive as those recorded by media experts. But in calling the children by name and spending your time to accompany them in the following of Jesus, you will show them that you truly have them at heart, and you will help them not to confuse the figures of the saints and the episodes of the Gospel with the heroes on television.

The figures of value which you are asked to present have little in common with fantastic characters capable of any feat; rather you will speak of those involved in the simplest and most arduous undertaking: that of loving. You will thus speak of those who become priests or who consecrate themselves to prayer and works of charity, or of those who are married in the Lord. In short, you can counteract the image of television's "supermen" with the real heroes of everyday life, those who—without appearing on television—keep the world on its feet.

Educating children in the faith is an undertaking full of fascination and difficulties, because it must proclaim an absolute value to a generation so distracted as to believe that everything is relative.

It is thus a matter of a challenge of great importance, and its outcome will only be measurable many years from now. The immediate effect alone does not count. What truly matters is the edification of persons who welcome the Word that saves.

I am convinced of this: if, at first sight, an audiovisual seems more effective than your own words as a beginning catechist, perhaps this will not hold true ten years from now. By then some of your students will have forgotten all the audiovisuals you offered them, yet they will be ready to take your place as catechist, with the same fears and enthusiasm. In this way, the proclamation of the Gospel will continue because your simple and, at times, even timid and somewhat confused witness has convinced them that it is possible and wonderful to give their own contribution to the building up of the Church.

I accompany your service with my prayers, I am very grateful to you and bless you from my heart.

Letter to Two Newlyweds

Dear Daniela and Mark,

How strange these days must seem to you! After months of intense preparation and anxious expectation, after the tension and apprehension of recent weeks, after the solemn and fatiguing day on which you were the center of all the attention, after the rapture of the honeymoon, you are finally in your own home.

You were fortunate to find a home in the area you desired to live in. The far-sightedness of your parents has spared you the long and exasperating searches that take up so much of the time of many engaged couples.

Picturing a house and furnishing it is somewhat like planning life, and your ability to understand one another, which comes from love, is thus put to the test.

The discussions about where to put the pictures are still not over, and already at times it requires some effort to harmonize eating, dressing and sleeping habits, even down to such details as where to leave your slippers. But these are little things which give concreteness to the exploration of this new experience of living together.

With regard to the furnishings, there is one thing about which you have always agreed, and so you did not include a television set on the list of needed wedding gifts which you passed out to family and friends. It is with a certain pride that you tell your friends about this original choice you've made.

The choice to forego a TV is a choice for freedom. You wish to defend your evenings from unwanted guests who rob you of your time with absurd stories and banality. For you, the time together at table, sharing the events of the day, becomes a time of genuine relaxation. No scheduled TV program forces you to cut short your conversation.

And, after supper, the prayer which as an engaged couple you sought with intense desire can be transformed into a peaceful moment in which all misunderstandings and hopes are purified by the mercy of God.

I know very well that your decision not to own a television does not mean you have shut yourselves off from the world and its problems. I find your idea of making use of the television of Mark's mother for programs that interest you, very significant. Your visits bring life to a house that could otherwise be too lonely, and Daniela finds the opportunity to become acquainted with her mother-in-law. Naturally this is possible because no one is adamant about watching his/her own program; so the television can be shared as a common good. For the rest, you prefer to read and discuss the newspapers to obtain information.

Because the habit of owning one's own television has become so deeply rooted that it seems impossible to renounce it, your choice might seem exaggerated to some.

To me, instead, it offers a possibility to be freer. I would like to encourage many others to seek this freedom, despite the cultural pressures and force of habit. Perhaps one day, when you have older children, there will be motives for reconsidering this choice. However, I am happy to imagine that when I come to visit you it will be easy to take part in your discussions and to join you in prayer, without causing you uneasiness because of an interrupted program or the embarrassment of having nothing to say. In fact, those who are accustomed to thinking, to praying, to reading, to dialoguing, always have interesting things to share in a conversation.

Instead, a grave danger to the quality of a conversation is the passivity induced by many hours spent in front of images which disappear without leaving any thoughts behind, and in which conversation is often restricted to trite topics. And, confidentially, I find triteness boring.

I am happy to conclude with the wish that the anxious and even somewhat dazed happiness of these first days of married life may always preserve the freshness of your love. I also hope that the intensity of the spiritual life that you are happy to develop may always fill your life together, so that you need not seek in the television a comfortable alibi for that interior emptiness which prevents you from having something to say to the persons you love most.

Letter to a Grandmother

Dear Grandmother Theresa,

The cold winter weather and the pains that have been bothering you for months force you to live in long periods of solitude during this time. I think, therefore, that you will be pleased to receive a letter in which I can assure you of my affectionate remembrance and my prayers.

Elderly people often have the impression of being forgotten by the society which they served during their working years. At times they even feel neglected by the children and grandchildren to whom they have dedicated their lives. I would like the Christian community to be able to express its nearness to grandparents too. When Jesus is at the center, no one is far away.

Often, in thinking of persons who find themselves in your situation, I try to imagine how you pass the time. You are fortunate because you live close to married children, and the grandchildren pass by every day at least to say: "Hi, Grandma Theresa." Sometimes, when their mother is busy, they stop there to do their homework.

But the evenings are long and sleep never comes. How then does Grandmother Theresa occupy her time?

Since the television has become the established guest in every home, you can find in its tireless talking every evening an easy alternative to silence. TV's endless succession of ever new images also offers you an escape from the routine aspects of your life.

Time spent in watching television is not always time lost. It is marvelous that even the possibility to visit distant countries is offered to persons confined to their homes.

Even when our eyes are too tired to read the newspapers, the problems that afflict persons and nations cannot remain foreign to us. And if infirmities prevent us from participating in the Eucharistic celebration on Sunday, the word of the Lord and his praises continue to offer comfort by reaching your home, thanks to the radio and television.

You really feel like part of a big family when you can say the Rosary and be certain that you are praying with countless other people tuned in to the same wave length on the radio.

There is, however, the danger of letting yourself be led into an attitude of inertia, by which, instead of using the instrument to know about and share in the life of our times, you are led outside of reality into an artificial and deceptive world. There are television programs in which vulgarity predominates and in which interest is captured by episodes of betrayal, wickedness, and violence.

Even being a grandmother is a condition in which holiness is a grace and a struggle, dear Grandmother Theresa!

So I offer you, too, my encouragement to keep yourself free and lively. When the bad weather is over, I am sure that you will overcome the temptation to laziness in order to experience again the joy of meeting friends and of sharing prayers and happiness.

But not even in the winter months is it right to fill the time by fantasizing about the endless complications of the episodes recounted on the *soap operas.*

I know that the missionary group has already asked for some of your famous little crocheted works for a benefit sale. And when the grandchildren come to do their homework at grandma's house, they stay more willingly if, when prying around the kitchen, they discover a freshly baked cake!

So the relationships of friendship, the cultivation of intelligent and useful hobbies, and the desire to do some good preserve one's vivacity even in advanced age. They allow one to see the contrast between activity and the inertia and laziness to which a bad use of television can lead. There is still much good to be done!

And if one day I come to visit you, dear Grandmother Theresa, I would be pleased to find you with a rosary in your hand and a smile on your lips, witnessing to the fact that being old is not a sufficient reason for letting oneself be overcome by sadness and living as though the call to holiness were reserved to others.

Meanwhile I offer you my best wishes and recommend myself to your prayers.

Letter to Baby Jesus

Dear Baby Jesus,

Your presence accompanies each day in the lives of all our families with an encouraging smile. However, during the Christmas season many signs help us to remember you with greater affection. Even in the barest houses the simple faith [of the family] finds a corner of beauty to say thanks to you because you have made yourself so close to us. And in the houses in which there is too great an accumulation of goods, nostalgia for simplicity reserves a corner to offer you an invitation.

The imagination that decorates your crib expresses the desire to have you as guest, at least for a while, because every home needs you, even when families do not know it.

I once saw a crib built inside an old television set; the boy who had the idea even won a contest. And so you too became an inhabitant of our modern "global village," of this planet on which radio and television cancel distances and give us the impression that we live everywhere and that we are informed about everything.

Perhaps the boy who placed the stable inside the television wanted to express the conviction that you, dear Baby Jesus, are the most important good news and that you alone deserve to be the center of attention.

I have often asked myself why you were born at such

a distance and why the most important event in history occurred in such an unknown place. What did you want to tell us with this discretion, entering on tiptoe, without raising your voice, without causing a stir in the street?

I have learned that we can only know what we love, and to truly receive news means to take charge of it, as of a responsibility. For this reason you sought to make known your mystery to those who—like your Mother and the disciples—have accepted your invitation to live with you and for you.

For this reason you loved to call your friends aside and listen to their questions and invite them to stay with you. This is how your good news spread, as an inviting fraternity to which all have been called by name, even to the ends of the earth.

Even now the lights of your crib are seen in many homes while entertainment centers are brightly lit. The mystery of your silence remains hidden while the television sputters out its messages and provokes viewers with its advertising.

However, when the lights are turned out and the children are invited to say their prayers around the crib, even the clumsiest Nativity figures are able to help us recognize the important news, the things that really count in life.

Your silent patience awaits even parents. When late in the evening they can finally go to rest, you speak to them the comforting words of truth: well-being is not enough to make us happy; marvelous products, offered in the most attractive ways so as to attempt to satisfy the desires of the human heart, are not enough to ensure peace in the life of a family.

You have found a home even in a television set, thanks to a boy's intuition. From this unusual dwelling you recall that everything can serve the good if the heart is free and the modest eye overcomes the temptation to indiscreet curiosity, inertia and sensuality.

Dear Baby Jesus, perhaps children are still used to writing Christmas letters to you to ask a gift or present a promise. If you dwell willingly not only in the ancient villages of your land but also in our "global village," I too can dare to ask of you a grace for myself and for all the families united with me in prayer.

Give us a lively desire for you,
the desire to meet you as a friend
meets a friend,
and defend us from too many distractions.

Give us a heart open to the truth that saves,
to the love that unites,
to the joy that illumines our homes,
and free us from the dull search for the superfluous.

Grant us a reconciled gaze
that knows how to see the good possible everywhere
and makes wise use of it,
giving thanks in everything.
Amen.

Christmas Letter to Families, Milan, November 1991

CHAPTER 16

Teach Us to Pray as a Family

One Evening at Supper

After your telephone call of last year I was finally able to accept the invitation to have supper at your house.

Before we began to eat, I said a short prayer, but I noticed that this action was a bit new for you. The topic emerged again in the conversation after coffee was served, when I asked: "Do you pray together as a family?"

An embarrassed silence followed. Someone ventured an answer: "Sometimes." Another said: "Last year on November first we said the Rosary for the deceased."

"And then we ate chestnuts," the little one recalled. "However," added the mother, "you could teach us how we can pray together more often."

That is how this little book was born. It contains some reflections on prayer and some practical exercises. Write to me if they have helped you, so we can improve it and help many others. I wish you good prayer together as a family!

Why Pray as a Family?

The embarrassment caused by my question: "Do you pray together as a family?" certainly comes from practical difficulties. Let's explore some of them.

Why pray, if prayer is such a rare and difficult experience? Let's leave it to priests and saints! Why pray, when as husband and wife we have so little time to talk to one another and when we only see our children in the evening? Why pray, when we are tired and nervous, and the television seems to offer a relaxing program? Why pray, when we really know so little about God, and we have not yet read the entire Gospel through? Why pray, if our brothers and sisters ask for help, if words are not enough to express charity because charity requires deeds?

These and other questions test our good will to put aside some time to remain with the Lord.

"Teach Us to Pray" (Lk 11:1)

The best attitude in view of these difficulties is that of the disciples who, after having seen Jesus return from prayer happy and relaxed, asked him: "Lord, teach us to pray" (Lk 11:1).

Jesus is the real teacher of prayer, and we sit close to his disciples and listen to his Word.

First of all, Jesus reassures us: "For where two or three are gathered in my name, I am there among them" (Mt 18:20). It is marvelous to discover the presence of God in a family that learns how to pray!

Jesus never forgets us; he knows and shares our every problem. He will accompany us in our efforts to learn how to dialogue with the Father. "Many parents," writes Cardinal Colombo, "complain that they do not know how to pray, that they cannot succeed in establishing the custom of prayer in the family, that they are unable to persuade their children to participate in it. Perhaps they have never asked this gift from the Holy Spirit with humble constancy and great trust" (*L'originalità cristiana della famiglia*, 22).

The prayer of a mother and father with their children is thus a great occasion for experiencing the extraordinary closeness of God (cf *Familiaris Consortio*, 59).

Silence

The experience of prayer is linked first of all to the ability to maintain silence within ourselves, to attempt to isolate ourselves from the noise and distractions of the city in order to find the echo of God's voice.

In the Gospel of Matthew, after having taught his disciples the Our Father, Jesus said: "Don't worry about your life, what you'll eat or about your body, what you'll wear" (Mt 6:25). The very condition for prayer is a certain silencing even of desires and regrets.

Let us recall what happened in the home of Martha and Mary at Bethany. A sudden visit from Jesus with his disciples sent Martha into a state of agitation, and she began to prepare something to eat. Mary, instead, remained at the feet of the Master to listen to his every word. To the protests of the busy sister, Jesus replies: "Martha, Martha, you're anxious and upset over many things, but one thing is necessary. Mary has chosen the better part" (Lk 10:41-42).

To set aside a daily hour for prayer is thus to choose, as Mary did, the one thing necessary. It means we have understood that the encounter with God is the most important and meaningful news of our day.

The Presence of God

In the Bible we read that "the Lord used to speak to Moses," the leader of the people of Israel, "face to face" (Ex 33:11).

It is wonderful to experience this intimacy in our prayer: to feel the breath of the Lord, to hear the sound of his footsteps in our garden.

In order to know a person well we cannot be content

with just hearing about them. We need to converse with them face to face. Even an exchange of greetings can be enough to begin to have an idea of one another.

The extraordinary thing about our dialogue with God is that, if in the beginning we seem to begin to speak to God, at a certain point we find ourselves talking *with* him, and finally we discover that to pray means to listen to God who speaks with us!

Praise God Because He is Great

We will learn to pray when we learn to contemplate the depths of things with an unselfish eye. We are no longer accustomed to looking at reality without the interested gaze of one who has to gain something from every situation.

Contemplation appears to be an investment without returns, and we do not want to make losing investments.

Only those who have the courage to "throw away" time in prayer also have the possibility of penetrating the mystery of the divine Presence with their own gaze. Then amazement is changed into joy, and as in the Psalm our lips can murmur: "O Lord, our Sovereign, how majestic is your name in all the earth!" (Ps 8:9). Praise is the immediate response that rises to our hearts when we look upon the greatness of God.

If you have ever seen a baby laugh in response to the smile of his mother, if you have happened to stop to look at the sky, a woods, a brook, which struck you because of something you called "beauty," if the desire to sing or to run came to you all at once because of something you called "joy," if you ever asked yourself in wonder why those who are close to you love you, you can understand what it means to praise!

Thank God for He is Good

Being born in a Christian country is a grace, but it

can become a "limitation": we no longer marvel at the gift of God.

Praying means being aware that we are his gift. The Lord gives us many things every day, through nature and through our encounters with our sisters and brothers. Parents and children give one another many things, even without thinking about it, and all this comes from God. The greatest gift is Jesus. With his death and resurrection he has given back to us the hope of a life without end.

When Jesus left this earth to return to the Father, he made us a tremendous promise: "Stay here in the city until you have been clothed with the power from on high" (Lk 24:49). It is the Spirit of God who today suggests to us the truest words of our prayer.

Pray with and for Others

To pray does not mean to isolate ourselves from the world, it does not mean to escape from daily responsibilities.

Praise and thanksgiving raise a very concrete question in our heart: what does God want from me? What does he want from our family, from our parish community?

Prayer becomes acceptance of the role that the Lord has entrusted to you as parents or as children, to me as bishop, to priests as consecrated persons, to lay persons as builders of the city.

In the Garden of Olives, Jesus prayed: "Father...not my will but yours be done" (Lk 22:42). Dialogue with God brings to maturity our readiness to put aside our small interests so as to enter onto the paths of God, to go out to meet our sisters and brothers.

Our choice to pray as a family thus helps us live the communitarian and fraternal dimension of prayer (cf *Familiaris Consortio*, 62).

Prayer will accustom us to look at the world with the eyes of God. It is extraordinary to hear a husband pray for his wife, that the Lord may help him to love her more and more; or to hear a mother who prays for her own children, that they might grow like the child Jesus, not only in the sight of men but especially in the sight of God; or to hear the prayer of a child for his sick, elderly grandfather. Truly God can dwell in the hearts of his people!

Prayer then extends beyond the confines of our family to embrace the pain of those who suffer in body or in spirit; to share the hopes of those who invoke justice and freedom; to sustain the search of those who are drawing closer to God and to enlighten the hearts of those disillusioned persons who are drifting away from his Church.

In his Gospel John tells us that Jesus, on the eve of Holy Thursday, just before leaving his friends, prayed for those whom God had entrusted to him: they were yours and you have given them to me. I pray for them because they belong to you (cf Jn 17).

This is the attitude that should also characterize our prayer for our dear ones. They belong to God, it is he who has entrusted them to us, and who has placed some persons at our side, so that together with them we might attain the joy of his Church.

At this point I would like to suggest:

Three Simple Ways of Praying as a Family

1. In the first place, it is a question of using again the common, daily prayers which each of us learned from our families and which we cherish as an inheritance of the Faith: *praying together with the words that we know.*

2. In the second place, I would like to dwell on the Psalms, the common, daily prayers that set the rhythm of the day for every family of Israel: *praying the Psalms together.*

3. In the third place, it seems to me useful to offer some suggestions about *praying a passage of the Gospel together.*

Praying Together with the Words That We Know

Morning and Evening Prayer

The precious patrimony of Christian faith, the "common prayers," must not be lost.

At one time we learned them in the family—Christian education began before explicit religious instruction: it was an "ambient," a sum total of big and small things, of meetings, of relationships, of words and of silence. From this environment sprang family prayer, which was not so much "making the children pray," as "praying with them."

Certainly there were not the same difficulties as today—Because they worked close to home, people did not return late at night; and perhaps the reasons for going out in the evening were less frequent at one time.

We learned to pray as a family and so, through daily repetition, the prayers were written in the hearts and the lives of the children.

They were easy and simple times—Prayers created a common way of addressing the Father of all, helping us with their clear, understandable language.

Everyone knew these prayers by heart—It happens to us too at times that we want to pray and we do not know how to express the desires of our hearts to the Lord.

It is true that words are not always necessary to pray:
—There are "silences filled with love" that possess an even greater depth than words which are only the support of our feelings toward God.

There are, however, days on which we need to be sustained and helped in prayer. By inserting us into the simple and living tradition of entire generations who have prayed and still pray them with faith, these common prayers help us in our poverty, and suggest motives for prayer that go beyond our fragile and self-centered petitions to the Lord.

They were also called "daily prayers"—Every day was begun and concluded in the name of the Lord, with the sign
of the cross.

Morning and evening are two moments in which
time makes itself felt in a more evident way. Persons perceive that they are travelers, that their destiny is death,
and that their vocation is to the life that knows no end.

At the same time, the symbolism expressive of the
Christian mystery, such as light and darkness, is linked to
these moments of the day.

The light of the coming day arouses in us the remembrance of the resurrection of Christ, which took
place at dawn.

The evening disposes us to await his glorious return.

They Can Still Be Prayed Today

a) I am, then, teaching you an initial, practical and
very simple way of praying together. It consists in saying
together some of the ten formulas that we know and
which I am including here.

Do not recite many of them. One or two, read slowly,
is enough. Before beginning make the sign of the cross,
and then allow space for some moments of silence. You
should be able to hear the tick of the clock, or the hum of
the refrigerator or of the washing machine. This silence
disposes us to feel the presence of God.

Then one person slowly intones the first part of the
prayer, and the others join in a low voice. Tell the children
not to shout the prayers. God listens to us just the same.

At the end, pause again and conclude with the sign
of the cross.

b) A variation of this first way, which you can try after
you have learned to pray slowly, consists in stopping at the
end of the prayer and asking if someone wants to emphasize a phrase. Each one repeats an invocation of the

prayer (for example, "thy kingdom come") that seemed more important to him or her at that moment, or that corresponds to a particular grace for which he/she would like to pray.

The others can repeat it together so as to give strength to that invocation.

c) The Rosary prayed and meditated together as a family expands on this form of simple prayer, beginning at least with a decade of the rosary. "There is no doubt that...the Rosary should be considered as one of the best and most efficacious prayers in common that the Christian family is invited to recite. We like to think, and sincerely hope, that when the family gathering becomes a time of prayer, the Rosary is a frequent and favored manner of praying" (Paul VI, *Marialis Cultus*, 54; cf *Familiaris Consortio*, 61).

How to Pray a Psalm Together

The Value of the Psalms

Among the books of the Bible, the Book of Psalms has a very particular value: it includes 150 prayers written on several occasions by different persons of the people of Israel.

One evening we will seek to pray together choosing one of these ancient and beautiful compositions.

The psalms were written centuries before the birth of Jesus and represent an extraordinary witness to faith in God. At times they refer back to the great events of the history of the Hebrew people, such as the passage through the Red Sea and the Covenant on Mount Sinai. Other psalms, instead, describe some personal dramas, such as the conversion of a sinner or the suffering of a sick person.

Still others are serene prayers of praise to God. They

reveal the profound sensitivity of the ancient Hebrews and their ability to perceive the powerful hand of the Creator in the harmony of creation.

All the psalms arise from the daily experience of a people who, with simplicity and passion, describe the friendship of God with his people by using the images familiar to them. The Lord, from being a Shepherd who guides us through the most difficult paths, becomes the One who defends us in battle from the assaults of our enemy.

The prayer of the psalms has a long tradition behind it. The people of Israel sang them at all the religious ceremonies, to the accompaniment of the zither or other musical instruments.

But the verses of these songs were also on the lips and in the heart of the simple Hebrew man who, from dawn to dusk, set the rhythm for all the moments of his day with prayer.

Jesus often prayed with the psalms. When he was twelve years old he went as a pilgrim to the Temple of Jerusalem, and sang the psalms provided for the journey: "I was glad when they said to me, 'Let us go to the house of the Lord!' Our feet are standing within your gates, O Jerusalem" (Ps 122).

The Gospel tells us that Jesus attended the synagogue at Nazareth on Saturday and therefore joined in the reading of the Bible and the recitation of the psalms.

Again, Jesus was faithful to the celebration of the Hebrew Passover and therefore to the song of the great "Alleluia," with its refrain: "For his steadfast love endures forever" (Ps 136).

If we carefully reread the account of Jesus' Passion, we can see the citation of many psalms. Finally, his last words on the cross are suggested by the psalms: "My God, my God, why have you forsaken me?" (Ps 22) and "Into your hands I commit my spirit" (Ps 31).

The community of the first Christians, guided by the Holy Spirit, made the prayers of the psalms their own, applying to their Lord and to themselves what is said in the psalms about the people of God, Jerusalem, the King, the Temple, the Promised Land, the Kingdom, the Covenant.

The Hebrew prayers become the prayers of the Church, the new Passover is the Lord who died and rose, the eternal Covenant is the Eucharist.

Within the tradition of the Church each psalm receives a title that helps us understand it, and it is introduced by an antiphon which adapts the psalm to the mystery of Jesus celebrated throughout the liturgical year.

What can the psalms say to us of the twentieth century? I believe that they contain at least three secrets:

— the ability to perceive God's activity in the world, as an expression of the Lord's closeness to and friendship with his creatures;

— the ability to read in depth the heart of the human person, to bring every joy and every problem back to the trust and hope of those who believe in God;

— the ability to read the history of a people, to discover in it the realization of the plan of God who through Israel calls all people to salvation.

How Do We Pray a Psalm?

1. Our decision to pray a psalm one evening should lead us first of all to choose a suitable psalm.

Each psalm is suited to a particular situation of our life. Perhaps we are experiencing a moment of joy or of sadness; perhaps we are passing through a period of particular closeness to God, or on the other hand it may be that we have never felt him so far from our life.

The psalms are a faithful mirror of the person's feelings, and our every attitude is reflected in one of them.

This evening we want to experience the Lord's presence in our midst, and we have a great desire to communicate with him. For this reason I believe it is a beautiful thing to experience praying with Psalm 137.

2. We should all have the text in front of us; we arrange ourselves in a circle, either standing or sitting, so as to have a concrete sign of our communitarian action.

We place ourselves in a prayerful atmosphere with the sign of the cross accompanied by a moment of silence. We should now fix our attention on the real presence of the Lord in our midst, and know that we are beginning a dialogue with him.

3. Now one of us reads the psalm calmly:

> *"I give you thanks, O Lord, with my whole heart;*
> *before the gods I sing your praise;*
> *I bow down toward your holy temple*
> *and give thanks to your name*
> *for your steadfast love and your faithfulness;*
> *for you have exalted your name and your word*
> *above everything.*
> *On the day I called, you answered me,*
> *you increased my strength of soul.*
>
> *All the kings of the earth shall praise you, O Lord,*
> *for they have heard the words of your mouth.*
> *They shall sing of the ways of the Lord,*
> *for great is the glory of the Lord.*
> *For though the Lord is high, he regards the lowly;*
> *but the haughty he perceives from far away.*
>
> *Though I walk in the midst of trouble,*
> *you preserve me against the wrath of my enemies;*
> *you stretch out your hand, and your right hand delivers me.*
> *The Lord will fulfill his purpose for me;*

your steadfast love, O Lord, endures forever.
Do not forsake the work of your hands" (Ps 138).

The first reading of the psalm has given us the possibility of entering into the spirit of the prayer we have chosen. It has placed before us the intentions of the author and the general meaning of his prayer.

4. Now we will take the psalm from the beginning, and all together, very calmly so as to have a truly choral prayer, we begin to read it in a subdued voice.

Here we must seek to make the words that we are reading our own. It is as though each of us puts him/herself in the author's place this evening and, in this home, spoke this prayer to the Lord for the first time.

5. Let us now have a moment of silence, in which each one chooses the word and phrase of the psalm that has caught his/her attention. This is a means for penetrating the psalm more deeply, rather than stopping at the surface. In this way we want to make each detail, each image resound within us, so as to grasp the essential core of its message and the universality of its framework.

6. Without any specific order we pray in turn the particular word or phrase chosen, always leaving a brief pause after each:

"You have heard the words of my mouth..."
"The Lord regards the humble..."
"Your fidelity and your mercy..."
"You give me life again..."
"I want to sing to you..."
"I called and you answered me..."
"The Lord will accomplish his work..."

7. We have identified ourselves with the author of the psalm and we have penetrated its meaning. Now the mind leaves room for the voice of the heart. The most beautiful images and expressions of the psalm become

our prayer; they spontaneously suggest some simple intentions:

—This evening we are learning how to pray, and *you, Lord, have listened to the words* of our mouths; help us to treasure this marvelous experience.

All: *"Lord, your kindness endures forever!"*

—Lord, your *fidelity* is great, but we often do not entrust ourselves to your word and we behave badly; enable us to accept your pardon and to experience your mercy.

All: *"Lord, your kindness endures forever!"*

—Lord, you called each one of us into existence, and each day *you give us life again*; help us to respect the life of others, especially that of the weakest, of babies and the elderly.

All: *"Lord, your kindness endures forever!"*

—Lord, I am happy; *I want to sing to you* together with all the children of the world!

All: *"Lord, your kindness endures forever!"*

—A family in our neighborhood is experiencing a period of sadness because of the loss of a dear one; Lord, in sorrow *they have called upon you,* hear their prayer and strengthen them in this trial.

All: *"Lord, your kindness endures forever!"*

—Our children are very young. They still have a long way to travel in life, they have many choices to make. Lord, *complete* in them the work you began on the day of their Baptism.

All: *"Lord, your kindness endures forever!"*

We conclude our prayer as we began it, with the sign of the cross. With this we want to sum up all the words of our prayer so as to present them to the great family of God *the Father, the Son and the Holy Spirit.*

8. I suggest some other psalms with which you can pray together:
—to give thanks: Psalms 5, 18, 30, 115;
—in moments of illness: Psalms 7, 22, 38;
—for bereavement: Psalms 130, 12, 16;
—to invoke God's help: Psalms 17, 143;
—to glorify and adore God: Psalms 92, 135, 145;
—to ask pardon: Psalms 25, 51;
—to express trust: Psalms 23, 139.

Let's Pray Together a Passage from the Gospel

You all have at least the Bible in your home, or the four Gospels. In fact, it is very important that each member of the family, after their First Communion, have their own personal copy of the four Gospels. To each of the young persons whom I meet I give the small book of the Gospel read during the liturgical year. It does not belong in a bookcase but near the daily newspapers or on the night table. The Gospel is, in fact, the "book of life."

Christian families should not limit their reading of the Gospel to the Liturgy of the Word at Mass, but should use it for their own reading, even "to pray together." Otherwise we risk agreeing with those who affirm: "God doesn't say anything to me."

Instead, God does speak. He has essential things to say to the people of today, he has much to say to you as a family, to you as a person.

Someone will tell me: "It is very difficult to pray the Gospel!" The greatest difficulty lies, perhaps, in the fact that we are too used to thinking that what counts in prayer is having something to say to God. Above all, praying means letting God tell us what he wants to communicate to us. Listening, more than speaking, is what counts.

In Simple Listening and Reflection

I would like to suggest to you a method for praying the Gospel as a family. It is very simple: it comprises four moments.

1. The first act to fulfill together is a moment of *silence* and the recitation of a *prayer*.

We could pray this way: "Help us, Jesus, to listen to your Word so that always and everywhere we can be a living Gospel."

2. Then we need to *choose a passage* from the Gospel. This passage can be suggested, on particular occasions, by one or more members of the family, taking into consideration the suggestions of the children also. In any case it is very useful to use the passage offered by the Sunday liturgy or by the lectionary of the day.

I'm suggesting a passage by way of example: Mark 4:35-41, where the evangelist tells the story of Jesus calming the storm.

"That day when evening had come he said to them, 'Let's cross over to the other side.' After dismissing the crowd, they took him as he was, in the boat, and other boats were with it. A violent wind squall came up, and the waves were breaking over the boat so that by this time the boat was already filling up. Yet he was in the stern, sleeping on the cushion. So they woke him and said to him, 'Teacher, doesn't it matter to you that we are going to die?' Then he woke up and rebuked the wind, and said to the sea, 'Silence! Be calm!' The wind ceased and there was a profound calm, and he said to them, 'Why are you afraid? Do you still not have faith?' Then they were seized with fear and said to each other, 'Who is he, then, that both the wind and the sea obey him?'"

3. This passage is to be read slowly by one person. At

the end, pause for a moment of silence, so that each one can reread the text on their own; then those who wish may read aloud those words or that verse that struck them. For example: "Why are you afraid?"—"A great windstorm arose and the waves beat into the boat"—"The wind ceased"—"Who then is this, that even the wind and the sea obey him?"

4. These words sound like a prayer. Repeating them is one way of entering into the text, of allowing the word and power of Jesus to enter us.

Gradually we reach the point where we can change the phrase into a prayer: "Jesus, we want to stay with you, even in the storm." "We are not afraid if you are with us."

The prayer is concluded by reciting slowly together the Our Father. The whole prayer time does not take more than several minutes.

Meditation Together?

This second way of praying as a family can be practiced once in a while, for example on the vigil of a feast, or on a birthday, and after the family has had some practice with the preceding method.

It consists in posing four questions to the text, after having listened to it in silence: Who are the principal characters? What are they doing? What are they saying? Each one seeks the answers to these questions, sharing what they feel about this passage. Then we conclude with the question: "What is this passage saying to me?" and with prayer.

1. Who are the principal characters in the story we have read? In the passage chosen there are five: a lake, a boat, the storm, the disciples, Jesus. Even the children can easily be involved in singling them out.

It will be the task of the older family members, whenever possible, to make the *situation* described in the gos-

pel passage current. In the passage from Mark it is easy
enough. Each of us aspires to reach the other bank joyfully, that is, to spend life in serenity, as if it were the
peaceful crossing of a lake. The continual effort is that of
keeping afloat and of journeying toward new and fascinating discoveries. Often, however, we are forced to deal with
storms, in which we become very afraid of shipwreck and
failure. The disciples of Jesus experienced the same sen-
sation, and not only during the episode of the storm on
the lake.

2. What do these characters do? In the gospel passage chosen, the *lake* (the events of life) is transformed
from friend to enemy by the storm. The *boat* (the supports
of life) is taking in water from all sides, and at first the
disciples anxiously try to fix the situation, and then are
overcome by panic and confusion. *Jesus* is sleeping...
almost indifferent and withdrawn. But a simple word
from him is enough to restore calm at once. The disciples
who lacked faith and were afraid, discover that they have
here a much greater Person than they realized.

3. What do the characters say? In the passage under
consideration, we do not find conversations but exclama-
tions and questions.

The disciples: "Teacher, doesn't it matter to you that
we are going to die?" Jesus addresses the wind and the sea:
"Silence! Be calm!"

Then he turns to the disciples: "Why are you afraid?
Do you still not have faith?"

The disciples: "Who is he, then, that both the wind
and the sea obey him?"

It is a dialogue between God and man about how to
face the stormy situations, the crises, of life.

Like the disciples we are tempted to blame God: "If
God is a friend, why doesn't he intervene? Why is he
hiding, almost as though our anxious attempts to remain

afloat mean nothing to him?" In reply God says: "Why are you troubled? I am here! Why do you have so little faith?"

His intervention causes the question to arise spontaneously: "Who is this?" What do we think of Jesus?

4. Then comes the most important question: What is this passage saying to me? Every episode in the life of Jesus contains within it the question which the Master, in another passage (Mk 8: 29), poses to his disciples: "Who do you say that I am?"

If up until now your family has sought to reflect "in the" Faith (it is the Faith which unites you to meditate together), it is important to make a further step: the communication "of" Faith.

Each one, even the children, shares with their dear ones what the Lord has revealed to them about themselves and what God expects of them, that is, his concrete will in the present moment of life.

I myself would like to share with you what Jesus has said to me in this gospel passage, while I was thinking of you. In this fascinating but tempestuous time of ours, it is not hard to find persons who are disoriented, full of fear, who do not feel protected, who are distrustful, resigned, at times desperate.

Genuinely heroic efforts often run the risk of being submerged in the crisis situations we are passing through. Many feel that even God is absent, like Jesus in the storm, far away, like one who doesn't seem to care much about our stubborn, exhausting floundering. "If there is a God, he should not let things go on like this."

The passage from Mark is truly "evangelical," that is, "beautiful news," because it contains an exceptional and profound motive for hope: God may seem absent but in reality he is in the boat with us.

And again: he alone is God! Nothing, not even the most tremendous storm, is stronger than he. And he uses his strength to fight with us against every power that attempts to overwhelm the human person.

God, then, is more powerful than crises.

The Lord gives us the possibility of strengthening these convictions during the approaching Christmas season.

We shall go in church for the Eucharistic celebration and we will celebrate because the Lord assures us that he is "Emmanuel," that is, God with us, the "*living bread that is broken*"—God for us.

I am persuaded that phenomena such as the social and political disengagement, the materialism practiced by those who are only concerned with enjoying life, the anxious search to save what can be saved, the hasty classification of many situations as "lost causes"...are all phenomena that hide a lack of real hope.

The powerful and strong love of God is the secure boat that does not eliminate the difficulties of the storm, but reassures us that in the end it is man who will come through, because the one, invincible Lord is with him.

"Why are you afraid? Do you still not have faith?" Don't you know that "I'll be with you all the days until the end of the age"? (Mt 28:20)

The only real fear is that of not possessing the faith that gives rise to hope.

If we have faith, if we listen to his Word and put it into practice (Mt 7:24-27), all kinds of adversities may break out, but we will remain standing because our life is anchored on the rock of God.

Do we have this kind of faith?

The *Prayer of Intercession* will come spontaneously at this point, to ask the Lord for the strength to live what he has enabled us to understand together.

Let each person formulate a prayer intention to which all can respond with an invocation similar to that used in the liturgical assembly for the Prayer of the Faithful: "Hear us, O Lord!"

The time spent after supper with this friendly family has passed quickly. I have limited myself to pointing out some methods for a brief period of prayer together, for prayer that can be practiced even where there are many distractions. Other beautiful things about family prayer can be read in the apostolic exhortation on the duties of the Christian family in the world of today, *Familiaris Consortio* (59-62). Certainly it is wonderful to think that there are families in the diocese who recite some part of the Liturgy of the Hours!

In union with all the prayers offered in our homes, I conclude with a prayer:

> *"Lord Jesus, you chose a family*
> *in which to come and remain among us;*
> *bless this family which has listened*
> *to the word of its bishop.*
> *Send away illness and sadness.*
> *Bless this family with attention, patience,*
> *reconciliation, peace.*
> *Grant that next Christmas*
> *you may find us all gathered around your table."*

I bless you! Blessed Christmas to all!

Christmas Letter to Families, Milan, November 1984

CHAPTER 17

The Gospel of Life

Introduction

Dearest friends, at the beginning of this prayer vigil, we invoked upon us the "protective hand of the Father, the friendship of Jesus and the power of the Holy Spirit...." At the same time we want to remember the liturgical feast of the Presentation of the Lord in the Temple.

We are gathered together for a solemn moment, which involves and challenges all of us. In fact, with this celebration *we officially open the diocesan regional Conference, "Birth and death today. The Churches of Lombardy for a new culture of human life."* The bishops of Lombardy have planned this conference for some time and announced it to the faithful of the churches of our region with their letter of September 8, 1991....

The significant moment that we are living—and the journey that will follow—is part of a renewed attention and commitment to the life of the human person.... In our reflection we want to let ourselves be urged on by the theme which the Italian bishops have proposed for this

Day for Life: "The right to life, foundation of democracy and peace." We realize the importance of the high stakes and the responsibility of putting into action an initiative that corresponds, at least minimally, to the recommendations and invitations that emerged from the recent *Special Assembly of the Synod of Bishops for Europe*. The synod Fathers, in fact, in their *Closing Statement* said, among other things: "Since the right to life in many nations of modern Europe, both East and West, is seriously violated, especially in the case of abortion and euthanasia, our Synod recommends to the individual churches and in particular to the Conference, the annual celebration of a 'day or week for life' in all the communities and parishes. With time, it could, by common agreement, be scheduled for the same day or the same week.... By means of a common action coordinated with the cooperation of the public authorities, we must strive for the elimination of everything contrary and truly damaging to human dignity, such as pornography, the sale and use of drugs, and organized crime" (n. 10).

We thus feel ourselves in step with the journey of the Church in Italy, the Church in Europe, and even with the journey of the *universal Church*, because our Conference is also a precious occasion for preparing to receive that papal document on the value of life which the Cardinals, gathered in Rome for the extraordinary Consistory in April 1991, asked the Holy Father for.

In this reflection of mine I would like to respond with you to some questions:

1. What are the motivations for this conference?
2. What is its goal? What does it want to be?
3. How do we want to begin it today?
4. What are the steps to be taken during the coming months?

The Urgent Need for a New Evangelization

1. The bishops of Lombardy wanted this Conference not only to respond to an historical need that we all believe is very serious (it was recently announced that Italy is in the last place, among the nations of the world, as regards the birth rate). They also wanted to emphasize *the very mission* that the Church has received from Jesus. As the Pope said in his letter of May 19, 1991, to all the bishops, the Church "has received from Christ the Gospel of life and feels responsible for proclaiming this Gospel to every creature."

It is the same clear awareness that emerged from the Synod of Bishops. It is the awareness of all the synod Fathers of being called to continue the work undertaken by the Second Vatican Council "to offer again to the men and women of Europe the liberating message of the Gospel" (*Closing Statement*, 3). Because Europe needs "to be enabled to decide once again about its future in the encounter with the person and message of Jesus Christ" (n. 2). Herein lies the necessity of *retelling the central message of the Gospel with all its consequences*, of announcing a God who is living and close to us, who communicates himself to us in an experience of communion which has already begun and which opens up to the certain hope of eternal life. "The center of this evangelization is: 'God loves you. Christ has come for you.' If the Church preaches this God, it does not speak of an unknown God but of the God who has loved us to the point that his own Son became man for our sake. It is the God who approaches us, who communicates himself to us, who makes himself one with us.... The Lord has promised this communion not only in this life (Mt 28:20) but above all as victory over sin and death through participation in his resurrection (cf Rom 6:5; 1 Cor 15:22) and as friendship without end, face to face with God (cf 1 Cor 13:12)" (n. 3).

This is, in synthesis, the "Gospel of life": the Gospel

of the communication that God makes to man about his living in fullness, the announcement of the primacy of divine life and of the orientation of every human life toward this goal.

It is from this profound, renewed awareness, in which we must first of all let ourselves be evangelized, that the Conference is born. We feel the irrepressible need to witness to the consequences deriving from the certainty of having the very life of God within us.

2. However, our Conference is also *attentive to the situations around us*, which manifest the urgent need for this mission of the Church.

This is not the moment to describe the present-day social and cultural situation surrounding human life, with all its complexities, ambiguities and contradictions. A rich and interesting interpretation was offered to us last November 23 by Professor Campanini.... It is enough for me to recall what Cardinal Camillo Ruini synthesized in his introductory report to the Synod: "While today, as never before, we find ourselves faced with signs of attention, care and promotion of the life of the human person and of the 'quality' of that life, often the attitude toward generation, suffering and death is characterized by rejection, lack of respect and violations which appear incompatible not only with the Gospel but with the primordial nature and rights of our being and with integral human experience. The persistent tragedy of abortion, the growing incentive toward the legalization of euthanasia, the tendency toward experimentation and application of new technologies in the sphere of human life which leave aside moral criteria, unfortunately—despite the noble and vigorous attempts to react—characterize the present European panorama" (n. 7).

As a background to all this there is the *eclipse of the religious and moral sense* with regard to the offenses against life, which the Pope recalled in his above-cited letter to all the bishops: "If the widespread phenomenon of the elimination of so many human lives—unborn or approaching their end—is so serious and disturbing, no less serious and disturbing is the fading of moral sensitivity in consciences. The laws and civil norms not only make this dimming manifest but even contribute to strengthening it."

Thus the entire social-cultural system in which we live is in question. Here comes into play our society's ability, or lack of ability, to recognize the truth about man and to promote the authentic human ecology of which John Paul II spoke in *Centesimus Annus* (cf n. 39). For this reason we believe it is extremely important to proclaim the Gospel of the life that God offers to man in its fullness, now and forever.

For a New Culture of Human Life

What does this Conference, then, want to be?

1. It wants to put into effect *a great strategy for life*, for a new culture of human life, respectful of the dignity and the life of every person. In harmony with the document of the Italian bishops—*Evangelization and the culture of human life*—our Conference would like to promote the realization of "a cultural change, capable of causing our society to emerge from materialism and subjectivism, and of leading it to rediscover and live the whole truth about the human person and life" (n. 42). A formidable task, which we can take on only by trusting in the power and the mercy of God.

However, we would like our intention to be well understood. We are not moved by a spirit of revenge or of conquest with regard to the world in which we live. We are not nourishing any plan for the "restoration" of a happy past that was totally respectful of the person and which, it seems to us, never existed. While we do not tire of repeating that unconditional respect for the right to life of every human person, from conception to natural death, is one of the pillars on which civil society rests, together with the Pope we want to assure everyone that "when the Church recalls this truth, it does not want to introduce a Christian state: it wants simply to promote a human state, a state which recognizes as its primary duty the defense of the fundamental rights of the human person, especially that of the weakest" (*To the participants at the Convention for study of "The right to life and Europe*," December 18, 1987). We are not, therefore, striving for the Church's power over society.

2. Rather, we are moved by the *love without reserve* which we bear for every man and woman and for the whole of our society, which we want to be ever more just, happy, and authentically human! We realize with trepidation and a renewed sense of responsibility that *this* is the society to which we are sent, of which we are a part and with which we share every happening. We want, therefore, to bend with love and sympathy over our cities and our modern civilization. This love and sympathy, however, do not close our eyes to what is problematic or negative within us and around us.

We want, rather, to look at everything and every event with the sincere will to live and to judge the various situations in depth. It is in this spirit that, as the Italian bishops have written, we feel "today more than ever the responsibility to proclaim to all, in words and actions, the dignity of the human person...that the life of each person comes from God; that life is a vocation to love and to the gift of self; that life must always find welcome and care in each moment of its existence, especially in the principal moments of its beginning and its death" (*Message for the Day for Life*, n. 2). In the same spirit, we repeat that "abortion, like homicide, is never a right. Euthanasia can never be a sign of compassion. Crime, the consumption and sale of drugs, the abuse of minors, any violence against persons, blackmail, and kidnapping are all attempts on life" (*Message*, n. 3).

3. Within the logic of what I have just quoted, the Conference wants to be an opportune moment to help us Christians and our communities *question ourselves about the culture of human life with which we are in contact,* which we are able to announce, witness to and promote, and which we are called more and more to develop.

What is the culture of human life that is diffused in our churches today and what do our churches do to serve human life? What pastoral concerns should our churches activate so as to better serve human life?

Here are the two fundamental questions which we must seek to respond to during this year. The challenge is to succeed, even in a pluralistic, technological and modern society such as ours, to proclaim, witness to, celebrate and serve the life of the person as a great and marvelous gift to be respected, defended and promoted.

The possibility of adequately responding to the challenge will depend first of all on our prayer, our personal conversion, and consequently on the responses we know how to give to the two questions formulated above.

4. At the same time, the Conference also wants to lead us to a *serious and deep confrontation* between Catholics and non-Catholics, believers and non-believers, concerning the fundamental questions about human life; in the areas where thought is developed, as in the various professional, daily spheres in which we live and act and in which we express our commitment. The Conference—as I emphasized last November 23—should thus be "an act of courage on the part of the churches of Lombardy, which do not want to remain closed in on themselves, like a group of

well-intentioned persons who love values. Rather, they want to reach the whole of civil society, to reach the reality of the country as it is, with its shadows, its darkness, its tragic points, which are precisely those which threaten life, which cause a culture of death and darkness to emerge." And we should do all this with a "style of charity, attention, love, interest, presence and participation."

The Inestimable Gift of Life

From now on let us begin to act according to that style and to lay the bases for a new culture of human life by asking ourselves, in the light of the word of God which has been proclaimed, *who man is, where he comes from and where he is going*, seeking to know the mystery of God, Creator of heaven and earth, of things visible and invisible.

Let us raise our praise to God for the greatness of the human person.

Praise to God for the Greatness of the Human Person

"*O God, our Creator and Father, we praise and bless you because you are great and because you communicate life to us. We thank you because you have made us marvels, you have knit us in our inmost being. You have created our inmost being and have formed us in our mothers' wombs. Stupendous are your works; you know us inside and out.*"

The most spontaneous attitude of the person towards his own life is one of *wonder and amazement*. And our song of praise, whose roots and deepest motivations are well expressed in Psalm 138, is a song to the mysterious action of God who is "knitting" and "forming" the human creature within the mother's womb.

God knows man right from his most mysterious beginnings; he knows the fetus which no human eye can discern because, right from the beginning, he is the Lord of man's loins, of his inmost being, that is, of what is most secret in man. Thus the human person belongs to God right from the womb; herein lies the ultimate foundation of his greatness and of the greatness of his life.

The eye of the Lord not only perceives a being that is invisible to the human eye, but foresees, beyond what is as yet unformed, the adult of tomorrow whose days are already written in his book. In this perspective, man is the marvel, the greatest miracle of God; he is one of the glorious, revealing actions of God himself. The human embryo is already a sign of the creative love of God, a manifestation of his creative imagination, of his splendor; it is the prefiguring of a plan, it is the introduction to one of the pages of the "book of life," it is the beginning of a vocation. Truly great is the mystery of the human person created by God. We must, first of all within ourselves and then in others, promote a contemplative spirit, a profound reverence before the unspeakable mystery of God which is shown right from the conception of each human life!

Each Person Is a Sign of the Living God

In praising God we must also perceive that the *dignity of the human person is almost divine.* For this reason we ask ourselves, with the psalmist: "When I look at the heavens, the work of your fingers, the moon and the stars that you have established; what are human beings that you are mindful of them, mortals that you care for them?" And with the psalmist we want to respond with joy and gratitude: "Yet you have made them a little lower than God, and crowned them with glory and honor. You have given them dominion over the works of your hands; you have put all things under their feet" (Psalm 8: 4-6). The greatness of the human person and his life lies in having been made "a little lower than God." The indestructible dignity of each of our lives is rooted in being made participants in the very life of God. In the Letter to the Romans, St. Paul writes: "For those whom he foreknew he also predestined to be conformed to the image of his Son, in order that he might be the firstborn within a large family. And those whom he predestined he also called; and those whom he called he also justified; and those whom he justified he also glorified" (Rom 8:29-30). It is in the mystery of the predestination of Christ that the mystery of the person is revealed in its fullness, the mystery of every person, whether powerful or weak or defenseless, rich or poor, man or woman, adult or child, already born or just conceived. From this mystery emerges the religious dimension and the specifically christological dimension of the "Gospel of life." In each child that is born and in each person who lives, we recognize the image of the glory of God, a sign of the living God; each person appears as an icon of Jesus Christ.

What we have said is not a humanistic exaltation or an apotheosis of the person. It is, instead, once again the amazed exaltation of that which makes the human person a unique and unrepeatable being, that is, the grace of God, his love, his concern for the human creature. In this regard I recall the very beautiful words of St. Gregory of Nyssa: "The human person who, among all beings, counts for nothing, is dust, grass, vanity, when once adopted by the God of the universe as his child, becomes a family member of this Being, whose excellence and greatness no one can see, hear or comprehend. What word, thought or outburst of the spirit can exalt the superabundance of this grace? The human person surpasses his nature: from mortal he becomes immortal, from perishable, imperishable, from ephemeral, eternal, from man he becomes god" (*De Beatitudine* VII: PG 44, 1280).

In the Cross of Jesus: the Meaning of Suffering and Death

Together with the praise of God and admiration for the dignity of the human person, we also need to develop our understanding of the *meaning of suffering and death*.

For this we have prayed and continue to pray:

"Grant, we beseech you, that we may learn that the name we are to give every sorrow and suffering of man is the cross of Jesus. Thus, even the life of those who are struck by illness, by solitude and marginalization, such as that of the elderly and of those about to die, will have meaning."

This means referring to the cross of Jesus, contemplating Jesus crucified, the sign of God's love for every person, sign of each person's need to be loved, even when his/her life appears externally to be deprived of meaning.

The cross of Christ is the certain response to this need for love, because it is the place of the full and unreserved manifestation of God's love for man. Whenever persons find themselves in the most atrocious suffering and tribulation, in extreme solitude, abandoned and rejected by everyone, the cross of Jesus will make them repeat with firm hope and with gratitude the words of Paul: "Who will separate us from the love of Christ? Will hardship, or distress, or persecution, or famine, or nakedness, or peril, or sword?...No, in all these things we are more than conquerors through him who loved us," because nothing "will be able to separate us from the love of God in Christ Jesus our Lord" (cf Rom 8:35-39).

Referring to the cross of Jesus means above all looking on the suffering of Jesus and learning to give it a name. As Fr. Giovanni Moioli, a great theologian whom the Lord called to himself after a terrible illness, taught, in suffering we can live the attitude of resistance and surrender and rediscover the salvific meaning of suffering and dying. "I do not surrender to suffering," he wrote, "but to God, to this strange closeness that seems a distance.... This surrender of myself to God keeps away desperation and rebellion, and the titanic struggle against suffering. Within I am poor, abandoned: this is surrender to the mystery of God."

"Herein lies the whole secret of trust, of hope, of confidence. This, which seems a surrender, is in reality an extraordinary strength. Thus surrender arouses resistance...the resistance of entrusting, of knowing how to endure pain because another is supporting you; of being patient in suffering, because it is the patience of God, because I await God. In this sense 'I have patience' before God. And I even know how to make a gift of suffering. It is the resistance of prayer, of continuing to speak, to dialogue with God.... It is an act of love not only for God but of love for and donation to our neighbor" (*La parola della croce: The Word of the Cross*, Edizioni Viboldone, Milan, 1985, pp. 58-59).

Respect for Life: Foundation of Democracy and Peace

1. I would like to recall a final aspect of this theme of the dignity of the human person, taken from the message of the Italian bishops for the XIV Day for Life: *respect for life is a foundation of democracy and peace*. In fact, the bishops write: "We invite each and every person to recognize that 'the right to life is a foundation of democracy and peace.' This is the testimony that comes to us from the past and present history of our country, of Europe and of the world" (n. 1). They add: "There cannot be a true democracy if we do not recognize the dignity of each person and if their rights and duties are not respected" (n. 1).

The recent history of many European countries testifies to this: when we do not recognize the transcendent dignity of the person, we fall fatally into an open or subtle form of totalitarianism, and democracy cannot flourish. The Pope emphasizes this in *Centesimus Annus*: "If one does not acknowledge transcendent truth, then the force of power takes over, and each person tends to make full use of the means at his own disposal in order to impose his own interests or his own opinion, with no regard for the rights of others. People are then respected only to the extent that they can be exploited for selfish ends. Thus, the root of modern totalitarianism is to be found in the denial of the transcendent dignity of the human person who, as the visible image of the invisible God, is therefore by his very nature the subject of rights which no one may violate—no individual, group, class, nation or State. Not even the majority of a social body may violate these rights by going against the minority, by isolating, oppressing, or exploiting it, or by attempting to annihilate it" (n. 44). I wanted to quote these words of John Paul II the other day at Davos, a small town of Switzerland, on the occasion of an international Congress on world economy, before the personalities of great nations which are still closed to these realities and do not recognize the freedom and dignity of each human person.

2. Reflections similar to those on freedom in relation to respect for life must be developed on the *theme of peace.* The sound of arms, which have covered with blood the peoples and European countries very close to us in the land of Croatia, must certainly cease so that we can speak of peace and build peace. But the silence of such sounds is not yet peace. In fact, peace involves justice and solidarity and is their most genuine fruit; peace is real only when the common internal and international good is achieved and, thus, when it respects and promotes the dignity of each and every person. "There cannot be true peace," our bishops write, "if not in justice and solidarity, and therefore in full respect for the rights of the person, of peoples and of nations" (*Message for the Day for Life,* n. 1). As a consequence, respect for the right to life has priority, for all other rights rest and are grafted on it; because when the possibility of living is taken away from the person, the

possibility of exercising every other right is excluded.

As Paul VI said in his *Message for the World Day of Peace* in 1977: "If you want peace, defend life.... To have an authentic and happy peace we must defend life, improve life, promote life.... Every crime against life is an attempt against peace, especially if it corrupts the customs of the people, as often today, with horrible and often legal ease, there comes about the suppression of unborn life through abortion."

And again: "The discourse can be prolonged by listing the hundred forms by which offenses against life today seem customary, where individual wrongdoing is organized so as to become collective, to assure itself of the conspiracy and complicity of entire classes of citizens, to make private revenge a vile collective duty, terrorism a phenomenon of legitimate political or social affirmation, police torture an effective method of public force no longer directed to re-establishing order but to imposing an ignoble repression. It is impossible that peace flourish where the security of life is compromised in this way. Where violence rages, peace ends. Instead, where the rights of the person are truly professed and publicly recognized and defended, peace becomes the joyful and active atmosphere of social life."

Here then are some of the profound ideal motivations that urge us on in the journey of the Conference: the situation in which we find ourselves, the commitment to proclaim the Gospel, the offering of praise to God the Creator, respect for the dignity of the human person, the meaning of suffering and death enlightened by the cross of Jesus, the values of freedom and democracy, love for peace.

A Journey that Continues

In the coming months we shall have to insist on this direction, taking up again and developing the reflections which I have offered you because *the journey must continue.* But how?

It must continue through the constant and intelligent commitment of each and every one, of each of our Christian communities, first of all with *prayer.* The formula which we recited together should be recited individually and in common at all the Eucharistic assemblies each first Sunday of the month.

In the second place, the journey must continue through *reflection* on the themes of life and the culture of life. To this end, in addition to going back to today's meditation, I especially invite the priests and parish pastoral councils to deepen and develop the rich suggestions of the "Gospel of life" contained in the talk given last November 23 by his Excellency Bishop Dionigi Tettamanzi, which will soon be available. I also ask each pastoral council to dedicate at least one of its sessions during the year to reflection on these themes, letting themselves be aided by an outline prepared for this purpose, which will be sent as soon as possible. I invite the parishes, Catholic Action, the associations, groups and movements to study and to promote moments of more specific catechesis on the themes of life, taking inspiration from the second part of the document of the Italian bishops, *Evangelizzazione e cultura della vita umana* (*Evangelization and the culture of human life*).

The places of cultural development, the various professional unions, and cultural centers are urged to promote initiatives for a *high profile cultural confrontation*, even with those who do not share the Christian faith but who are equally concerned about the future of man and society.

Let those who in different forms already offer a *pas-*

sionate service to the human person and human life continue in this generous task; let them find greater forms of coordination and know how to draw other vocations, especially among the young.

I recommend that *families* go back to being, as the Pope says in *Centesimus Annus,* "the sanctuary of life...the place in which life—the gift of God—can be properly welcomed and protected against the many attacks to which it is exposed, and can develop in accordance with what constitutes authentic human growth" (n. 39). To this end, families need to be the first to rediscover and live this vocation and mission of theirs. But it is also necessary that, on the social level...the family be promoted and fostered as a natural society founded on matrimony, avoiding interventions that tend to place the family institution on the same level as other kinds of living together. It is especially necessary that everything possible be done so that the family may truly become the center of every social policy.

In the unfolding of our Conference, other *common appointments* will also await us, especially in the coming autumn, for which precise indications will be given. In the meantime each one is asked to become *humble and courageous witnesses to the value and dignity of life.* The "mandate" which we will celebrate at the end of this Vigil, is intended to be a reminder and a commitment for all, in the desire that the text of the Letter of the bishops of Lombardy and the message of the Permanent Council of the Italian Episcopal Conference, may reach every family of the Diocese. I have personally sent these documents to the public authorities and to the representatives and leaders of civil society, in the conviction that the theme of human life cannot fail to be of concern to those engaged on the social, political or institutional level, and that politics cannot remain neutral or indifferent to the right to life of every person.

Conclusion

Everything that we do, live and propose during the course of the Conference and the fruits that will arise from it, are a sign—I repeat—of that great love for each person which we have learned from our God and from his Son Jesus.

We want to recognize and honor each and every person, whom we contemplate in the light of Jesus who was born, died and is risen. It is the same invitation, full of wonder, that Paul VI addressed to everyone for Christmas of 1967 and which I would like to have resound again at the beginning of our Conference:

> Let us honor the newborn life of the person!
> It is the creature of God,
> impressed with his image and likeness,
> conceived in the love which makes of two beings,
> man and woman, only one life,
> brought into the world not without suffering
> on the part of the mother,
> but for the joy of the world.
>
> Let us honor infancy.
> It too is a creature of God,
> and a motive of happiness for society.
> The infant is called to the mysterious rebirth of Baptism,
> a pledge of the life that does not die.
>
> Let us honor the woman,
> equal to man in dignity,
> called to the beauty and to the privileged love
> of consecrated virginity,
> or more often to that sacrosanct love of married life
> and to the incomparable ministry of motherhood.

Let us honor the child,
whose brother is the young Jesus,
who "grew in wisdom, age and grace before God and men."

Let us honor the man
in the fullness of his adulthood,
who finds in Jesus the model of work,
of social living,
of wisdom that sees beyond the senses
and beyond temporal phenomena.

Let us honor the human person in his infirmity,
who receives from Christ the succor of human compassion,
healing care,
and the gift of the merit which makes him similar
to Jesus crucified and gives value to suffering.

Let us honor humanity,
fallen and sinful,
for whom the life-giving love of Christ had preference
—for us almost inconceivable—and for whom Christ
reserved his admirable restoration.

Let us honor the person,
whomever he or she may be,
in whom the likeness of the divine image of Christ
is reflected wherever the need
for comfort and help is greater.

Let us honor the person
who advances in the conquest of the earth and the universe;
God has destined him/her to such an end.

And finally let us honor
the life that has passed away in justice,
to whom Christ guarantees his peace
and his marvelous resurrection.

The wish, the prayer, the task, is that our churches may be capable of giving this "honor" to the human person. May blessed Cardinal Andrea Carlo Ferrari help us in our journey. May the most holy Virgin, who accompanied Jesus to the temple and in whom we place all our trust, assist us: "Mary, mother of the Life, accompany us and sustain us, so that we may know how to recognize and guard, in the face of every human person, the sign of the living God whom you received in your virginal womb. Amen."

Homily for the opening of the Conference of the churches of Lombardy: "Birth and death today." Milan, February 1, 1992

CHAPTER 18

Brief Prayers

Introduction

We always begin with the sign of the cross, introduced by the father or mother or by an older member of the family.

If there is only one copy of the book, a child—especially one who is preparing for First Communion or Confirmation—reads both the introduction and the text of the prayer.

All respond: Amen.

If there are copies for everyone, then it would be well if an adult reads the introduction, and one of the children reads the prayer.

All respond: Amen.

Those who wish to pray more at length can conclude with the Our Father, Hail Mary, or say the Angelus (included at the end).

Prayers for Every Day of the Week

A very brief prayer that can be used on any day.

May you be blessed,
O Lord,
for this bread
which we share
as a sign of your love!
Through Christ our Lord. Amen.

    or:

May you be blessed, Father, God of the universe!
Through your goodness
we receive this food.
May we partake of it together in joy
and serve you with a sincere heart.
Through Christ our Lord. Amen.

Thursday

    Jesus says: "Where two or three are gathered in my
name, I am there among them" (Mt 18:20).

Lord Jesus, our God,
full of goodness and mercy,
be present at our table,
and make us witnesses of your love in the world.
You who live and reign for ever and ever. Amen.

Friday

    Jesus says: "No one has greater love than this, to lay
down one's life for one's friends" (Jn 15:13).

O God our Father,
to nourish your people
with eternal life
you accepted the offering

that Jesus our brother made
of his life on the cross.
Grant that we remember
his glorious death
in the certainty of sharing
in his resurrection.
Through Christ our Lord. Amen.

Saturday

"[The disciples of Jesus] were constantly devoting themselves to prayer, together with certain women, including Mary the mother of Jesus" (Acts 1:14).

We bless you, Lord Jesus.
Make us worthy of participating
in your heavenly banquet;
we pray to you with trust
through the intercession of the Blessed Virgin Mary,
your Mother and ours.
You who live and reign forever and ever. Amen.

Prayers for Certain Feasts During the Year

For Christmas Day

We thank you, O Lord,
for having gathered us around this table
on this feast day.
You have made yourself one with us.
Come sit at our table
and preserve the joy of this day.
You who live and reign
forever and ever. Amen.

For New Year's Day

We thank you, O Lord of the ages!
At the dawn of this new year
you gather us around the table
so that we may wish one another a happy beginning.
We pray:
may your gaze brighten our journey
through all the days to come.
Through Jesus Christ your Son our Lord. Amen.

For Easter

May you be blessed, God our Father,
King of heaven and earth,
Lord of life and of death,
for this Easter day.
May the light of the risen Christ
shine on us forever.
He who lives and reigns
forever and ever. Amen.

For Pentecost

Lord our God,
today you sent your Spirit
on the Apostles
and on the whole Church
to spread the Gospel throughout the world.
Be with us at our table
and put your words on our lips
and in our heart.
Through Christ our Lord. Amen.

For All Souls' Day

O God our merciful Father,
today we remember all our deceased brothers and sisters.
Grant them your pardon!

Give them the joy and light of your home
and reunite us with them in the eternal day.
Through Jesus Christ your Son,
Lord of the living and the dead,
who lives and reigns with you
forever and ever. Amen.

For a Feast of Our Lady

We thank you, O Father,
for this food
which we share together on the day
of the feast
of the Mother of your Son.
May she who brought joy to the wedding feast of Cana
bring peace of heart
to us who participate in this meal.
Through Jesus Christ, Son of Mary,
who lives and reigns forever and ever. Amen.

Prayers for Different Occasions in the Life of a Family

For the Baptism of a Child

We thank you, O Lord,
because you have given ...... (name)
new birth through water and the Holy Spirit.
Grant that, in growing up among us,
he/she may come to know and to love you.
Through Christ your Son and our Lord. Amen

For the Mother's Birthday

O Lord our Father,
you gather us today around this table
to celebrate the birthday of our mother.

We thank you for her presence
and her care,
for her joy and her affection.
Watch over her,
as you watch over us.
Keep her in good health
and let her happiness increase
because of us.
We ask this through Christ our Lord. Amen.

For the Father's Birthday

Our Father who art in heaven,
we thank you
on this day of our father's birthday.
Keep him in good health,
make him serene in his work
and with us all,
in Christ your Son and our Lord. Amen.

For the Birthday of One of the Children

Bless, O Lord, this food
which we share together
in joy on the birthday of ...... (name)
Our wish is that he/she may grow every day
in knowledge of you
and in love for everyone.
Through Christ our Lord. Amen.

For the Birthday of a Family Member

We thank you, Father,
for the gifts which you give each day to ..... (name)
Sustain him/her with your love!
May the joy of this birthday
fill his/her whole life.
Through Christ our Lord. Amen.

For a Feast Day

Lord, today we are celebrating
the feast day of .... (name)
May the Saint whose name he/she bears
obtain for him/her the grace
to be of service to many brothers and sisters
and to always be happy.
We wish this wholeheartedly
and ask it of you, our Father,
through Jesus Christ our Lord. Amen.

For a Happy Occasion

Lord our God,
source of our joy!
You do great things for us.
We thank you with a sincere heart
and we ask you to lead us from the joy of this day
to that of eternal life
Through Christ your Son and our Lord. Amen.

For the Visit of a Friend

O Lord our God,
today the joy of our meal is greater
because you give us the gift of welcoming a friend.
May we grow in this friendship
so as to always be able to give you thanks.
Through Christ our Lord. Amen.

For the Day of First Communion

O Lord our God!
Today we celebrate at this meal
because Jesus has given himself to us
as the bread of life.
We thank you for your great goodness.

Grant that, by participating at the Eucharistic meal,
we may grow every day in your love
and in love for all our sisters and brothers.
Through Christ our Lord. Amen.

For the Day of Confirmation
Lord our God,
today we meet at this table with joy
because you have given us your Holy Spirit.
Grant that we may open to him the doors of our home
and of our heart.
Make us witnesses of the Gospel of Christ
who lives and reigns forever and ever. Amen.

On the Eve of an Exam
Bless, O Lord, this food of ours.
May it sustain in their daily effort
those who are preparing for exams.
May it enable them to face the exams
with a serene and trusting spirit.
Through Christ your Son our Lord. Amen.

To Obtain an Important Grace
Lord, all-powerful God,
by gathering us around this table
you make us understand
that you love us and think of us.
We recommend to you the intention
that we have greatly at heart.
May we soon be able to rejoice
because you have heard us.
Through Christ our Lord. Amen.

In Time of Suffering

O God, infinitely good Father,
through the sufferings of Jesus
you opened for us the way to life.
Be with us at this time
(of difficulty, fear, anguish).
Teach us to carry our cross with hope
in union with the mystery
of the death and resurrection
of Jesus your Son and our Lord. Amen.

For a Sick Person

O God our Father,
your Son Jesus Christ
has taken upon himself our ills.
Hear our prayer
for one who is sick.
May we all soon rejoice at his/her recovery.
Through Jesus your Son, friend of the suffering,
who lives and reigns forever and ever. Amen.

For One Who Is About to Take a Long Trip

Lord our God,
you fill every place with your presence
and no one can ever go far from you.
Protect ... (name) during his/her journey.
Be with him/her in difficulties,
that he/she may return to our table with joy.
We ask this through your Son Jesus
who is way, truth and life
forever and ever. Amen.

At the Moment of a Death in the Family

Lord our God,
through the death of your Son Jesus
you conquered death
and through his resurrection
you give us life again.
Be with us in this sorrowful moment
when we mourn the death of .... (name).
Receive his/her soul into your peace.
Increase our faith!
We know that those who are no longer with us
at this table are not far from us
because they have believed and hoped in you.
May we all be united one day
at your banquet in heaven.
You who give life to all the deceased
and reign forever and ever. Amen.

Our Father

Our Father,
who art in heaven,
hallowed be thy name.
Thy kingdom come,
thy will be done on earth as it is in heaven.
Give us this day our daily bread,
and forgive us our trespasses
as we forgive those who trespass against us;
and lead us not into temptation
but deliver us from evil. Amen.

Hail Mary

Hail Mary, full of grace,
the Lord is with you.
Blessed are you among women,
and blessed is the fruit of your womb, Jesus.

Holy Mary,
Mother of God,
pray for us sinners
now and at the hour of our death. Amen.

The Angelus

V. The angel spoke God's message to Mary,
R. and she conceived of the Holy Spirit.
Hail, Mary.

V. "I am the lowly servant of the Lord:
R. let it be done to me according to your word."
Hail, Mary.

V. And the Word became flesh
R. and lived among us.
Hail, Mary.

V. Pray for us, holy Mother of God,
R. that we may become worthy of the promises of Christ.

Let us pray.

Lord,
fill our hearts with your grace:
once, through the message of an angel
you revealed to us the incarnation of your Son;
now, through his suffering and death
lead us to the glory of his resurrection.
We ask this through Christ our Lord. Amen.

Milan, 1987

══════ St. Paul Book & Media Centers ══════

ALASKA
  750 West 5th Ave., Anchorage, AK 99501; 907-272-8183
CALIFORNIA
  3908 Sepulveda Blvd., Culver City, CA 90230; 310-397-8676
  5945 Balboa Ave., San Diego, CA 92111; 619-565-9181
  46 Geary Street, San Francisco, CA 94108; 415-781-5180
FLORIDA
  145 S.W. 107th Ave., Miami, FL 33174; 305-559-6715
HAWAII
  1143 Bishop Street, Honolulu, HI 96813; 808-521-2731
ILLINOIS
  172 North Michigan Ave., Chicago, IL 60601; 312-346-4228
LOUISIANA
  4403 Veterans Memorial Blvd., Metairie, LA 70006; 504-887-7631
MASSACHUSETTS
  50 St. Paul's Ave., Jamaica Plain, Boston, MA 02130;
  617-522-8911
  Rte. 1, 885 Providence Hwy., Dedham, MA 02026; 617-326-5385
MISSOURI
  9804 Watson Rd., St. Louis, MO 63126; 314-965-3512
NEW JERSEY
  561 U.S. Route 1, Wick Plaza, Edison, NJ 08817; 908-572-1200
NEW YORK
  150 East 52nd Street, New York, NY 10022; 212-754-1110
  78 Fort Place, Staten Island, NY 10301; 718-447-5071
OHIO
  2105 Ontario Street (at Prospect Ave.), Cleveland, OH 44115;
  216-621-9427
PENNSYLVANIA
  214 W. DeKalb Pike, King of Prussia, PA 19406; 215-337-1882
SOUTH CAROLINA
  243 King Street, Charleston, SC 29401; 803-577-0175
TEXAS
  114 Main Plaza, San Antonio, TX 78205; 210-224-8101
VIRGINIA
  1025 King Street, Alexandria, VA 22314; 703-549-3806
GUAM
  285 Farenholt Avenue, Suite 308, Tamuning, Guam 96911;
  671-649-4377
CANADA
  3022 Dufferin Street, Toronto, Ontario, Canada M6B 3T5;
  416-781-9131; 1-800-668-2078